Harper's Comparative Government Series

MICHAEL CURTIS, EDITOR

FRENCH POLITICS
AND
POLITICAL
INSTITUTIONS

FRENCH POLITICS
AND
POLITICAL
INSTITUTIONS

ROY PIERCE
THE UNIVERSITY OF MICHIGAN

HARPER & ROW
Publishers

NEW YORK, EVANSTON, AND LONDON

For my mother and father

Library of Congress Catalog Card Number: 68-16209

CONTENTS

v

Appendixes

LIST OF FIGURES

LIST OF MAPS

LIST OF TABLES

ACKNOWLEDGMENTS

I gratefully thank the people, research organizations, and publishers whose generous help and cooperation have contributed to this book.

Georges Dupeux kindly read the first three chapters and saved me from making several errors; if any remain there, it is because I did not always heed his advice. Credit for the maps and figures belongs to Leslie R. Thurston, who drew them.

The *Institut Français d'Opinion Publique* gave me permission to print the data which appear in Tables 10 and 11. The *Fondation Nationale des Sciences Politiques* gave me permission to print the data which appear in Table 13 and some of the data which appear in Tables 8 and 12, as well as to base Figure 1, in part, on data which it has published.

The Librairie Armand Colin gave me permission to print the data which appears in Table 3, as well as to base Figure 1, in part, on data which it has published. The Free Press gave me permission to use certain data which appear in Chapter Seven.

The scholars on whose work I have drawn in preparing this book are named in the footnotes and the bibliography. The latter contains three works, however, which appeared too late to be taken into account in this book: Richard F. Hamilton's *Affluence and the French Worker in the Fourth Republic*, Mark Kesselman's *The Ambiguous Consensus: A Study of Local Government in France*, and Duncan MacRae Jr.'s *Parliament, Parties, and Society in France, 1946–1958*.

I alone am responsible for the opinions expressed in this book and for whatever errors it may contain.

ROY PIERCE

MAP 1. The Departments of Metropolitan France.
SOURCE: Institut National de la Statistique et des Études
Économiques, "L'Espace Économique Français," *Études et
Conjoncture*, Numéro spécial, Imprimerie Nationale and Presses
Universitaires de France, Paris, 1955.

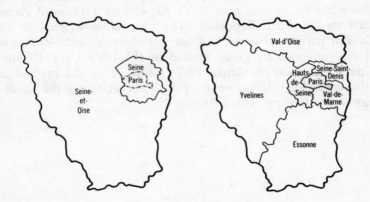

MAP 2. Administrative Reorganization of the Paris Area
(Left, Old; Right, New).

SOURCE: La Documentation Française, *Répertoire Permanent de l'Administration Française, Année 1965*, Imprimerie des Journaux Officiels, Paris, 1965, p. 253.

ADDENDUM

At the fourth national congress of the UNR-UDT, at Lille, in November, 1967, the name of the party was changed to the *Union des démocrates pour la Ve République* (Union of Democrats for the Fifth Republic). The new name adopted by the Gaullist party was similar to—but not identical with—the name of the parliamentary group formed by the UNR-UDT Deputies after the election of March, 1967 (see p. 167), and marked another stage in the discontinuity of the nomenclature of the Gaullist movement (see pp. 122–124).

CHAPTER ONE

The French Political Tradition

FRENCH POLITICS is fascinating. This is no doubt because of what Charles de Gaulle referred to in 1946 as France's "perpetual political effervescence." French politics seems always to be in ferment, and ferment is exciting. There is suspense over the outcome of each new sequence of developments, and those developments themselves pose interesting problems for the scholar who seeks to understand them.

There are several aspects to the "effervescence" to which Charles de Gaulle referred. One aspect is that the very nature of the political system—what the French call the *régime*—is a subject of continuing political dispute. France has a long and checkered history of experimentation with different régimes. Another aspect is the existence of a multiparty system which expresses a variety of political conflicts and leads to a continuing process of combination and recombination of parties in the search for electoral and parliamentary majorities. A third aspect is the best known and most frequently commented upon one of all: the ministerial instability which was characteristic of the Third and Fourth Republics.

None of these phenomena can be fully explained and understood with reference to French political history alone, but neither can any of them be fully explained and understood without reference to that history. In all societies which permit free political organization and expression, contemporary politics reflects what men did long ago. The influence of the past is, perhaps, particularly important in France, which has experienced numerous convulsive events throughout its political history. French political attitudes,

1

and the behavior based on them, reflect not only the burning issues of the day, but also burning issues of days past.

Institutional Instability

Since 1789, France's political leaders have not been able to arrive at general agreement over the kind of political institutions by which the country should be governed. No single régime has ever enjoyed the kind of legitimacy which the English constitutional monarchy has enjoyed since the late seventeenth century. The politically active and aware segment of the population has never, at any given time, been agreed that the political system in operation was the right and proper system for France.

Since the overthrow of the Old Régime—a process begun in 1789 and completed with the execution of the King in January, 1793—France has lived under two monarchies, two empires, five republics, the Vichy régime (which started out as a twentieth-century effort to restore the governing patterns and social order of the Old Régime and ended up as an imitation and vassal of the German Nazi régime), not to mention several short-lived variants (see Table 1).

It would, however, be an error to place too much emphasis on the simple fact of the turnover in régimes without regard for the duration of those régimes. The Third Republic, which emerged relatively late in the post-Revolutionary period, lasted for 70 years while the two monarchies which preceded the Third Republic together lasted for only 34 and the two empires which preceded it together lasted for fewer than 30. There can be little doubt that it was the Third Republic, and not the monarchies or empires, which divided France least.

And while the record of instability of French régimes is striking if one compares it with the English record, it appears less aberrational if one compares it with the records of other continental countries, such as Germany and Italy (see Table 2). In one sense, the more appropriate comparison is with England, because Germany and Italy are countries which were not unified until 1870, while France has been a unified nation for centuries, just as England has. At the same time, there are considerations which suggest that the comparison with the other continental countries is the more appropriate one to make.

The political forces which have operated in the continental countries have been more similar to one another than those of any one of them have been similar to the forces at work in England.

TABLE 1. French Régimes in Modern Times

Dates	Régime
Before 1789	The Old Régime
1789–1792	Revolutionary and Counterrevolutionary Struggles
1792–1799	The First Republic
	1792–1795: The Convention
	Radical Republican Rule, 1792–1794
	Conservative Reaction, 1794–1795
	1795–1799: The Directory: Moderate Republican Rule
1799–1814	The Age of Napoleon
	1799–1802: First Consul
	1802–1804: Life Consul
	1804–1814: The First Empire
1814–1830	The Bourbon Restoration: Constitutional Monarchy and Traditional Authoritarianism
1830–1848	The July Monarchy: Orleanist Constitutionalism and Emerging Business Interests
1848–1852	The Second Republic
1852–1870	The Second Empire: Louis Napoleon
1870–1940	The Third Republic
1940–1944	The Vichy Régime
1944–1946	Provisional Government of Charles de Gaulle
1947–1958	The Fourth Republic
1958–	The Fifth Republic

We will see in a moment that France's institutional instability is rooted in the revolutionary crisis of 1789. French revolutionary armies carried the revolutionary principles of 1789 into other continental countries, including what later became Germany and Italy, and these set off political conflicts similar to those which were to operate in France. Similar forces, in other words, tended to produce similar results, although it should be noted that France, unlike Germany and Italy, never produced a strong fascist party and was governed by Nazi-style leaders only briefly, toward the end of World War II, when France was wholly occupied by German armies (see Chapter Two).

French experience with war has also contributed to its institutional instability. The impact of war upon the nature of political

TABLE 2.   French, German, and Italian Régimes, 1870–Present

France	Germany	Italy
Third Republic, 1870–1940	Second Empire, 1870–1918	Constitutional Monarchy, 1870–1922
	Weimar Republic, 1919–1933	Fascist Régime, 1922–1943
Vichy Régime, 1940–1944	Nazi Régime, 1933–1945	Provisional Government, 1943–1946
Provisional Government, 1944–1946	Allied Occupation, 1945–1949	Italian Republic, 1946–
Fourth Republic, 1947–1958	Bonn Republic, 1949–	
Fifth Republic, 1958–		

systems is an important phenomenon of modern times. Military invasion, defeat, or occupation often results in a change of régime. Sometimes a defeated or occupied nation is more or less constrained by the victor to change its political system. Sometimes a leadership group exploits the new conditions created by the war to bring about a change of régime. Even a nation which is victorious in a war may experience a change of régime as a result of new forces set into motion by the war itself.

The German Weimar Republic was established as a result of Germany's defeat in World War I; the economic consequences of that war contributed to the rise of the Nazi movement; the defeat of Germany in World War II made possible both the West German Bonn Republic and the East German Communist régime. Italy was among the victors in World War I, but the Fascist régime was born out of conditions created by the war. Twenty years later, Italian military defeat in World War II tumbled the Fascist régime and cleared the way for the establishment of the Italian constitutional republic.

French experience with war has been much more similar to that of the other continental countries than it has been to that of England. France, like Germany and Italy, and unlike England, has been invaded, defeated, and occupied in modern times. In the speech in which de Gaulle referred to French "political effervescence," he also referred to the fact that France had been invaded seven times in 150 years. Several of the changes in régime which France has undergone were precipitated by the fortunes of war.

The Bourbon Restoration of 1814 occurred because Napoleon's armies had been defeated and there were 200,000 foreign troops around Paris; the new King arrived in France in the "baggage of the allies."

One scholar has written appropriately that the Third Republic "was an experiment which began and ended amid the sound of gunfire dying away round Sedan."[1] The Second Empire came to an end when MacMahon's army was defeated and Louis Napoleon captured by the Germans. The Third Republic would probably have eventually been established in any case, but the military defeat of the Empire provided the Republicans with an opportunity to establish the Republic. And the Third Republic itself came to an end as the result of another military defeat. Demoralized Members of Parliament voted to abolish the Republic while about one-half of French territory was occupied by the Germans. This experience led the framers of the Constitution of the Fourth Republic to include a provision prohibiting amendment of the Constitution while foreign troops occupied any part of Metropolitan France and the framers of the Constitution of the Fifth Republic to include a provision prohibiting any amendment of the Constitution while the integrity of the territory is in jeopardy.

The Vichy régime fell with the Liberation of Paris in 1944, and the way was cleared for the establishment of the Fourth Republic.

The military record alone does not explain France's long history of institutional instability. A régime may resist the consequences of defeat and even of occupation if it enjoys a high level of legitimacy. Norway and Denmark, for example, were invaded and occupied by the Germans during World War II, but they did not

[1] David Thomson, *Democracy in France, The Third and Fourth Republics*, Oxford, Fair Lawn, N. J., 1958, p. 9.

alter their régimes as a result. But where the legitimacy of the régime is in question, the régime is vulnerable to external shocks, and this has been the French experience.

French régimes have also been overturned without the stimulus of foreign war. France has an indigenous revolutionary tradition which harks back to the Revolution of 1789. Both the Bourbon Restoration and the July Monarchy were overthrown by revolution, and the First and Second Republics were overthrown by military coups. The Fourth Republic came to an end because its leaders feared that either a military coup or a Communist revolution would occur if they did not call Charles de Gaulle back to power; but it should be noted that even in 1958, the conditions which led to the collapse of the existing régime included an external shock in the form of the Algerian war.

The record of institutional instability has had important consequences for French political life. The very instability of the past creates conditions conducive to instability in the present. Each change of régime produced discontent among groups which had identified with and prospered under the previous régime, and in sedimentary fashion, layers of support were built for each French régime. The result has been that each régime is threatened by reactionary forces in the literal sense of the term: groups which want to restore some past form of political organization. Until the end of the nineteenth century, Republicans, Monarchists, and Bonapartists competed with one another within each régime, and the establishment of the Vichy régime demonstrated how strong nostalgia for the distant past remained even in 1940.

Vichy was discredited at the Liberation, although it continued to have some partisans during the Fourth Republic. The forces of reaction did not disappear in 1944; they simply began to take on a new form. Just as the Third Republic contained advocates of monarchy or empire, the Fourth Republic contained advocates of the Third. Today, the Fifth Republic contains an opposition which would like to return to the institutions and practices of the Fourth Republic.

The fact that the régime has been changed with some frequency in the past encourages expectations that it will be changed again. This not only sustains the nostalgia of reactionaries who would like to restore some past régime; it also encourages the hopes of radicals who would like to establish a new régime. In this respect, the kind of comfort which Monarchists or Bonapartists during the Third Republic could derive from French historical experience was no different from the kind of encouragement which Communists or other radicals can derive today from the same experience. Monarchists could not openly identify themselves with the revolutionary tradition, because their consciousness of themselves as a political force was shaped during the revolutionary era after 1789 when they were the targets of the revolutionaries. The Communists, however, as unrevolutionary as they appear to be, can and do appeal to the revolutionary tradition of which many Frenchmen are proud.

No French régime has enjoyed unchallenged legitimacy. Each one is threatened by reactionaries or radicals or both. Efforts are made by dissident groups to weaken the existing régime and exploit its difficulties in order to create conditions which would make it possible to replace it with another political system. The leaders of each régime have to expend much energy not only in the conduct of Government policy but also in the defense of the régime against its opponents. It is not the record of instability which creates opposition to each régime, but the record of instability gives encouragement to the opposition which it might not otherwise have.

Conflicting Social and Political Ideals

The major reason why French political leaders became so sharply divided over the question of the régime is that the circumstances of the revolutionary era made it difficult for them to view the political system in purely instrumental terms. When a political system enjoys legitimacy in a liberal environment, it becomes essentially an instrument for reducing tensions within the country and between that country and other countries. French political leaders throughout the nineteenth century, however, were unable to regard the political system as an agency for considering and conciliating conflicting claims about how society should be organized. Instead, they identified different political systems with different forms of social organization. No régime could become an arena for the settlement of social conflicts when the advocates of each competing set of social ideals believed that a particular régime was indispensable to the attainment of those social ideals. The result was that institutional and social conflicts were almost inextricably combined throughout the nineteenth century.

Two principal and opposing sets of political and social ideals emerged out of the revolutionary era following 1789, oscillated throughout the nineteenth century and even into the twentieth, and still linger in the attitudes of certain groups in France today, although one of them is virtually extinct and the other much less extensively and vigorously held than formerly. Because of their long duration, both sets of ideals can be called traditional. One is authoritarian; the other is democratic.

TRADITIONAL AUTHORITARIANISM

French traditional authoritarianism represents the heritage of the Old Régime in both its political and social manifestations. In fact, as we have already said, its political and social elements cannot be separated. They both spring from the central principle of hierarchy based upon birth rather than the principle of equality which permits mobility through talent and election. Politically, it is monarchical; socially, it is aristocratic.

It also places a high value on the social and political role of the Catholic Church as a support for both the social and political structure. Accordingly, Church and state should, in this conception, not be separated, but rather the state should aid the Church.

And while this cluster of attitudes is properly labeled authoritarian, the label should not be taken in its twentieth-century connotation of police-state brutality. According to the traditional view, authority would be freely accepted out of affection and respect, and obedience would proceed not from force but from custom. Traditional authoritarianism advocated decentralization of the political system. Various local leaders might be authoritarian in their own right, but the central state would be essentially weak.

This authoritarian ideal underlay the Restoration monarchy between 1814 and 1830. It was less characteristic of the July Monarchy between 1830 and 1848, as that régime was more receptive to the elective principle (although not to universal suffrage) and more hospitable to commercial and business, as opposed to aristocratic, interests. But it was this earlier authoritarian ideal which endured longest in the minds of opponents of the Third

Republic. Of course, it became increasingly anachronistic. As expressed by a group like the *Action Française*, which was formed
in 1905 and remained active during the remaining years of the
Third Republic, its affirmative aspects became almost completely
submerged beneath the vituperation which that group poured on
the Third Republic and its leaders. Monarchy had relatively few
supporters by the 1930s, but the other elements of the authoritarian ideal continued to attract admirers, and traditional authoritarianism was the doctrinal underpinning of the first years of
the Vichy régime.

The traditional authoritarian ideal disappeared as a significant
political force with the collapse of the Vichy régime itself. There
are, however, vestigial patterns of social organization in France
which resemble this traditional social ideal. They are to be found
mainly in the agricultural regions of the west where the people
are strongly attached to the Catholic Church.[2] It was reported
in 1958 that the proportion of mayors whose names included the
preposition *de*, indicating that the name derives from landed property, exceeded 10 percent only in four departments (see Map 1),
all in the west (Loire-Atlantique, Maine-et-Loire, Mayenne, and
Vendée). The proportion was between 3 percent and 9 percent
in twelve other departments; nine of these were in the west.[3] In
a work published in 1913, André Siegfried referred to certain
family names regularly associated with national politics in the
department of Vendée.[4] A Deputy bearing one of those names
was elected to the National Assembly at each post-World War II
election until 1958.

TRADITIONAL DEMOCRACY

French traditional democracy developed in opposition to traditional authoritarianism. While the social ideals of tradi-

---

[2] Since the beginning of this century, the number of priests in France has
been declining while the French population has grown. In the department of
Vendée, in the west, however, the ratio of priests to inhabitants has increased.
In 1904, there was 1 priest for every 776 inhabitants; in 1965, there was 1
priest for every 622 inhabitants. *Le Monde*, September 8, 1965.

[3] Jacques Fauvet, Henri Mendras *et al.*, *Les Paysans et la politique dans
la France contemporaine*, Armand Colin, Paris, 1958, p. 35, Map. 13.

[4] André Siegfried, *Tableau politique de la France de l'Ouest sous la Troisième
République*, Armand Colin, Paris, p. 28.

tional authoritarianism rested on the notion of hierarchy, the traditional democratic social ideal rested on the concept of equality. While traditional authoritarians advocated the hereditary principle as the basis for leadership selection, traditional democrats advocated popular sovereignty. Traditional authoritarians advocated an hereditary monarchy; traditional democrats placed their faith in elected assemblies rather than in any form of executive power.

Instead of sympathizing with the claims of the Catholic Church, traditional French democrats were vigorously anticlerical and advocated the separation of Church and state. This does not mean that traditional democrats were necessarily antireligious; many, and perhaps most, of them were not. It does mean, however, that they opposed using state resources for support of the educational activities of the Catholic Church.

Conceptually opposed and historically enemies, traditional authoritarians and traditional democrats shared one major attitude in common. Both groups opposed the power of the central government. The traditional authoritarian ideals were inspired by the kind of social and political organization which antedated the centralization of governmental power by the monarchy. The traditional democratic ideal distrusted governmental power because its proponents identified it with the abuses against which they fought in their revolutionary efforts during the nineteenth century. Neither traditional ideal was favorably oriented toward the use of governmental power for the purpose of achieving social reforms. Traditional authoritarians and traditional democrats both believed that the central state should be weak, except in the persecution of their opponents. Each group sought a political system which would express and symbolize its social ideals, but neither conceived of government as an instrument for the continuous pursuit of specific, socially desirable objectives. Traditional authoritarians conceived of authority as decentralized, benign, and softened by religion. Traditional democrats were opposed to every form of authority except that of an elected assembly. Both ideals were obviously marked by strong utopian strains. It must be said, however, that the traditional democrat had the merit of believing in a system which survived for 70 years, while the traditional authoritarian clung to what, by 1848, had already become a mirage.

JACOBINISM AND BONAPARTISM

There are few generalizations about anything as complex as French politics which do not require qualification. Traditional French democracy was overwhelmingly opposed to state authority, but there have always been French democrats who were oriented toward political achievement, in the sense that they believed it was essential to employ the power of the state to promote positive social goals. There is a strain of French democratic thought called Jacobinism which is intensely nationalistic and which has never hesitated to harness the power of the state in the pursuit of its objectives. The political history of the Third Republic is as studded as that of any other nation with leaders of strong will and authoritative behavior: Gambetta, Ferry, Waldeck-Rousseau, Combes, Clemenceau, and Poincaré.

Moreover, the accomplishments of the Third Republic until well into the twentieth century can stand the test of comparison with those of other European nations. Free compulsory elementary education and freedom of association were adopted early. French industrial production per capita grew at a faster rate between 1901 and 1913 than did that of either Germany or Europe as a whole;[5] and between 1919 and 1929 France made a more rapid economic recovery from World War I than did either Germany or England.[6] The arts flourished and freedom of expression was assured.

It remains true, however, that the dominant outlook among French democrats was hostile to the exercise of state power. The main advocates of a positive state in France during the nineteenth century were the Bonapartists. The Bonapartists accepted the democratic concept of social equality, insofar as it meant widening the social bases from which talent could be drawn for the service of the state. They acknowledged the concept of popular sovereignty but preferred to implement it through the plebiscite rather than through the election of a powerful legislature. They rejected doctrinaire anticlericalism: the first Bonaparte signed a concordat with the Church and the second one invaded Italy to liberate Rome from the anticlerical Italian republican forces.

[5] Raymond Aron, *France, Steadfast and Changing*, Harvard, Cambridge, Mass., 1960, p. 45.
[6] Raymond Aron, *Dix-huit Leçons sur la société industrielle*, Gallimard, Paris, 1963, p. 322.

Most of all, Bonapartists strengthened the state and wielded its powers for purposes as diverse as the conquest of Europe and the rebuilding of Paris. They also crushed political liberty. Far more than the traditional authoritarians, it was the Bonapartists who created the image of abusive executive power against which traditional French democrats sought to protect the French people.

CONTEMPORARY INSTITUTIONAL CONFLICTS

Traditional authoritarianism has all but disappeared, and the old conflict between hereditary social stratification and social equality has been displaced by more modern issues concerning the distribution of wealth and methods of producing economic growth; but a conflict over the nature of the political system endures. This conflict is complex because it is not simply polar, but it is clearly related to French traditions.

De Gaulle and his supporters prefer a presidential régime of the kind which was created under the Fifth Republic. It is not surprising that some commentators refer to Gaullists as Jacobins while others see them as belonging to the Bonapartist tradition. Like the Jacobins and Bonapartists, the Gaullists are achievement-oriented. They are nationalistic, they favor a strong centralized state with an authoritative executive, and they do not hesitate to use state power to pursue ambitious programs of which they approve. They accept the principle of popular sovereignty, but instead of confining its application to the election of a legislature (as the Jacobins did), they have applied it through referendums and extended it to the election of the President, which has incited their opponents to draw comparisons with Bonapartist plebiscites.

The opponents of the Fifth Republic are not united with respect to their own institutional preferences. They object to what they call the "personal" character of the régime, referring to de Gaulle's dominant position, and they object to certain of the institutions of the régime. But while some democratic opponents of the Fifth Republic are traditional democrats, many of them are not, in the sense that they are as achievement-oriented and as much in favor of a strong and authoritative executive as the Gaullists are. But they do not have a common conception of an institutional structure to offer as an alternative to the Fifth

Republic. They make various institutional proposals,
technical kind, but these do not spark any large respo
the public at large. The only strong democratic tradition
they can rely is the traditional one.

For if traditional authoritarianism has virtually disappea   ...e
traditional democratic attitudes have not. After all, it was the
latter which triumphed over the former with the consolidation of
the Third Republic. The traditional democratic view endures
most strongly in the southern half of the country, primarily in
the southwest and along the Mediterranean coast. This area is
the historic center of strength of those politicians who, during the
Third Republic, embodied and propagated the traditional democratic attitudes. The same area remains today the seat of the
strongest opposition to the political conception of the Gaullist
Fifth Republic (see Map 4).

The present, of course, is not the past. The conditions are
different, the specific issues are different, and, naturally, the men
are different. Different groups may be linked to historic traditions
but they cannot be identified with them. Gaullists are not literally
either Jacobins or Bonapartists, and most French democrats are
probably not the traditional French democrats of the last century.
But France does not have a tradition of achievement-oriented
democracy which can accommodate itself easily to a strong, independent executive or to a strong state, and for that reason, contemporary conflicts often look like reproductions of the conflicts
of earlier times.

The Multiparty System

The main characteristic of the French party system is the
multiplicity of the parties. Modern political parties, organized in
order to give some kind of coherence to the electoral efforts of
like-minded Members of Parliament, were not formed in France
until the beginning of the twentieth century, but well before
then French politics had developed along multigroup or multi-
factional lines. And the tendency toward multiparty politics has
stubbornly resisted those intermittent periods when free political
organization was eliminated or repressed, as during the reigns of

the two Bonapartes and during the Vichy régime. After each of these hiatuses in free political competition, factionalism and multi-party politics returned.

The contemporary French party system has been shaped by three revolutions: the political, social, and religious revolution of 1789, the industrial revolution of the nineteenth century, and the Russian Bolshevik revolution of 1917. The first set into motion three great issues which have been involved in party politics in France ever since: the question of the régime, the question of the relationship between state and Church, and the question of social organization. The second exacerbated French economic problems and gave new dimensions to the social question. The third produced an entirely new group, whose supporters were susceptible to appeals based on traditional French partisan claims, but whose leaders were dedicated to a new and different set of political objectives.

There was a variety of groups throughout the nineteenth century which wanted to establish a democratic republic, and they are known collectively as the Republicans. They gained strength as the century progressed. They succeeded in establishing the Third Republic in 1870 and consolidating it by 1879 because their opponents were divided. Their opponents included the Bonapartists and two groups of Monarchists, one loyal to the heir of Charles X, who had reigned during the Bourbon Restoration (1814–1830), the other loyal to the heir of Louis Philippe, who had reigned during the July Monarchy (1830–1848).

The issues dividing these groups have already been discussed in terms of their conflicting political and social ideals. By the turn of the century, the Monarchists and Bonapartists no longer were significantly represented in Parliament (although they had active and latent support in the country), and the multigroup nature of French politics started operating within the republican framework. The divisions among Republicans had counted for less than their common opposition to the Monarchists and Bonapartists before the Republic was established and while it was not yet secure, but once all, or almost all, parliamentary groups accepted the republican label, the divisions among the Republicans themselves came to the fore.

These divisions revolved around religious and economic questions. It is not possible to state with certainty which was the more important of the two, although there is good reason to believe that the predominant issue was religious.

THE CLERICAL QUESTION

The words "droite" and "gauche" ("right" and "left") are the two most frequently used words in the French political vocabulary, but they defy objective definition in every sense but one: their relation to religion, or what is known as the clerical question. Few Frenchmen doubt that anticlericals are on the left and clericals are on the right. The clerical question, therefore, is not only a main source of political conflict in France but is also the only generally accepted concrete referent of the major symbols of political conflict in France.

Religion is a political issue in France for historical, philosophical, and probably also psychological reasons. The Republicans of the early years of the Third Republic were anticlerical because of the heritage of almost a century of conflict between the Church and Republican forces. French Republicans identified with the revolutionary movement which had overthrown the Old Régime, but that movement had also ended some of the privileges which the Church had enjoyed under that régime, when Church and state were intimately associated. In the eyes of the Church, the revolutionaries and their Republican heirs appeared as opponents of religion, and in the struggle between competing political and social ideals which lasted throughout the nineteenth century, the Church and its staunchest followers opposed the Republicans and supported the Monarchists. The Catholic Church did not acknowledge the legitimacy of the Third Republic until 1892, and many French Catholics continued to oppose the Republic long after that date. The Republicans, on the other hand, distrusted even the Catholics who rallied to the Republic and took advantage of every opportunity to humiliate the Church. Shortly after the turn of the century, the Republicans launched an onslaught on Church schools and religious congregations which brought a protest even from such an unimpeachable Republican as Waldeck-Rousseau. The clerical question became a political question because the Church was involved in the political struggles of the nineteenth century.

The concrete expression of the clerical question is in the field of education. Until early in the Third Republic, religious instruction was given in state schools, but this practice was ended by the Third Republic (although not in Alsace-Lorraine, where the early Third Republic laws did not apply because the area was annexed to Germany at the time, and where the school laws were not applied when the area was returned to France after World War I, with the result that religious instruction continues to be given in the state schools there). The substance of the clerical question, therefore, involved the socialization of French youth. Catholics regarded the educational role of the Church as essential to the maintenance of the Catholic faith, while Republicans regarded a secular school system as essential to the maintenance of the Republic. Throughout the Third Republic, anticlericals insisted on having control of the Ministry of Education, and the parish priest (*curé*) and the state primary school teacher (*instituteur*) were symbols of the clash over the clerical question.

More recently, the issue has turned on whether state aid should be given to private schools which, in practice, are virtually all Catholic schools and which in 1958 accommodated some 17 percent of French school children, mainly in western France. Two relatively recent laws, the Barangé law passed in 1951 and the Debré law passed in 1959, permit state subsidies for Catholic schools under certain conditions. On both occasions, however, the issue was strongly contested, and it is by no means certain that these laws will not be revised one day.

The philosophical and psychological aspects of the clerical question are less evident than the historical one but may well be of equal importance. Anticlericalism has its intellectual origins in the Enlightenment, which represented an emphasis on reason over faith and valued above all the freedom of the mind from dogma. We have already seen that French traditional democrats were not achievement-oriented in the sense of wanting to employ the resources of the state to pursue positive programs of social or economic reform; but they did cherish freedom of criticism. Democrats in this tradition viewed the Church as a constraint upon the freedom of the mind, and they could regard themselves as more progressive even than those devout Catholics who were more favorable than they were to programs of social and economic reform.

The psychological aspect of the question is the most difficult to assess, but it is probably quite real. Republicans opposed authority in almost every form. We will see in a moment how they did all they could to keep the agents of state power—presidents, premiers, and ministers—in a permanent position of subordination. The Church also is a symbol of authority. It is likely that French Republicans viewed the Church as an institution which, like the others, had to be subordinated to the only form of authority which they accepted, because it was diffuse: that of a popularly elected assembly.

The clerical question is still among the most important issues to which French voters respond. It is deeply embedded in the consciousness of many French men and women, laden with emotion, and susceptible of exploitation for partisan purposes. When the Fifth Republic was established, for a while there was a kind of moratorium on normal party politics. The scene was dominated by the Algerian war and people waited for de Gaulle's intentions concerning its settlement to become clear. When the first stirrings of normal political life occurred, it was the clerical question which aroused them. Anticlericalism, under the label secularism (laïcité), is still a central point of doctrine for the elementary public school teachers' union, the Syndicat national des instituteurs (SNI). Religion was a major factor in voting behavior at the presidential election of 1965 (see Chapter 6, p. 162). The issue has also left its imprint on French social patterns. There is evidence to suggest that there are two distinct recruitment patterns for white-collar workers in state and private enterprise: the civil service recruits in the anticlerical southwest and central regions while Parisian business recruits workers for similar jobs in the more strongly Catholic north, west, and east.[7]

To be anticlerical is not the same thing as being anti-Catholic or even non-Catholic. A survey made in 1961 classified 34 percent of the adult population as regular practicing Catholics, 33 percent as occasional practicing Catholics, 18 percent as nonpracticing members of the Catholic tradition, and only 10 percent as unbelievers and 5 percent as members of other faiths. Of the total sample, however, only 47 percent were in favor of private schools, while 37 percent were opposed (although some of those opposed gave as their reason lack of qualified teachers, which implies

[7] Michel Crozier, The Bureaucratic Phenomenon, The University of Chicago Press, Chicago, 1964, pp. 277–278.

no doctrinal hostility to private schools), and 16 percent did not reply to the question.[8]

ECONOMIC AND SOCIAL CONFLICTS

The Republicans had always been divided between groups which were more or less radical and those which were more or less conservative concerning the extent to which they believed that the government ought to regulate the use of property and redistribute the nation's wealth through taxation and spending. These differences naturally became prominent when the Republicans were no longer struggling to establish the Republic, but had to assume responsibility for governing it.

Most of the early Republicans were dedicated to the institution of private property (unless it were owned by the Church), although a few of them were socialists. As French industrial and urban development took place during the nineteenth century, the socialists grew stronger, and in 1905 a unified Socialist Party was formed. The differences between Republicans had earlier involved matters of degree; now they involved matters of principle. The result was that while Republicans like those who formed the Radical Party in 1901 were emotionally and rhetorically close to the Socialists, with whom they shared both republicanism and anticlericalism, they found it easier to agree on economic and social policies with the more conservative groups. During the Third Republic, these included the *Alliance démocratique* (formed in 1901 as a counterweight to the Radical Party) and the *Fédération républicaine* (formed in 1903). The *Alliance démocratique* was, in the main, both republican and anticlerical, but its voters did not respond to the same kind of emotional slogans which the Radicals and Socialists employed. The *Fédération républicaine* was a clerical group attached to hierarchical concepts of social organization.

In 1920, the Socialist Party split when part of its membership decided to join the Third International which had been formed by the Russian Communist Party. The group which split from the Socialists formed the French Communist Party, and this resulted in not simply still another party but a whole new set of problems for the other parties. The Communist Party drew votes from people who responded to the kind of republican and anti-

[8] *Sondages,* 1962, no. 1, pp. 30–31, 51.

clerical appeals made by the Socialists and the Radicals, but its aim was to destroy the democratic republic, not to strengthen it.

The French party system today is not identical with that of the Third Republic. Parties which existed then exist no longer, new parties have appeared, and the balance of strength of the old parties has been altered. But the system retains some of the fundamental characteristics which it acquired early in its history. It is a multiparty system based on various and deep cleavages. The question of the régime, the clerical question, economic and social issues, and pro- and anti-Communist attitudes are the foundations of the system, and French partisans occupy an arena which is rife with conflict.

In 1957 and 1958, a study was made of leading French personalities, including Members of Parliament, in order to discover the factors to which they attributed their success. The replies from union leaders and politicians led the study's author to make this comment: "As they see themselves, these men have a lively ardor of conviction, and they struggle for an ideal and for the defense of their ideas, whatever their orientation is; they are dedicated to a cause which absorbs them completely, and loyalty to their faith plays a large role in their pride. . . . Many of them display the temperament of religious believers, and as they belong to different and sometimes very antagonistic confessions, one can take a better measure of the harshness of the political struggles which can result."[9] This self-image of French politicians understates their adaptability to their estimates of the electorate's changing moods, but it illustrates the intensity with which political cleavages can be expressed in France.

Ministerial Instability

The phenomenon which most people associate with French politics under the Third and Fourth Republics is no doubt ministerial instability, the frequent turnover of Cabinets. This phenomenon can be illustrated by comparing the number of French and English Cabinets and Premiers (or Prime Ministers) during similar periods.

Between the time of the consolidation of the power of the

[9] Alain Girard, *La Réussite sociale en France*, Presses Universitaires de France, Paris, 1961, p. 160. Author's translation.

French Republicans in 1879 and the fall of the Third Republic in 1940, France was governed by a succession of 94 Cabinets, with an average life of 8 months. During the same period, 44 different persons held the post of Premier, occupying the position for an average tenure of 16 months. In Great Britain, during the period between 1880 and 1940, there were only 21 Cabinets, with an average life of almost 3 years, and only 11 persons served as Prime Minister, occupying the position for an average tenure of more than 5 years. Of the 94 French Cabinets of the period, only 8 remained in office for two years or more (none after 1928) and only 10 remained in office between one and two years.[10]

During the life of the Fourth Republic, from 1947 to 1958, the same comparison holds. Omitting the five Cabinets which remained in office for less than a month, and including the last Cabinet of the Republic, 18 Cabinets held office during the period and their average life was the same as that of the Cabinets of the Third Republic—8 months. Fifteen different persons held the post of Premier and occupied the office for an average tenure of 9 months. Two Cabinets remained in office for more than a year (but none more than 16 months). Between January, 1947, and June, 1958, France was in the midst of a Cabinet crisis for 281 days, or the better part of a year.[11] For England, it is possible to extend the comparable period from 1945 until 1963 without affecting the number of Cabinets or Prime Ministers, of which there were only five and four respectively. The average life of these five English Cabinets was 43 months, and the average tenure of these four English Prime Ministers was 54 months.

Still, it is important not to exaggerate. There was a great deal of continuity of personnel and of policy throughout the numerous French Cabinet crises. Most of the crises produced a reshuffling of personnel rather than major shifts in policy, and in this respect they are more properly comparable to reorganizations of an English Cabinet than to changes in administration (although French Cabinets were also reorganized by the Premier from time to time *between* Cabinet crises). At any given time there was

---

[10] Jacques Ollé-Laprune, *La Stabilité des ministres sous la Troisième République, 1879–1940*, R. Pichon & R. Durand-Auzias, Paris, 1962, pp. 231–236.

[11] The data on French Cabinets and crises during the Fourth Republic is from Serge Arné, *Le Président du Conseil des Ministres sous la IVe République*, R. Pichon & R. Durand-Auzias, Paris, 1962, pp. 300–306.

a small pool of *ministrables*—former Ministers who were leading candidates for a return to office—among whom major posts were rotated. These senior men served for long periods of time, although not always continuously, and they often served in the same post. Even when posts changed hands, there was often continuity of party control of that post.

Between 1879 and 1940 there were 94 French Cabinets, but 45 of them included at least one-half of the members of the previous Cabinet; on 16 occasions the outgoing Premier succeeded himself in the same post; and there were only 12 occasions when the new Cabinet did not contain a single member of the previous one. More than 10 percent of the French Ministers who were appointed more than once served for more than five years. Six men together served for 34 years as Minister for Foreign Affairs; seven for 32 years as Minister of Finance; and five for 23 years as Minister of Agriculture. Between 1920 and 1940, the Radical Party controlled the Ministry of the Interior for 12½ years, the Ministry of Education for 12 years, and the Ministry of Agriculture for 10 years.[12]

Most of the same considerations apply also to the Fourth Republic. No French Premier succeeded himself during the Fourth Republic, but between January, 1947, and June, 1958, the new Premier came from the previous Cabinet on 16 of 21 occasions, and at no time was there a complete turnover in the composition of the Cabinet. The Ministry of Foreign Affairs was occupied by only two men, from the same party, for all but a few weeks of the period from September, 1944, to June, 1954. Between the Liberation and the end of the Fourth Republic, the Minister of the Interior and the Minister of Education were almost always either Radicals or Socialists.[13]

A comparative study of ministerial personnel in Great Britain and France between 1945 and 1957 has shown that the average rate of appointment of new men as Ministers was almost identical in the two countries.[14] Changes of Government and ministerial

[12] Ollé-Laprune, *op. cit.*, pp. 67, 231–236, 259, 288–289.

[13] For the composition of the Cabinets of the Fourth Republic, see Philip M. Williams, *Crisis and Compromise; Politics in the Fourth Republic*, Longmans, London, 1964, Appendix 3.

[14] Mattei Dogan and Peter Campbell, "Le personnel ministériel en France et en Grande-Bretagne (1945–1957)," *Revue Française de Science Politique*, VII (April–June, 1957), 338, 340, and VII (October–December, 1957), 796.

reorganizations in England were less numerous than Cabinet crises and Cabinet reorganizations in France but, on the average, after each personnel change, 72 percent of the English Ministers remained in the ministry and 71 percent of the French Ministers remained in the Cabinet, most of them continuing to hold the same posts. But if the rate of introduction of new Ministers hardly differed in the two countries, it is still true that changes in the composition of the ministry were made more frequently in France than in Great Britain and that French Premiers rotated in office at a much faster rate than English Prime Ministers.

REASONS FOR MINISTERIAL INSTABILITY

Ministerial instability during the Third and Fourth Republics was partly a reflection of the traditional democratic outlook and partly the result of the difficulty of governing a country with a multiparty system based on deep cleavages.

It reflected the traditional democratic view in that it implemented the subordination of the executive to the popularly elected assembly. The early French Republicans, in particular, were deeply suspicious of executive power. The institutions which they created might have permitted a stable and authoritative executive to develop, but they followed unwritten political rules which made the legislature the main locus of political power and subordinated the executive to the legislature.

Parliament prevented the presidency from becoming a source of strong executive leadership under the Third Republic by driving the first three Presidents (and later a fourth) from office and by almost always passing over candidates for the office who could be expected to wield its powers vigorously. The first President of the Fourth Republic was a prominent figure who exercised considerable influence from the office, but he incurred hostilities in doing so and his successor, who was not a nationally known leader at the time of his election, preferred to play a more modest role until the last days of the régime, when he threatened to resign if Charles de Gaulle were not made Premier.

Ambitious, strong-willed, and popular leaders could become Premier, but the price which Parliament exacted for this concession to the necessity for leadership was frequent rotation in office. The Constitution of the Third Republic gave the President the power to dissolve the Chamber of Deputies, with the consent of the Senate, and if it had been exploited skillfully, the dissolution power might have helped to restore the balance between the executive and the popularly elected chamber. But President Mac-Mahon abused the power in 1877, and the Senate became populated with politicians as mistrustful of executive power as were the Deputies of the Chamber. No further use was made of the dissolution power until 1955 (by then under different constitutional rules), and Premiers were obliged to perform their duties under the jealous eyes of Deputies who rarely allowed them to hold their posts for more than a year at a time. Premiers who wanted to return to office were made to understand that they should exit gracefully when the parliamentary tide began to turn against them.

As time passed, French political leaders came to doubt the wisdom of these practices. By the time the Fourth Republic was established, many French politicians, particularly those from urban and economically modern areas, were convinced of the need for positive governmental action in order to overcome or prevent economic and social problems. Under the Fourth Republic, Premiers often refused to depart from office without a fight, exhausting their constitutional powers and their energy in efforts to forestall a decisive vote against them. The dissolution of 1955 is illustrative in this respect, although it failed to alter the situation. By that time the problem of instability was caused more by the divisions among the parties and their leaders than by doctrinaire antagonism to executive power. Still, the extent to which the old practices were symbols of higher values appears clearly in the remark made in 1959 by Vincent Auriol, who had been the influential first President of the Fourth Republic, that liberty would be gone when there were no more ministerial crises.

Ministerial instability also reflected the difficulty of governing with a divided leadership. Under the multiparty system of the Third and Fourth Republics, no single party came close to winning a parliamentary majority by itself. French Governments always depended upon a coalition of parliamentary parties for their majorities, and the Governments themselves were almost always coalitions, in that they contained representatives of two or (and usually) more parties.

It required arduous political bargaining among the parties to establish the terms on which coalitions could be formed, and the bargaining generally produced agreement over only a limited number of questions and for a relatively short period of time. The emergence of a new problem or the expiration of the sort of "contract" which the coalition members had been able to agree on earlier would require the start of a new round of bargaining. The fact that the groups were numerous meant that several different coalitions were almost always possible, and the fact that Premiers were rotated frequently meant that there were almost always several candidates available to lead a new coalition, even if it might differ only marginally in composition and policy from the previous one.

In these circumstances, Cabinet crises became as much a central feature of French political life as the multiparty system or the constitutional bodies, and they were conducted with as much form and ritual as parliamentary operations themselves.[15] The provocation of a Cabinet crisis was a stage in the bargaining process among the groups of a coalition in much the same way as a strike or a lockout is a stage in the bargaining process in industrial relations. References made to the need for "arbitration" by critics of the practice were not without relevance to the problem. In order to emphasize how much importance it attached to its particular demands, one group would withdraw from the coalition and cause a crisis. The seriousness of French Cabinet crises varied widely, depending upon the importance of the issues at stake and the diversity and intensity of the various groups' attitudes toward them. Whether the crisis was serious or not, its form was almost always the same. Bargaining among the partners in a coalition over what that coalition should do was transformed into bargaining among potential partners in a new coalition over what the composition and policies of the new coalition should be.

[15] On the ritual of Cabinet crises, see Williams, *op. cit.*, chap. 29.

CHAPTER TWO

From the Third Republic
to the Fifth Republic

FOR ABOUT THE FIRST 50 YEARS of the Third Republic, the economic and social characteristics of France were quite compatible with the intense suspicion of political power which defined the traditional French conception of democracy and which was reflected in presidential weakness and ministerial instability.[1]

France was a major power and an industrial nation in the nineteenth century, but it was the least industrialized and urbanized of the industrial nations and the one with the largest percentage of its population engaged in agriculture and living in rural areas and small towns. The demands of the agricultural and small-town population were minimal and did not require the continuous and active intervention in social and economic affairs which can be accomplished only by a stable and authoritative executive. Farmers seemed content to produce for local markets made secure by a tariff wall; much of French manufacturing was done on a small scale in the family-owned and managed firms; and France's numerous small shopkeepers were not inclined to assume the risks of expansion which might have gotten them into the kind of trouble from which only governmental intervention could extricate them.

Absorbed in their own affairs, these groups—which were dominant in the electorate—asked little of the government in the form of positive action, although they might ask much of the Deputy in the form of local protection against such intervention in their affairs as the central bureaucracy did undertake. In a

[1] This analysis follows that presented by François Goguel, *France Under the Fourth Republic*, Cornell, Ithaca, N.Y., 1952, chap. 5.

society such as this, which perceived little need for the exercise of governmental power to achieve social goals, politics could be confined to the symbolic struggle between the local priest and the elementary school teacher. Cabinets might come and go, but these mysterious political rites, only dimly understood by most French men and women, had little direct bearing upon the course of people's lives.

In this respect, there is truth to the frequent assertions that the turbulence of French politics during the Third Republic was a superficial phenomenon which contrasted sharply with the stable social foundations on which it rested.

But if there is truth to the notion that a stable society underlay an almost artificial political instability, it is not the whole truth. Economic development was producing social consequences with important political implications. French cities were smaller than English cities, but they were growing. The industrial working class was less numerous proportionately than the English or German working classes, but a large working class was forming. Most farmers and businessmen may have been producing on a small scale for local markets, but economic units were growing larger and extending their activities. The harmonious operation of an increasingly complex society was becoming increasingly dependent upon the adjustment and control of relations among various domestic groups and between France and other nations.

These developments were creating social problems which required the attention of the political authorities, but the suspicion of political power which dominated the political system limited the capacity of the political leadership for innovation in the light of new and changing social needs. Moreover, there was little immediate incentive for the leadership to act in order to meet these needs, as the majority of the population lived in conditions which encouraged their political representatives to keep the government weak. The provinces were suspicious of the industrial cities, and the provinces dominated Parliament.

The urban areas and the industrial working class were politically represented. France has an old indigenous socialist tradition; unions were made legal early in the 1880s; a unified Socialist Party was formed in 1905; and the Communist Party was created in 1920. But the working-class parties were without significant influence in the policy-making process until late in the Third Republic. In part, this was because they represented only a minority of the population and because the electoral system tended to operate to their competitive disadvantage. In part, it was because they acted in a manner which reduced the political influence which they might otherwise have been able to wield.

The Socialist Party was Marxist in inspiration; it was convinced of the reality of class conflict; and many of its leaders were convinced that it would be impossible for the working class to achieve any significant social and economic gains short of the party's winning undivided political control of the nation. Many Socialists did not want to enter coalition Governments with the bourgeois parties because they did not believe that any results of lasting value could be achieved by doing so. The Socialist Deputies sometimes supported bourgeois Governments, but the Socialists did not fully participate as a party in a French Government until 1936, when the Socialist leader, Léon Blum, formed the Popular Front Government which rested on the support of the Socialists, the Communists, and the Radicals. It may be that the rigid outlook of the Socialists before 1936 was essential if they were to compete successfully with the Communists for working-class votes, but it also made the Socialist Party appear revolutionary when in fact it was not. The policy frightened the middle-class parties and voters without providing any compensation in the form of direct satisfaction of working-class needs.

It is doubtful whether the Communist Party was interested at all in achieving immediate, direct benefits for its supporters. The Communist Party was interested primarily in building its organizational strength for an eventual conquest of power and in supporting the Soviet Union. The party never participated in a Government during the Third Republic and it did not support one until 1936, when the Popular Front Government was formed. Communist support of the Popular Front Government was made possible by a new turn in Russian foreign policy after 1934, when Russia's fear of Nazi Germany led it to encourage the participation of Communists in coalition Governments in France and elsewhere.

Various factors, therefore, account for the inadequate representation of urban and working-class interests in the policy-making process before 1936. The inadequacy of this representation not only

worked hardships on the people concerned but was also dangerous
for the stability of the political system. Attention to the needs of
the industrial workers could not be postponed indefinitely, but
they had been postponed long enough to make the Popular Front
coalition, which took form between 1934 and 1936, appear to its
opponents as a revolutionary movement when in fact it was simply
reformist.

The Crisis of the Thirties

The potentially disruptive forces boiling beneath the surface of
French politics erupted during the 1930s, and the comparative
political calm which France had enjoyed throughout the Third
Republic was destroyed. The major impetus for what was to appear as a breakdown of the political system came from the depression, but it was heightened and reinforced by other events as
well: Hitler's advent to power in Germany, the emergence of the
Soviet Union from its international isolation and the emergence of
the French Communist Party from its domestic political isolation,
and the succession of international crises which formed the pro-
logue to World War II.

The impact of the depression did not strike France until 1932,
and its economic consequences were not as severe in France as in
Germany, England, or the United States. But unemployment
increased and the standard of living dropped, particularly among
farmers and the middle-class groups.[2] French Governments had
been far from stable in more favoring circumstances; they became
even more precarious in the face of the economic crisis. Between
1931 and 1940 the average life of a Government was 5 months,
compared to 8 months for the Third Republic as a whole. Governments of all political orientations were poorly informed about
economic matters and made unwise decisions, with the result that
by 1939 France was to make the poorest economic recovery of the
Western industrial nations. The most decisive error was probably
the decision made in the early 1930s, and not reversed until 1936,
to pursue a deflationary policy. This was economically unwise at
a time when strategic pump-priming might have been helpful and

[2] Georges Dupeux, *Le Front Populaire et les élections de 1936*, Armand
Colin, Paris, 1959, pp. 24–40.

the devaluation of the franc was a national necessity, and it had serious political consequences, as the prospect of reduced incomes and pensions probably helped to swell the ranks of discontented veterans' organizations and other groups which were emerging in opposition to the Government and, in some cases, to the régime itself.

The French parliamentary system came under strong critical attack during the 1930s, in almost every case for its failure to deal more authoritatively with the problems of the times. There was nothing new about opposition to the régime, nor was there anything new about the formation of new groups outside the arena of normal party competition for purposes of attacking the régime. Since the founding of the *Action Française* in 1905, its traditional authoritarians had poured invective on the Republic, and the emergence of antiparliamentary movements—usually referred to as leagues—had been a recurrent French political phenomenon since the early 1880s. But during the 1930s, the opposition to the régime came from more varied sources, ranged more widely and took on more contemporary and dangerous aspects than had that of earlier times.

Opposition generated among groups which had normally supported the régime, as in the case of those socialists—called the Neo-Socialists—who adopted the slogan "Order, Authority, Nation" in order to convey their conviction that a coherent national effort was required by the domestic and international crises of the period. Some of the leagues which, with the toughs of *Action Française* and the support of certain veterans' organizations, took to the streets in February, 1934, were inspired by the Italian Fascist or even the German Nazi model more than by traditional French models of political organization. The germination of the Popular Front alliance intensified anti-Communist demagogy and contributed toward reinforcing the atmosphere of crisis. A variety of ephemeral organizations were formed for the purpose of criticizing the régime and the society.[3]

A movement to revise the Constitution along lines which were eventually to be adopted when the Fifth Republic was established in 1958 was spearheaded by two prominent political figures in

[3] See Stanley Hoffmann, "Paradoxes of the French Political Community," in Stanley Hoffmann *et al.*, *In Search of France*, Harvard, Cambridge, Mass., 1963, pp. 21–34.

1934.[4] André Tardieu, a reform-minded Conservative who had been Premier three times between 1929 and 1933, and Gaston Doumergue, a Radical who had been President of the Republic from 1924 to 1931 and who was called back from retirement to head the Government in 1934 after an antiparliamentary street demonstration in Paris resulted in some 15 deaths and over 1000 injuries, undertook campaigns to strengthen the executive relative to Parliament. Both men urged that the executive be given the power to dissolve the Chamber of Deputies without the consent of the Senate and that the right of the Deputies to initiate financial legislation be restricted. Tardieu also proposed that the executive be authorized to hold advisory referendums, a method by which the executive could appeal directly to the people over the heads of refractory Members of Parliament. The clamor for constitutional reform was sufficiently loud for both chambers of Parliament to set up committees on state reform, and the committee of the Chamber of Deputies adopted a set of proposals similar to those advocated by Doumergue. Doumergue's Government fell when he lost the support of the Radical Party, however, and constitutional revision was shelved.

Whether reforms of the kind urged by Doumergue and Tardieu could have strengthened the Republic is questionable. French Governments were weak because they were divided and unsure of themselves, and many of the same mistakes which they made, both in domestic and foreign policy, were also made by other Western governments which were more united and more stable. The Republicans' doctrinaire antagonism to authority was a serious weakness in the light of the problems which required governmental decisiveness, but it was not unreasonable for Republicans to refuse to permit the Chamber of Deputies to be dissolved in 1934, when the opponents of parliamentary democracy appeared to be stronger than ever.

Moreover, the critics of the Third Republic were as divided and mutually incompatible as the Republicans themselves. They included socialists and capitalists, pacifists and militarists, clericals

[4] See Nicholas Wahl, "The French Constitution of 1958: The Initial Draft and Its Origins," *American Political Science Review*, LIII (June, 1959), 379–380; and Jean Gicquel, "Le problème de la réforme de l'État en France en 1934," in Jean Gicquel and Lucien Sfez, *Problèmes de la réforme de l'État depuis 1934*, Presses Universitaires de France, Paris, 1965.

and anticlericals, traditionalists and fascists, people who had never participated in the system and people who had achieved the highest posts it could offer. Each group which criticized the régime in the name of authority had its own conception of how that authority should be exercised and of the ends toward which it should be directed. The critics of the régime were neither more united nor stronger than the régime's defenders, as the elections of 1936 were to demonstrate. For at that election, the coalition of Communists, Socialists, and Radicals won a majority of the seats in the Chamber of Deputies, and Léon Blum then formed the Popular Front Government.

The Popular Front Government enacted some overdue reforms, particularly in the sphere of labor relations, but the new coalition was no more successful in confronting the international crisis —now intensified by the outbreak of the Civil War in Spain and German occupation of the formerly demilitarized Rhineland— than earlier Governments had been, and it proved to be just as fragile. The Radicals, despite their name, were too conservative to support the Government indefinitely and they provoked its fall a year later.

The Popular Front Government left an atmosphere of bitterness in its wake. Many of its opponents regarded it as bolshevist and many of its supporters regarded all opposition to it as fascist. Foreign and domestic attitudes became intermingled so that some opponents of the Government began to see virtues in fascism and nazism that they had not seen before, while some supporters of the Government overlooked indefensible aspects of Communist rule in Russia. Yet for all that, by the time World War II broke out in 1939, the French political crisis appeared to be over. There were no more demands for constitutional revision, and it seemed almost as though France had returned to its old political routines. The illusion was shattered by the German army.

The German army succeeded in accomplishing what the domestic opponents of the Third Republic had failed to do: it broke the self-confidence of the leaders of the Republic. Military defeat came to France in May, 1940, and that summer, Frenchmen were offered an historic choice. They could either follow Charles de Gaulle, who had broadcast an appeal from London to continue resistance to the Germans, or they could follow Marshal Pétain, who had signed an armistice with the Germans. The overwhelm-

ing majority of the politicians of the Third Republic opted for
Pétain by voting in July to give him full powers and to authorize
him to prepare a new constitution for France. Only a few of the
Members of Parliament who voted to destroy the régime which
they had embodied were actually opponents of that régime; many
of them had belonged to the Popular Front majority (although
no Communists voted for Pétain; the Communist Party had been
outlawed in September, 1939, and its Members of Parliament un-
seated early in 1940). But most of the Members of Parliament
had become defeatist. They believed that Germany would win the
war with England, and they followed the lead of Pierre Laval,
who argued that if they did not establish a new régime modeled
on the authoritarian dictatorships, the Germans would impose
one on them.

With about one-half of France occupied by the Germans, most
French Deputies and Senators lost confidence in themselves and
in the future. They abdicated their powers and their responsibilities
to an 84-year-old Marshal, and they could not conceive of Germany's defeat. In the light of this situation, one may perhaps say
that the most serious consequence of ministerial instability during
the Third Republic was that it had habituated French political
leaders to giving priority to the daily negotiations among members
of the Government and between the Government and Parliament
that were necessary if they were to stay in office, thereby exhausting
energies which might otherwise have been spent in considering
France's future.

The Vichy Régime

The Vichy régime was not a homogeneous political system for
the simple reason that it reflected the diversity and the contra-
dictions of the opponents of the Third Republic.[5] At various times
the leadership of Vichy included former Ministers or Members
of Parliament of the Third Republic (including Pierre Laval, the
dominant figure of the Vichy régime). For the most part, however, the men of Vichy had either opposed the Republic, been
deliberately excluded from its posts of political power, or had not

[5] This analysis follows that presented by Stanley Hoffmann in "Aspects du
régime de Vichy," *Revue Française de Science Politique*, VI (January–March,
1956), 44–69.

known how to reach those posts through the political processes which the Republic provided. The Vichy régime evolved considerably during its few years of existence, as different groups became dominant. The range of inspiration and acts between 1940 and 1944 was far wider than that which the shifting coalitions of the Third Republic had ever produced.

The initial conception of the régime, which was labeled the National Revolution and which gave the régime its distinctive overt characteristics for about two years, reflected the French traditional authoritarian political and social ideals. The Vichy régime dismantled the characteristic institutions of the Republic and sought to replace them with other institutions more in accordance with ideals which derived from early nineteenth- and even eighteenth-century France.

Vichy did not restore the monarchy, but Marshal Pétain, undeterred by the fact that he held his own position by virtue of a decision of a popularly elected Parliament, proceeded on the assumption that he was entitled to name his successor. Although his powers of decision were faltering by early 1941 and he was losing his grip on the conduct of affairs, he was the legal source of all authority under the régime. The principle of popular sovereignty was abandoned: elections were abolished for all assemblies except the local councils of towns with fewer than 2000 inhabitants. Parliament was adjourned, departmental and *arrondissement* councils were suspended, as were the councils of 163 larger cities and towns and, in 1941, political party activity of any kind was suspended.

The rights and guarantees accorded by the Third Republic were abolished. The Republican motto of *Liberté, Égalité, Fraternité* was replaced with *Travail, Famille, Patrie* (adopted, it must be added, by the last Parliament of the Third Republic). The customary and legal protections against abusive police power disappeared, the rules governing the civil service (including those protecting judges) were suspended, and more than 2000 civil servants were purged inside of six months. The press was censored. Anti-Jewish measures were adopted early and progressively made more repressive.

The secular character of the Republic was reversed. The teacher-training schools—called normal schools—were closed, free secondary school education was abolished, and state aid to Catholic schools was restored. This emphasis on religion was part of a larger effort to establish a form of moral order based on preindustrial social concepts. Traditional French authoritarianism had been in favor of decentralization and Vichy also was theoretically in favor of the development of "natural" communities, such as the family, the occupational group, and the region. But while families are natural groups, occupations and regions require organizational bases, and these Vichy only unevenly supplied. Decentralization never was achieved because the electoral principle which it requires was abandoned. The régime hoped to achieve occupational organization through a form of corporatism, but before it could set up its own "natural" organizations it had to abolish those labor unions and employers' associations which had developed under the Third Republic. The régime was not sympathetic to socialism, of course, but neither was it sympathetic to modern capitalism. It preached a return to the pastoral virtues and promoted working the land into a high moral principle.

By 1942, the National Revolution was bankrupt. It could hardly have been otherwise, for what it tried to do was impossible. The conception of France which underlay the National Revolution was compatible only with a preindustrial society, oriented toward a universal Church, without group loyalties extending beyond one's occupation and without the experience of participation in a national, free, and secular community. The kind of society envisaged by the early leaders of Vichy emerges spontaneously in favoring conditions or it does not exist at all.

The early leaders of Vichy were neither pro-German nor inspired by totalitarianism, yet the régime evolved increasingly toward collaboration with the Germans and toward the establishment of institutions and practices more similar to those of twentieth-century dictatorships than of eighteenth-century traditionalist monarchies. The Germans occupied one-half of France from the start, and after November, 1942, when the Allies invaded North Africa, they occupied the remainder of France as well; and they made increasingly severe demands for collaboration on the Vichy Government. The Germans also subsidized and encouraged the pro-German and committed French Nazi sympathizers, who were centered mainly in Paris and not at Vichy, thereby exercising a form of blackmail over the Vichy leaders, who knew the Germans might replace them with even more pliant types.

The early Vichy leaders did not want to establish a single-party system, but their inability to make their archaic conception of a new French order work spontaneously led them to create a number of strategic points of social and economic control. Unschooled in the arts of totalitarianism, they never fully exploited these instruments of power themselves, although these were seized upon by pro-German Frenchmen without scruples who used them to secure eventual control of the régime. The Vichy régime was so unworkable in the conditions of occupied France that parts of its administrative apparatus were at the direct service of the German occupiers and other parts of it were in complicity with Resistance forces.

The Vichy régime never succeeded in establishing its conception of order even though it probably had the tacit support of most of the French population at the start. Its Governments were hardly more stable than the Governments of the Third Republic, and the head of state, Marshal Pétain, was as incapable of making decisive choices as less renowned leaders of Third Republic Cabinets had been. When it became apparent that the initial and commanding assumption of the men of Vichy that Germany would win the war was wrong, the régime took on a different aspect. Pressured by Germany for men and materials, the Vichy leaders were placed in a situation where they became increasingly the agents of a German government rather than a French one. Resistance efforts increased sharply in 1943, as Frenchmen took to the maquis in large numbers in order to escape being shipped to work in German factories. Finally, the German ambassador in Paris was naming French Ministers, and by the beginning of 1944 the French Cabinet consisted exclusively of pro-German adventurers. What had started out as an authentically French régime, based on an archaic but traditional French conception, became a satellite state run by men who were either so far committed that there was no turning back or so deceived by their limited vision that they believed either that Germany would win the war or that they could survive politically a German defeat.

The Resistance

While many Frenchmen chose to follow the route through Vichy to the armistice with Germany, and some even to collaboration with the Germans, others chose the Resistance. And just as the option for Vichy meant abandonment of the political system of the Third Republic, so eventually did the option for the Resistance. For if the Resistance organizations necessarily were hostile to the Vichy régime because of its acceptance of the armistice with Germany and its collaborationist policies, they were also antagonistic to the Third Republic, whose leaders and institutions they held responsible for the French military defeat.

The French Resistance was a complex phenomenon, as a variety of groups were organized separately and remained for some time without communication with one another. The main distinction is between Charles de Gaulle's Free France group, which was formed in London, and its networks of agents in Metropolitan France, on one hand, and the several internal Resistance groups which were formed separately in Metropolitan France, on the other. The internal Resistance may be further divided between the groups of the occupied zone, consisting of northern France and the entire Atlantic coast region, and the southern zone, which was not occupied by the Germans until the Allies invaded North Africa in November, 1942. The main groups in the occupied zone were the *Organisation Civile et Militaire* (OCM), *Libération-Nord, Ceux de la Résistance* (CDLR), *Ceux de la Libération* (CDLL), and the Communist-organized *Front National*, whose military arm was called the *Franc-Tireurs et Partisans* (FTP). The principal groups in the southern zone were *Combat, Libération-Sud*, and *Franc-Tireur*. The *Front National* operated in the southern zone also, but it was less active there than in the north.

Gradually, these groups were coordinated with one another and unified under the formal leadership of de Gaulle. The three main southern groups first coordinated their operations through the *Mouvements Unis de Résistance* (MUR), which was formed in March, 1943, and a coordinating committee for the northern zone was formed by the five large northern groups at about the same time. By May, 1943, all eight groups were represented in the *Conseil National de la Résistance* (CNR), whose first president was Jean Moulin, a former prefect who became de Gaulle's general delegate to the Resistance organizations in Metropolitan France.

Although the creation of the CNR meant the formal unification of the Resistance under the leadership of de Gaulle, it also marked the reappearance on the scene of the prewar political parties, because the Council was composed not only of delegates from the main Resistance groups, but also of delegates from six political parties and two labor unions. The decision to give such formal recognition to the political parties was opposed by many of the Resistance leaders, in particular by Pierre Brossolette, a young Socialist who, along with Moulin, had been a prime force in the unification of the Resistance. Moulin (and eventually de Gaulle) believed that it would be useful to have the French parties represented in the Council in order to demonstrate to France's allies—in particular to President Roosevelt—that de Gaulle was the leader of a united nation. Brossolette and other Resistance leaders, however, thought otherwise. Although Brossolette had made a similar gesture earlier by going to London in the company of a conservative political figure in order to emphasize that political distinctions were effaced by the Resistance, he came to believe that it would be an error to revive the old parties and that a new Resistance party should be formed in order to launch postwar France along new lines entirely.

This view was shared by many other Resistance leaders as well. Almost all of them, whether attached to de Gaulle at London or to the groups in France, were "new" men—men who had not occupied positions of prominence during the Third Republic. The earliest metropolitan groups were organized by junior officers, journalists, students, teachers, administrators, businessmen, young Socialists, trade unionists, and liberal Catholics, none of whom had played a major role before the war. Many of them had been critics of the Third Republic; some of them had participated in the revisionist current of the middle 1930s; and the liberal Catholics had been without influence in the anticlerical régime.[6] These men believed that France's older political leadership had failed completely. Few senior officers and no top-ranking political figure of the Third Republic had joined de Gaulle at London. The overwhelming majority of the Members of Parliament had voted full powers to Pétain, who had negotiated an armistice which the Resistance leaders regarded as shameful. The men of the Resistance risked their lives daily to maintain French honor and independence, and many of them felt that the Resistance groups, rather than the political parties, were best fitted to shape France's postwar régime.

[6] See Stanley Hoffmann, "Paradoxes of the French Political Community," *op. cit.*, p. 33.

Even before the formation of the CNR, however, political parties were making reappearances or being formed. Socialists, who were active mainly in the two *Libération* groups, had formed a *Comité d'Action Socialiste* as early as the spring of 1941, and while it contained only members of the Resistance, it was the beginning of the reconstruction of the Socialist Party. In the spring of 1943, the liberal Catholics—who were active mainly in *Combat*—began to think of creating the new party which was eventually to be the postwar *Mouvement Républicain Populaire* (MRP). And most importantly, the Communist Party had formed its own Resistance organization, *Front National*, and as early as October, 1942, the party's name was printed on Resistance tracts and manifestoes. The *Front National* was organized in such a way as to encourage non-Communists to join it, and it may well be that Moulin suspected the Communists of trying to absorb the other Resistance forces, in which case his formation of the CNR might have been motivated also by the desire to prevent such a development by demonstrating through the composition of the CNR that the *Front National* was only one of eight Resistance organizations and the Communist Party only one of six political parties.

Many men of the Resistance wanted not only to replace the personnel of the Third Republic but also to recontruct its political institutions. Accordingly, a great deal of consideration was given by the Resistance groups to the kind of political structure France should have after the Liberation. This was the period of what has been called "theorizing in the maquis,"[7] and proposals for new constitutions were produced at such a rate that it became a Resistance joke to say that "every *résistant* has his own constitution."[8]

There was not, of course, complete unanimity concerning the kind of political system France ought to have. The Communists did not participate in this preliminary constitution-drafting process, and the groups which did did not produce identical blueprints for the future. But there was something approaching unanimity in the way in which the groups that did propose new structures concentrated their attention on strengthening the executive in order to promote stability and authority. OCM proposed a system with

[7] Gordon Wright, *The Reshaping of French Democracy*, Harcourt, Brace & World, New York, 1948, p. 30.

[8] Henry Michel, *Les Courants de pensée de la Résistance*, Presses Universitaires de France, Paris, 1962, p. 376.

a popularly elected President and without a popularly elected national legislature; "Défense de la France" proposed a presidential system in which the President would be elected by an electoral college of some 1000 members and would have the power to dissolve the National Assembly. The principal planning group of the Resistance, the *Comité Général d'Études* (of which Michel Debré, the first Premier of the Fifth Republic, was a member), proposed to modify the system of the Third Republic by adding a provision for the dissolution of the Assembly by the President, although the MUR disapproved of the whole proposal, which did not depart very far from the institutions of the Third Republic. Leaders of the emerging MRP also recommended a stronger executive, and so even did leaders of the Socialist Party. Vincent Auriol, who had been Minister of Finance in the Popular Front Government of Léon Blum and who was to become the first President of the Fourth Republic, proposed in 1942 that the Assembly be automatically dissolved when it reversed a Government. Léon Blum himself, writing from prison, said that the parliamentary system was not the appropriate form of democratic government for France and that he personally inclined toward the American or Swiss systems with their separation of powers.

Some people, of course, believed that the institutions of the Third Republic should be retained, but they were in a minority. When General Giraud, one of de Gaulle's rivals for the leadership of the Resistance, indicated that he intended after the war to apply a Third Republic law (the Treveneuc law) which provided that power be vested in the departmental councils (*conseils généraux*) in the event of Parliament's inability to meet, his proposal met with the unanimous hostility of the Resistance groups in Metropolitan France. There was not unanimous agreement about the shape of the institutions which would replace those of the Third Republic, but it is apparent from the record that there was more widespread support for strengthening the executive relative to Parliament than had ever before appeared in Republican France.

The Constitution of the Fourth Republic

The discredit which had fallen on the Third Republic was reflected at a popular referendum which was held in October,

1945, under the Provisional Government headed by Charles de Gaulle. One of the questions asked at the referendum was whether the electorate preferred to re-establish the institutions of the Third Republic or to have a constituent assembly draft a new constitution. Most political leaders recommended abandoning the Third Republic; and the voters followed their lead by repudiating the Third Republic by an overwhelming majority. Some 96 percent of the voters indicated that they would prefer a new system, and the assembly which they elected at the same time went to work to draft a new constitution.

It became evident early in the deliberations of the Constituent Assembly that the parties which dominated it—the Communist Party, the Socialist Party, and the MRP—were not in fact going to make the reinforcement of the executive their primary constitutional aim. They all repudiated the Third Republic, but in institutional terms this repudiation took the form of rejection of the French Senate, the indirectly elected second chamber of Parliament, rather than rejection of close control of the executive by the legislature.

This attack on the Senate, which was made the scapegoat for the ills of the Third Republic, is perfectly intelligible. The Senate of the Third Republic has been called "the most important and characteristic institution" of that régime.[9] Its composition reflected closely what was probably the dominant body of opinion in the country; it was politically democratic but economically and socially conservative; it was firmly anticlerical but it was not socialist; it was opposed to the hierarchical social structure identified with prerevolutionary France but it was oriented toward maintaining the social equalitarianism of France's small towns rather than toward satisfying the economic needs of France's growing industrial areas.

The attack on the Senate was symbolic of a new mood in French politics created by the three large parties which dominated the first few postwar years. Socialist ideas had penetrated the Resistance movements, and the antagonism toward the old Senate was symbolic of the urge for social and economic reforms. The attack on an institution which was the expression of small-town France was in part also a reflection of growing awareness of the needs of a modern industrial nation. And the opposition of the

[9] Philip Williams, *Politics in Post-War France*, Longmans, London, 1958, p. 267.

MRP to this characteristic institution of the Third Republic was symbolic of a desire to displace the anticlerical bias of the Third Republic. The Catholics who formed the MRP had proven in the Resistance that they were no less loyal to France than the anti-clericals; they wanted to demonstrate further that they were no less democratic and social-minded. It is comprehensible that they should have wanted to rid France of an institution which embodied anticlericalism.

While all three major parties wanted to abolish the Senate, they could not agree on other central constitutional questions. The Communist Party favored a system in which the executive would be subordinated to a single legislative assembly, and the Socialist Party preferred this solution to the separation of powers system which their leader, Léon Blum, had suggested might be more appropriate for France. De Gaulle indicated his displeasure with the turn that the constitutional debates were taking by resigning in January, 1946, although he did not carry his constitutional case to the public for another 6 months. The MRP, however, held out against the Communist-Socialist majority in the Constituent Assembly, although it did not so much take the position that the executive should be strengthened as that some checks—either in the form of bicameralism or of a system of control over the constitutionality of laws—should be placed on the power of a parliamentary majority.

When the Constituent Assembly finished its work and submitted the constitutional draft which it had prepared to a referendum in May, 1946, the draft was supported by the Communists and Socialists, but opposed by the MRP. The draft was defeated by about a million votes, probably largely because it was the product of a Communist-Socialist majority, and a Second Constituent Assembly was elected in June, 1946, to prepare a new constitutional draft.

This time, the Socialist Party did not hew so closely to the position taken by the Communists, but showed itself disposed to compromise with the MRP on various points. The net result was not the production of a constitution providing for a strong and independent executive, but rather a constitution which provided for a limited amount of control over the popularly elected legislative assembly through the establishment of a second chamber, called at that time the Council of the Republic, whose composition could be expected eventually to differ politically from that of the lower house, the National Assembly. But before this second draft had been completed, General de Gaulle broke the silence he had entered in January, 1946, by making the now famous Bayeux speech, in which he called for the establishment of a constitutional system providing for a strong and independent executive. The second constitutional draft was presented to the voters at a referendum, in October, 1946; it was supported by the three big parties but opposed by de Gaulle. The draft was accepted, but there were many more abstentions than there had been earlier, and while the legality of the electorate's adoption of the new constitution could not be doubted, there was some ground for later Gaullist assertions that the Constitution of the Fourth French Republic had been adopted without enthusiasm and amidst considerable popular indifference.

The Gaullist Revisionist Movement

Scarcely had the Fourth Republic gotten under way before it was confronted with a set of challenges which were to beset it for most of its existence. The Communist Party, which had participated in French Governments after the Liberation, went into the opposition in the spring of 1947. This meant the transposition into domestic French politics of the international Cold War, and from the spring of 1947 until the end of the Fourth Republic, French Governments were handicapped by the presence of between 100 and 200 Communist Deputies, who narrowed the spectrum of Deputies from which parliamentary majorities could be constructed. Premiers did not seek Communist support because of the kind of concessions they would have had to make to receive it, and they rejected Communist support even when it was proffered unconditionally because to accept it would have discredited them. But if Communist votes could not help a Government, they counted along with everyone else's when they were cast against Governments and their policies.

Even before the Communists departed from the Government and the majority, Charles de Gaulle had launched a new political movement, the *Rassemblement du Peuple Français* (RPF), for the purpose of building national support in favor of establishing a new régime. The RPF won about 20 percent of the popular votes at the election of 1951 and returned the largest parliamentary group in the Assembly. The RPF might have been able to bring the Fourth Republic to its knees and force the return of de Gaulle to power if its parliamentary group had, along with the Communists, systematically opposed every Government measure. The parliamentary group did not do so, however. Instead, it split in 1952, when some of its members decided to support the first Conservative Government since the war. By 1953, the remaining Gaullists were also showing signs of a desire to participate directly in the normal political life of Parliament, and in that same year de Gaulle severed all formal connections with the Deputies who had been elected under his banner and requested that they no longer use the RPF label. The General's followers formed a new organization, called the Social Republicans, and this group provided the nucleus of Gaullists who succeeded in turning the Algerian revolt of 1958 into a movement to bring Charles de Gaulle back to power on his own constitutional terms.

The crux of de Gaulle's analysis of the French political problem was that the Fourth Republic gave too large a role to France's multiple parties in the policy-making process. The center of power was the National Assembly, an arena of partisan activity; the Government was a coalition of partisans subordinated to the National Assembly; the President was powerless and chosen by the Parliament. In this system no decision could be made which was not the result of agreement among several parties.

In de Gaulle's view, the parties were too deeply divided to be an adequate source of public policy. They reflected what divided the nation, not what united it. The Government, in particular, was not a source of policy based on a coherent view of France's needs, but rather a field of party rivalry. De Gaulle believed that the Constitution of the Fourth Republic simply facilitated the expression of partisan rivalries, when what was needed was a constitution which would counteract them.

De Gaulle never spelled out in detail, during the Fourth Republic, the specific institutional structure he thought would best fit French needs. His principal recommendation was the creation of a presidency which would owe its election to some body larger than the Parliament and which would be empowered to appoint and dismiss Ministers, dissolve the National Assembly, and put certain questions directly to the people by popular referendum. The purpose of this proposal was to shift the initiative in policy-making away from the parties to the presidency and to make it possible for the President to appeal directly to the electorate if his policies met resistance in the Parliament.

De Gaulle's constitutional program, which sought to limit the power of the political parties, could hardly be very popular with them, and they did all they could to resist it. When, in 1953, the RPF was dissolved, it looked as though the General had been defeated. A year later, Moslem Nationalists launched a revolt against the French in Algeria which set into motion forces which were eventually to bring de Gaulle to power.

The End of the Fourth Republic

Before 1953, French political crises turned principally on domestic policy. After 1953, they turned mainly on overseas policy. There is no intrinsic reason why overseas problems should have been more difficult to solve than domestic ones—the public was less concerned about overseas questions than about domestic ones—but they were. The tone of political debate became more than customarily acrimonious, a wave of xenophobic nationalism swept much of the political world, and the normally liberal political atmosphere became infected with a kind of French equivalent of McCarthyism.

Still, the Assembly managed to produce majorities to settle all the major overseas problems except one. The Indo-China war was ended in 1954. The European Defense Community treaty was rejected the same year. This decision produced bitterness which made it more difficult to settle later issues, but in 1954 France accepted German admission into the North Atlantic Treaty Organization and in 1957 joined the European Economic Community. Independence was granted to Morocco and Tunisia in 1956. The same year legislation was enacted which set France's African colonies south of the Sahara on the road to real, and not sham, self-government. The régime foundered, however, on the rock of Algeria.

Governments tried to crush the Algerian nationalists of the

Front de Libération Nationale (FLN), but they were unable to do so, even after most of the army had been stationed in Algeria. The groups which favored retaining French control over Algeria (including Gaullists) maintained their claims at such a fever pitch that the Assembly would not support a Government committed to negotiating with the FLN until it was too late. The Assembly gradually moved in the direction of negotiation, but at the same time, opponents of negotiation and opponents of the régime itself mustered their forces to oppose it.

On May 13, 1958, France emerged from the twentieth Cabinet crisis of the Fourth Republic by electing Pierre Pflimlin as Premier at the head of a Government which in all probability would have negotiated with the FLN. Earlier on the same day, a riot broke out in the city of Algiers under the leadership of people who wanted to prevent just such a development. A variety of groups, including not only the Gaullists but also Fascists and Pétainists who detested de Gaulle, tried to capture the momentum of the May revolt and harness it to their own purposes. The Gaullists alone were successful in doing so because the military leaders in Algeria threw their weight behind de Gaulle.

The military leaders did not support the Government in Paris because they were convinced that it intended to negotiate away what they still expected could be achieved: French control of Algeria. But they had no confidence in the local French leadership in Algeria either, and there is no evidence that any of them had personal desires to head a military Government for France. On May 15, General Salan, the Commander-in-Chief of French forces in Algeria, cried "Vive de Gaulle!" from the balcony before the Forum in Algiers, and a few hours later de Gaulle stated publicly that he was ready "to assume the powers of the Republic." The military in Algeria made preparations for an invasion of Metropolitan France, and various officers on the mainland prepared to assist it.

The Government in Paris lost all control of events. Its authority vanished rapidly and it recognized that no significant organized group except the Communist Party could be counted on to defend Metropolitan France from an invasion from North Africa. Jules Moch, a Socialist who was Minister of the Interior at the time, wrote shortly afterward that during those May days, "Prague, in

1948, haunted my sleepless nights as much as Madrid, in 1936."[10]
The two dangers of a Communist victory or a military dictatorship
were hardly equally likely, but fears of both prevailed. The leaders
of the Fourth Republic—President René Coty and former President Vincent Auriol, former Premier and Conservative leader Antoine Pinay, former Premier and Socialist leader Guy Mollet,
Premier Pierre Pflimlin himself—turned to de Gaulle as the only
person who could overcome the danger with which the country
was faced.

Turning to a nationally popular leader in order to solve a particularly difficult crisis was not a new practice for France. During
the Third and Fourth Republics the Parliament had periodically
called on strong or presumed strong leaders to assume leadership
when the customary policy-making process failed to produce a
workable solution to the problem at hand. Georges Clemenceau
had been given great powers during the final stages of World War
I, when it appeared essential to concentrate authority in the pursuit
of the war effort. Later, Raymond Poincaré was called in as
Premier to solve acute financial problems facing the country. The
call for Doumergue after the riots of 1934 and the call for Pétain in
1940 were acts in this same tradition.

The Fourth Republic resorted to the same procedure, but there
were signs that the leaders called upon to serve in difficult periods
were becoming more exigent in the terms they set for accepting the
responsibilities of leadership. Early in 1953, there was a long
Cabinet crisis during which President Auriol called upon both
Paul Reynaud, a senior statesman who had been the last Premier
of the Third Republic and who first gave Charles de Gaulle a post
in a French Government (and who was later to become a severe
critic of the Fifth Republic), and Pierre Mendès-France, a strong-
willed Radical who was to be the only Premier of the Fourth
Republic to produce a (short-lived) mood of enthusiasm for reform, to try to form a Government. M. Reynaud agreed only on
the condition that the Constitution be amended to give the
Government the unconditional authority to dissolve the National
Assembly, a condition which the National Assembly was unwilling
to accept. M. Mendès-France set a more sophisticated and probably also more potentially effective condition. He announced that

[10] Jules Moch, "De Gaulle d'hier à demain," La Nef (July–August, 1958),
10.

he would ask the Ministers who would serve in his Government not to serve in the next Government. He was also defeated in the Assembly. France's leaders were becoming less willing to be called upon in difficult circumstances only to be cast aside by the legislature once the period of acute crisis appeared to be over. Neither M. Reynaud nor M. Mendès-France, however, was strong enough to break the habits of the past.[11]

De Gaulle was strong enough and the situation gave him all the cards. With each passing moment during the last days of May, 1958, the fear of civil war grew, and it is almost certain that at one point de Gaulle blocked the invasion that was being prepared by prematurely announcing that he had begun to form a Government. Party leaders gathered the necessary votes, and on June 1, 1958, de Gaulle became the last Premier of the Fourth Republic by 329 votes to 224 and was given near-dictatorial powers. He returned to power according to constitutional forms, against the background of a threat of violence.

Chance had it that the constitutional amendment process had been set into operation earlier, and it was also possible without violating constitutional procedures to amend the amending article of the Constitution to give de Gaulle's Government authority to prepare a new constitution to be presented to the voters at a referendum.

The Constitution was drafted during the summer and adopted at a popular referendum in September. Elections for a new national Assembly were held in November. Charles de Gaulle was elected President of the Fifth Republic in December. The President appointed Michel Debré as Premier in January, 1959. France had a new régime.

[11] The two men's proposals are referred to in Philip Williams, *op. cit.*, p. 408.

CHAPTER THREE

Presidential Government

THE CONSTITUTION of the Fifth Republic does not make any reference to an "executive." Instead, it provides for a President and for a Government, consisting of the Premier and the Ministers, and confers on each of them various powers that are customarily regarded as executive in nature.

Conceptions of the Constitution

There was little ground for doubt, when the new Constitution was adopted, that of these two executive authorities, the President would be preeminent. De Gaulle had said in his Bayeux speech of 1946 that the keystone of the French constitutional system should be the presidency, and in 1958, Michel Debré, who was—after de Gaulle himself—the principal author of the Constitution of the Fifth Republic, repeated that the keystone of the new constitutional system would be the presidency. Still, it remained to be specified in what way the presidency would be the keystone, and on this point a conception of the Constitution was widely held for a brief period preceding and immediately following the adoption of the Constitution which was not borne out in practice.

THE PRESIDENT AS ARBITRATOR

According to this early conception of the Constitution, the Government—not the President—would be the chief policy-making authority, subject to the control of Parliament. The role of the President would be to ensure that the whole policy-making process—conducted by other constitutional authorities—operated smoothly and continually. In this interpretation, the President would not employ his constitutional powers to press for his own policy conceptions, but rather only to prevent or to repair break-downs in the operation of a system in which other agencies would have primary policy-making roles. The President would not be the chief policy-maker; he would be what was usually designated as the "arbitrator" of the constitutional system.

This interpretation of the Constitution rested in part on the two constitutional articles which define the roles of the Government and of the President. Article 20 says that "The Government determines and directs the policy of the nation." There could hardly be a clearer indication of governmental primacy in the policy-making process. Article 5 says that "The President of the Republic sees to it that the Constitution is respected. He ensures, by his arbitration, the regular functioning of the public authorities, as well as the continuity of the State. He is the guarantor of national independence, of the integrity of the territory, and of respect for Community agreements and treaties." This clause is vague and consequently "elastic," to employ a term important in United States constitutional development, but it also lends itself to the kind of interpretation described.

This interpretation rested also on the nature of several of the main powers conferred on the President by the Constitution. He was given the power to dissolve the National Assembly, a power which can be regarded as a way simply of settling a conflict between the Government and Parliament with which the President is not politically concerned. He was given the power to decide—when requested by other constitutional authorities—whether or not a referendum should be held, and this power can be similarly interpreted. He was also given extensive emergency powers, and these too can be fitted easily into an interpretation which holds that the President must be able to restore the system to working order without being an active policy-maker in his own right.

PRESIDENTIAL LEADERSHIP

The conception of the Constitution in which the presidency would be preeminent essentially in terms of majesty and dignity because of his role as ultimate protector of the constitutional process, but in which the presidency would not be a direct participant in the policy-making process, did not prevail for long. Early in the Fifth Republic, the presidency emerged as the dominant branch of the executive and assumed leadership in the policy-making process. Within four years, President de Gaulle had exercised every one of his principal constitutional powers and some constitutionally questionable ones as well. He asserted himself immediately as the chief policy-maker; he held two referendums on Algerian policy; he dissolved the National Assembly; and he exercised emergency powers. In a sharply contested move, he employed a referendum to amend the Constitution to provide for the direct popular election of the President. At the beginning of 1964 he affirmed that "the President is obviously the only one to hold and to delegate the authority of the State," and that "it should obviously be understood that the indivisible authority of the State is entrusted completely to the President by the people who elected him, that there is no other authority—either ministerial, civilian, military or judicial—which is not entrusted and maintained by him. . . ." In the fall of 1965 he stated that the President had, "during the past seven years . . . determined the orientation of French policy within and without . . ." At the same time, he also expressed the notion, curious in a country which has a representative legislature, that the President "is and is alone the representative and the mandatary of the nation as a whole. . . ."

De Gaulle's opponents have expressed indignation at this conception of the French presidency. At the same time, political leaders who believe that the presidency has encroached upon the proper constitutional sphere of the Government actually contributed to the situation which they deplore. In February, 1960, the Government asked Parliament to delegate some of its constitutional legislative powers to the Government, so that it would have broad powers to deal with the situation created by a revolt of French settlers in Algeria the month before (called the "revolt of the barricades" because the rebellious French barricaded themselves inside various points, including the University of Algiers). Parliament voted the delegation of powers, but only after making their use conditional upon the approval of the President, thereby indicating that they had more confidence in the President than they had in the Government.

It remains to be seen whether the dominant position of the President can endure beyond the incumbency of Charles de Gaulle.

With respect to the development of the presidency during that incumbency, however, one may cite the rhetorical question asked by Premier Pompidou during a debate in the National Assembly over the respective powers of the President and the Government: "Who can in good faith maintain that he did not expect to see General de Gaulle take the helm?" Or, if one prefers a more flowery phrase, one may cite de Gaulle's own question of a year later: ". . . who ever believed that General de Gaulle, once called to the helm, would be content with opening displays of chrysanthemums?"

De Gaulle as Chief Policy-Maker

THE "PRESIDENTIAL SECTOR"

The President has emerged as the chief policy-maker, but there is also a Government which plays a role in policy-making, and efforts have been made by various people to distinguish between policy spheres pertaining to the President and those pertaining to the Government. The most famous distinction of this sort was made by Jacques Chaban-Delmas, the President of the National Assembly, at the first congress of the Gaullist party, the *Union pour la nouvelle République* (UNR), which was held at Bordeaux in November, 1959. He referred to a "presidential sector" including Algeria and the Sahara, relations with France's African territories south of the Sahara, foreign affairs, and national defense, and to an "open sector" including everything else. "In the first sector the Government executes, in the second it conceives," he said.[1] M. Chaban-Delmas' remarks were in the context of distinguishing between those subjects on which, as he saw it, the UNR should simply follow the initiatives of the President and those in which it should develop its own policies, but this reference to a division of policy-making authority between President and Government by such a high-ranking official gained wide currency.

Such a distinction is too limiting and too categorical. When President de Gaulle referred in 1965 to his having "determined the orientation of French policy within and without," he cited economic, financial, and monetary stability, as well as overseas and

[1] *Le Monde*, November 17, 1959.

defense questions, as being among "so many Gordian knots" which had had to be cut, and in 1964 he had said that "there could be no watertight separation between the two levels at which, on the one hand the President, on the other he who seconds him [the Premier], daily exercise their respective functions." The President has been involved in such policy decisions as those affecting the relationship between Church schools and the state, the size of veterans' pensions, the major miners' strike of 1963, and corporation taxes. At the same time, there is an underlying accuracy to M. Chaban-Delmas' early remark. For in many matters, the President's role has been to settle differences among the members of the Government. In the four fields of what M. Chaban-Delmas called the "presidential sector," however, the President has constantly taken the initiative.

French policy concerning Algeria after June, 1958, was entirely the work of de Gaulle. It had to be. Not only was it the Algerian problem which de Gaulle had been called back to power to solve, but the last Cabinet of the Fourth Republic, which de Gaulle headed, and the first Cabinet of the Fifth Republic, which M. Debré headed, were as divided over Algerian policy as any earlier Fourth Republic Cabinet had been. Moreover, although Premier Debré loyally supported de Gaulle's Algerian policy as it developed, his own statements on Algeria were less liberal than those of de Gaulle.

The Cabinet was reorganized in February, 1960, to ensure that it contained only firm supporters of the President, but de Gaulle still faced resistance in Parliament, and in January, 1961, and April, 1962, he took his case to the electorate by way of popular referendums, in the first case to ratify the policy of self-determination for Algeria which he had announced in September, 1959, in the second case to ratify the agreement reached at Evian by the French and the FLN by which Algeria became independent. The initiative in both uses of the referendum came directly from the President.

Virtually all of France's former colonies are now independent, but when de Gaulle came to power in 1958 they were not. The Fourth Republic had laid the foundation for self-government in the colonies in 1956. In 1958, the policy which led to independence for the colonies was made by de Gaulle in as strikingly personal a way as he made French Algerian policy. During a tour of French African territories during the summer of 1958, in order to win

African support for the constitutional draft which was to be voted on at the referendum in September, de Gaulle announced that any French overseas territory which did not ratify the constitutional draft at the referendum would be regarded automatically as having chosen to become independent of France. In another speech, in Madagascar, he repeated that territories could "secede" from the Community by voting "No" at the referendum, and he added that even for those territories which voted "Yes," "procedures for revision are also envisaged for those who would like to follow their own destiny." The following day, in a speech in the French Congo, de Gaulle became more specific and said that a territory which accepted the constitutional draft could also at a later date become independent. Accordingly, the constitutional provisions relating to the Community—which de Gaulle virtually wrote in his African speeches—acknowledged the right of the overseas territories to become independent. By 1961, almost every former French African colony had become an independent state.

De Gaulle has made it clear that the President commands "when it is a matter of a subject whose importance involves everything," and that it is the President's "duty to trace out the nation's conduct in the essential domains." This means that the President commands in national defense and in foreign policy, which can hardly be separated from defense. In 1959, de Gaulle said, "The government's reason for being is, in any epoch, the defense of the independence and of the integrity of the Territory. It is in that that it originates. In France, in particular, all our régimes were born from that."[2] In de Gaulle's view, it is defense which involves everything; it is defense which is the essential domain.

Accordingly, it is the President who has shaped French foreign and defense policy under the Fifth Republic. The President attends "summit" meetings and communicates directly with the leaders of other nations. The "hot line" linking Paris to the Kremlin in Moscow is installed in the presidential palace. Article 21 of the Constitution declares that the Premier "is responsible for national defense," but by virtue of a Government decree of January 14, 1964, it is the President who holds final authority over the engagement of the nuclear striking force. Major policy decisions

[2] Speech at the Centre des Hautes Études militaires and to the three Écoles de guerre, November 3, 1959. *L'Année Politique 1959*, Presses Universitaires de France, Paris, 1960, p. 632. Author's translation.

have been announced in presidential addresses and at the presidential press conference. In fact, the distinguished annual, *L'Année Politique*, reported that there was general disappointment with the President's press conference of January, 1964, because it contained "no element of surprise."[3]

PRESIDENTIAL COMMITTEES

The main instrument through which the President supervised policy-making and reduced the role of the Government as a policy-making agency early in the Fifth Republic was the presidential committee. Some presidential committees were formalized by decree; others were constituted informally. There were presidential committees which included the President, the Premier, a small number of interested Ministers, some civil servants, and, occasionally, some military officers, to deal with Algeria, relations with the states of the Community, foreign affairs, defense, and African and Madagascan affairs. *Ad hoc* committees were formed to deal with other subjects as well.

By 1963, the presidential committees appeared to have fallen into desuetude, perhaps because the main lines of French policy had by then been fixed by the President and harmony between President and Government had been firmly established.[4]

The Referendum

The referendum was essential to de Gaulle's constitutional scheme because it provides an alternative to Parliament as the agency for legitimizing public policy. De Gaulle's analysis of French politics held that the parties were a screen rather than a transmission belt between the public and policy, and as Parliament is the arena of partisan representation, it was important that the executive be able to bypass Parliament in the policy-making process in cases where it believed that it could win popular but not parliamentary support.

The Constitution does not directly confer on the President the

---

[3] *L'Année Politique 1964*, Presses Universitaires de France, Paris, 1965, p. 12.
[4] Pierre Viansson-Ponté, *The King and His Court*, Elaine P. Halperin (trans.), Houghton Mifflin, Boston, 1965, pp. 41–42.

authority to hold referendums nor does it permit a referendum to be held on any subject. It does empower the President to submit to a popular referendum, either on the proposal of the Government during parliamentary sessions or on the concurrent proposal of the two legislative chambers, any Government bill affecting the organization of the public powers, entailing the approval of an agreement within the Community, or authorizing the ratification of a treaty which, while not contrary to the Constitution, would affect the operation of France's institutions (Article 11).

In actual practice, it has been the President, rather than the Government, who has taken the initiative in deciding whether to hold a referendum. This was made quite clear by the communiqué issued by the Council of Ministers on November 16, 1960, which said that "General de Gaulle indicated his intention of submitting, at the appropriate moment, to the country, by means of the referendum, a Government bill relating to the organization of the public powers in Algeria, pending self-determination."[5] The constitutional formalities have always been observed in that the Government has officially proposed that a referendum be held, but it was the President who took the initiative in each case. Parliament has never used its constitutional right to request a referendum.

There have been three referendums held under the Fifth Republic. This does not count the referendum of September, 1958, at which the Constitution of the Fifth Republic itself was approved, as this referendum was held under the constituent powers conferred upon de Gaulle's Government by the last Parliament of the Fourth Republic and not under the authority of the new Constitution itself. The first two referendums under the Fifth Republic, those of January 8, 1961, and April 8, 1962, concerned Algeria. The referendum of October 28, 1962, amended the Constitution to provide for direct popular election of the President. (See Table 3 for referendum results.)

The first two referendums were no doubt inspired by several motives. The referendum of January, 1961, at which the policy of self-determination for Algeria was approved, was probably designed less to bypass a parliamentary decision on the specific issue—which had already been approved by the National Assembly—than it was

---

[5] François Goguel, "Les circonstances," in François Goguel *et al.*, *Le Référendum du 8 janvier 1961*, Armand Colin, Paris, 1962, p. 27.

TABLE 3. Referendum Results, Metropolitan France, 1945–1962

	Oct, 1945[a]	May, 1946[b]	Oct, 1946[c]	Sept, 1958[d]	Jan, 1961[e]	Apr, 1962[f]	Oct, 1962[a]
Registered Voters	24,622,862	24,657,128	24,905,538	26,603,464	27,184,408	26,991,743	27,582,113
Voting	19,654,284	19,895,411	17,129,645	22,596,850	20,791,246	20,401,906	21,301,816
Abstentions	4,968,578 (20.1%)	4,761,717 (19.3%)	7,775,893 (31.2%)	4,006,614 (15.1%)	6,393,162 (23.5%)	6,589,837 (24.4%)	6,280,297 (22.7%)
Question 1							
Yes	17,957,868 (96.4%)	9,109,771 (47%)	9,002,287 (53.5%)	17,668,790 (79.2%)	15,200,073 (75.2%)	17,508,607 (90.6%)	12,809,363 (61.7%)
No	670,672 (3.6%)	10,272,586 (53%)	7,790,856 (46.5%)	4,624,511 (20.7%)	4,996,474 (24.7%)	1,795,061 (9.3%)	7,932,695 (38.2%)
Void	1,025,744	513,054	336,502	303,559	594,699	1,098,238	559,758
Question 2							
Yes	12,317,882 (66.3%)						
No	6,271,512 (33.7%)						
Void	1,064,890						

[a] Question 1: Do you want the Assembly elected today to be a constituent assembly?"
Question 2: An affirmative vote signified being in favor of limiting the powers of the Assembly according to a plan proposed by General de Gaulle.
[b] Ratification of the Constitution adopted by the Constituent Assembly elected in October, 1945.
[c] Ratification of the Constitution adopted by the Constituent Assembly elected in June, 1946.
[d] Ratification of the Constitution proposed by the Government of General de Gaulle.
[e] Ratification of the policy of self-determination for Algeria.
[f] Ratification of the Evian accords and grant of powers to apply them.
[g] Ratification of a Government bill amending the Constitution to provide for direct popular election of the President.

SOURCE: François Goguel and Alfred Grosser, *La Politique en France*, Armand Colin, Paris, 1964, pp. 269–272. (By permission.)

to demonstrate both to the *Algérie française partisans* (Frenchmen favoring French control of Algeria) and the Algerian nationalist leaders that de Gaulle's policy was widely supported by the French electorate. It was probably also intended to demonstrate to Parliament that the President's popularity was great and that it therefore should not seek to oppose him either on Algeria or other issues.

The referendum of April 8, 1962, at which the Evian agreements between the French Government and the Algerian nationalist movement were approved, was probably more directly inspired by the desire to demonstrate de Gaulle's personal popularity than the earlier referendum had been, as the Evian accords would probably have been ratified by the French Parliament, even though there was marked discontent in Parliament with de Gaulle's conception of the régime. Possibly, also, de Gaulle believed that a striking referendum victory would decisively legitimate the Algerian settlement and therefore reduce the possibility of its being used later as a political argument against him.

THE REFERENDUM OF OCTOBER, 1962

The referendum of October 28, 1962, is in a different category. This referendum amended the Constitution to provide for the direct popular election of the President. The constitutionality of the use of the referendum as provided for in Article 11 to amend the Constitution is highly questionable. Article 89 of the Constitution provides for amendments by procedures which may involve a referendum but which also require an affirmative vote by both houses of the legislature. At the time of the drafting of the Constitution, the Government's representative to the Constitutional Advisory Committee distinguished between the amendment of the Constitution and the matters provided for in what was eventually to become Article 11 of the Constitution. But de Gaulle had little hope of persuading the Parliament to pass a constitutional amendment to provide for the direct election of the President, and he carried out his plan despite the opposition of every French party except the UNR, the *Union démocratique du travail* (UDT)—a small group of labor-oriented Gaullists who later merged with the UNR—and a fraction of the Conservatives. An appeal was made by the President of the Senate to the Constitutional Council (see Chapter Four, pp. 80–81) to declare the use of Article 11 unconstitutional, but the Constitutional Council declared itself to be without jurisdiction in the matter.

Original Method of Presidential Election. Under the original terms of the Constitution of 1958, the President was elected by an electoral college composed of some 80,000 electors, consisting for the most part of delegates from or selected by the municipal councils. It was this kind of electoral college which overwhelmingly elected de Gaulle President in December, 1958, when his only opponents were a Communist Senator, Georges Marrane, and a token candidate, Albert Chatelet, supported by some small non-Communist groups opposed to de Gaulle (see Table 4).

TABLE 4.   Results of the Presidential Election of December 21, 1958 (Metropolitan France)

Registered Voters	76,359	
Valid Ballots Cast	74,391	
Charles de Gaulle	57,649	(77.5%)
Georges Marrane	10,125	(13.6%)
Albert Chatelet	6,617	(8.9%)

SOURCE: *Recueil des Décisions du Conseil Constitutionnel et de la Commission Constitutionnelle Provisoire, 1958–1959*, p. 49. Publié sous le haut patronage du Conseil constitutionnel. Imprimerie Nationale.

This method of election of the President was criticized by many people on the ground that such an electoral college, which gave disproportionately large representation to France's middle-sized cities, could not normally be expected to elect the kind of forceful and popular political leader who would be appropriate for the powerful presidency created by the new Constitution. It was believed that the college would consist mainly of middle-of-the-road politicians who would be likely to select an innocuous politician, without enemies and without clear policy objectives, thereby returning to the practices of the Third Republic. But the new method of election of the President did remove control of presidential selection from the Members of Parliament, where it had rested during the Third and Fourth Republics and, in any case, just as no one at the Federal Convention in Philadelphia in 1787 doubted that George Washington would be the first President of the United States, no one in France in 1958 doubted that de Gaulle would be the first President of the Fifth Republic, regardless of the electoral system employed.

In fact, the original system of presidential election under the Fifth Republic was a faithful translation of all de Gaulle's recommendations from his Bayeux speech of 1946 until 1961. Before 1961, de Gaulle had never said that he was in favor of direct popular election of the President; he had spoken only of creating an electoral college large enough to prevent the Members of Parliament from being decisive in presidential selection.

At the time of the drafting of the Constitution of 1958, Michel Debré rejected direct popular election of the President on two grounds. The first was that there was a risk that direct popular election might result in the selection of a President who had not been approved by a majority of the voters of Metropolitan France. In 1958, it was believed that France's colonies might remain within a French Community, and as the French President was also to be President of the Community, the electorates of all the countries of the Community would have to participate in the selection of the President. But the population of France's various overseas areas was almost as large as that of Metropolitan France, and this meant that those areas might be able to select a President against the wishes of a majority of French Metropolitan voters. The second ground was that it appeared difficult to make direct popular election of the President operate successfully while there was a large Communist Party. By 1961, the first potential difficulty no longer existed. A large Communist Party still existed, but its presence was evidently no longer regarded as an obstacle to the successful conduct of direct elections for the presidency.

The Decision To Amend the Constitution. In March, 1961, the UNR congress passed a motion calling for the popular election of the President, something it is not likely to have done without de Gaulle's approval. De Gaulle first referred to the possibility of changing the method of election of the President a month later, on April 11, 1961, when he referred to the "many" who thought "that the method of electing the President of the Republic by an electoral college limited only to elected representatives . . . would hardly be consistent for the person who will have to succeed me"; said that "it may be thought that he should be chosen by the nation through universal suffrage"; and said that he could put the question of his replacement on the agenda if he had the time and opportunity to do so. A year later, in May, 1962, he said that the election of the President by universal suffrage was not on the agenda at the moment.

By September, however, the question had been put on the agenda. An attempt was made on the President's life in August and, according to the President's remarks in a later speech, this determined him to make sure that his successor would have a solid electoral basis and that there would be a demonstration of popular support for the institutions established by the Fifth Republic. On September 12, de Gaulle announced to the Council of Ministers his intention to hold a referendum on the popular election of the President. On September 20, he went on radio and television to urge an affirmative vote, indicating that he had not been concerned about the method of election for himself because his nomination had been determined in advance "by the force of events." Moreover, he stated, "in view of political susceptibilities, some of which were worthy of respect, I preferred at that time for there not to be a kind of formal plebiscite as far as I was concerned." On October 4, 1962, President de Gaulle said that "from the very beginning, I knew that, before the end of my seven-year term of office, I would have to put it to the country to decide that it [the direct election of the President] be so."

When de Gaulle campaigned in favor of amending the Constitution by referendum to provide for the direct popular election of the President, he always spoke of the need for such a new electoral system in order to ensure that his *successor* would have the popular support necessary to enable him to carry out the duties of his office with proper authority. De Gaulle never said that he would not run for the presidency under the proposed system, but he did speak as though the new system of direct popular election would not apply to him, and high-ranking officials of the régime and the UNR said explicitly that the new system would apply only to de Gaulle's successors.

Whatever de Gaulle's intentions may have been in 1962 about running for re-election, his popularity was greater among the electorate than it was among the French political class from which the old presidential electoral college was drawn, and he would have faced a difficult electoral situation if he had run for re-election under the old electoral system. He had been elected in 1958 by an overwhelming majority of the presidential electoral college, but at that time the outcome of the Algerian problem was in doubt, a crisis atmosphere existed, and all parties and their leaders supported de Gaulle except the Communist Party and some small non-Communist groups of slight electoral significance. By late 1962 the situation had changed. Opposition to de Gaulle had grown among several of the parties, the Algerian problem was settled, and the crisis atmosphere was fast disappearing. The old presidential electoral college is similar to the electoral college for the Senate, and Gaullist strength in the Senate has always been much weaker than it is either in the National Assembly or among the public at large (see Chapter Four). No one can say what would have happened had the presidential electoral system not been changed, but the political situation late in 1962 was such that de Gaulle's chances for re-election by direct popular vote could have seemed much better than they did under the original presidential electoral system.

New Method of Presidential Election. As a result of the adoption of the constitutional amendment at the referendum of October 28, 1962, the French President is now elected for seven years by direct universal suffrage. Candidates must be nominated by at least one hundred citizens, whose anonymity is to be guarded, and who must be Members of Parliament, members of the Economic and Social Council, departmental councillors (*conseillers généraux*) or mayors of any city or town except Paris and its subdivisions, provided that the one hundred nominators of any candidate represent at least ten departments or overseas territories. The electoral system provides for two ballots. Election requires a majority of the valid ballots cast. If no candidate wins such a majority on the first ballot, there is a run-off election two weeks later, at which only two candidates may run. The two candidates who may run are those, among the candidates who ran at the first ballot and who still choose to run, who received the most votes at the first ballot. In other words, any of the candidates, even the two leaders at the first ballot, may withdraw from the race at the second ballot, but only those two candidates remaining who received more votes than any of the others who still want to run at the second ballot may do so. As there are only two candidates at the second ballot, the winner is assured of a majority of the votes cast.

The Dissolution Power

Article 12 of the Constitution of 1958 authorizes the President, after consulting the Premier and the Presidents of the two legislative chambers, to dissolve the National Assembly. The only limitations on the exercise of this power are that it may not be used while the President is exercising emergency powers (see below, in this chapter) and a new dissolution cannot take place within one year after the election of a National Assembly following upon a dissolution.

This is the least restricted dissolution power ever conferred upon the executive of a French Republic. During the Third Republic, the President could dissolve the Chamber of Deputies only with the consent of the Senate, and after President MacMahon's ill-fated dissolution in 1877 no President of the Third Republic again requested senatorial approval of a dissolution.

The Constitution of the Fourth Republic provided for the dissolution of the National Assembly only in conditions which, to a certain extent, it was possible for the National Assembly itself to prevent. Nevertheless, such conditions occurred in 1955, and for the first time since 1877, a Premier of the Republic dissolved the National Assembly. The dissolution of 1955 was not unpopular, and while the election of 1956 which followed produced an Assembly that was incapable of furnishing a solid majority, the dissolution may have helped to dispel some of the historic French fears of the dissolution power which hark back to the nineteenth century.

Like all the major presidential powers contained in the Constitution of 1958, the dissolution power has been used by President de Gaulle. Angered by the President's use of the referendum to amend the Constitution to provide for the direct popular election of the President, a majority in the National Assembly expressed its disapproval of the President's act by overthrowing the Government by a vote of censure on October 4, 1962. De Gaulle immediately invoked Article 12 and dissolved the National Assembly. The election for the new Assembly took place in November, 1962.

Emergency Powers

The Constitution of the Fifth Republic empowers the President to take "the measures required by these circumstances" in situations "when the institutions of the Republic, the independence of the nation, the integrity of its territory or the fulfillment of its international agreements are threatened in a grave and immediate manner, and when the regular functioning of the constitutional public authorities is interrupted" (Article 16). Before taking action, the President must consult the Premier, the Presidents of the two legislative chambers, and the Constitutional Council; he must inform the nation; he must consult the Constitutional Council about the measures he takes; and his measures must be directed toward restoring the capacity of the constitutional authorities to operate as quickly as possible. While the President must consult as indicated, he is in no way bound by the advice of others. The President alone determines whether the circumstances require the exercise of emergency powers. The only limitation which Article 16 imposes on the President is that he may not dissolve the National Assembly while he is exercising emergency powers. Parliament, however, meets by right while Article 16 is invoked (but see Chapter Four, pp. 98–99).

De Gaulle's insistence that the new Constitution provide for presidential emergency powers seems to have been based principally on the belief that if such constitutional powers had existed during the Third Republic, the collapse of the régime in 1940 might have been avoided. M. Debré invoked the possibility of an atomic war in his argument for creating presidential emergency powers. In fact, it was a repetition of events similar to those which had taken place in Algeria in May, 1958, which provoked President de Gaulle into employing the emergency powers provided for by Article 16 of the Constitution.

The same colonial and military groups which had succeeded in causing the collapse of the Fourth Republic also tried, under the Fifth, to force de Gaulle to adopt a policy aimed at retaining French control of Algeria and, when that effort failed, they tried to overthrow the Fifth Republic itself. The first manifestation of this resistance to the Fifth Republic came after the President announced a policy of self-determination for Algeria, and it took the form of the "revolt of the barricades" in January, 1960. The army in Algeria equivocated for a time in the face of this limited civilian uprising, but de Gaulle (wearing his uniform) addressed the nation over television, made conciliatory remarks to the army, remained firm on his policy, and succeeded in having the revolt suppressed and its leaders brought to trial.

Later, after the referendum of January 8, 1961, ratified the self-determination policy, a more serious insurrection took place in Algeria—the so-called "revolt of the generals." This revolt, led by four senior military officers, lasted only four days but it was the prelude to the formation of the *Organisation de l'Armée Secrète* (OAS) which was later to sow violence in Algeria on a large scale and, on a lesser scale, in Metropolitan France. De Gaulle met the challenge of the "revolt of the generals" promptly. It was in order to repress this revolt and to limit the danger of its consequences that he invoked Article 16.

Article 16 was invoked on April 23, 1961, and its application ceased five months later, on September 29. Eighteen presidential decisions were taken under the authority of Article 16, including the first, which put Article 16 into force, and the last, which ended its period of application. Police powers and the investigatory power of the examining magistrates were enlarged; certain publications were prohibited; military and civil service personnel could be removed or dismissed for participating in, facilitating, or encouraging subversion of the Republic; two special military courts were established to try persons accused of crimes or offenses against the security of the state; the pensions and seniority rights of dismissed military or civil service personnel were abolished; military and police officials could be put on special leave or dismissed; brigadier generals could be promoted to higher rank without regard to the normal rules of promotion; the permanent tenure of trial judges in Algeria was revoked, and both trial judges and prosecuting magistrates in Algeria could be kept without assignment at the disposition of the Minister. The application of these decisions to individuals (other than those brought to trial before the two special military courts) was not made public, so it is not possible to tell what the full impact of these measures actually was, but it is clear that the special powers taken under Article 16 provided President de Gaulle with the authority thoroughly to shake up the civil service, military, police, and Algerian judicial hierarchies.[6]

Problems of Constitutional Development

The Constitution of 1958, as amended by the referendum of October, 1962, created a hybrid institutional structure. The régime combines elements of the presidential (or separation of powers) system, the parliamentary system, and direct democracy. There is a popularly elected President with a fixed seven-year term of office who holds important constitutional powers. There is a Government which is authorized to exercise executive powers and which is responsible to the National Assembly. There is provision for popular referendums on certain subjects in certain circumstances.

During the incumbency of Charles de Gaulle, the presidency emerged as the dominant executive authority, but it is by no means certain that this will always be the case. Presidential leadership in France depends upon the willingness of the legislature to accept that leadership, and this, in turn, depends upon whether the electorate returns a majority to the National Assembly which will support the President's policies.

The President cannot use the referendum constitutionally unless the legislature or the Government, which depends upon legislative support, agrees to it. The President cannot resort to the ordinary legislative process to try to convert his policies into law unless the Government is willing to steer his measures through the National Assembly, where the support of a majority is necessary.[7]

De Gaulle was able to secure the cooperation of the Government in requesting that referendums be held, and the large display of popular support for his position at the two referendums on Algeria helped him to win the support of majorities in the National Assembly. On the one occasion when he and the Government lost the

[6] *Le Monde*, June 24, 1961, and October 1–2, 1961.

[7] There are circumstances in which the support of a majority is not needed, but rather only the absence of the opposition of a majority (see Chapter Four, pp. 93–94).

support of the National Assembly—over the referendum to provide for direct popular election of the President—the President dissolved the National Assembly. The election which followed, in November, 1962, returned a majority of Deputies prepared to support the President. But what if it had not?

One cannot say with any certainty what would have happened in the past if circumstances had been different, but the question highlights the possibility that the present balance of power within the constitutional framework may someday shift. The President may not constitutionally dissolve the National Assembly more than once during a 12-month period. If, after a dissolution, the electorate returned a National Assembly with a majority opposed to the President, executive leadership would revert to the Government, as the majority in the Assembly would be, in effect, in a position to select its own executive leaders. The President could be powerless for a year if Government and Assembly refused to cooperate with him. At the end of the year, the President would have to decide whether to dissolve the National Assembly again. If he dissolved again and won, he would once again become the executive leader. If he dissolved again and lost, he would be in the same position as before.

Some people have proposed that the Constitution be transformed into a presidential system on the American model, thereby abolishing the parliamentary aspect of the system completely. There would be no Government, but rather only a President and a legislature, completely separated in that the President could not dissolve the Assembly and the President would not require the support of a majority in the Assembly to remain in office.

Such a system would strengthen the Assembly, as it would have a veto power over presidential policy and would not be subject to any dissolution power, and for that reason it has been opposed by de Gaulle and his followers. But there is a further difficulty with that kind of system within the French political context. As it operates in the United States, the mutual dependence of President and Congress results most of the time in decisions reasonably acceptable to both. There are cases of complete stalemate, but they occur relatively infrequently. These conflicts have sometimes been severe, but they have not led to the destruction of one body's powers by the other. In France, the historic suspicion between legislature and executive has not so far permitted the creation of an atmosphere in which compromises could be expected continuously to be worked out between them while there remained the possibility for one agency to win a total political victory over the other.[8]

It may well be that this is a manifestation of a French cultural phenomenon. Michel Crozier has argued[9] that Frenchmen conceive of authority as absolute, and that this conception of authority accounts not only for those occasions when authority is exercised in France in such a fashion, but also for the intense suspicion of and elaborate protections devised against the exercise of authority in France. Furthermore, Crozier argues, this conception of authority makes it difficult for Frenchmen to bargain as among equals, because each holder of a share of authority sees that share as absolute and not subject to limitation through bargaining. There is much in the historic behavior of French politicians which can be accounted for by this cultural theory (see Chapter One, pp. 10, 17, 22–23). Whether or not this is the explanation for certain historical characteristics of French politics, however, those characteristics provide grounds for believing that any direct stand-offs which may develop between the President and the National Assembly, whether under the present constitutional system or a revised one, will not easily be resolved.

[8] The Second Republic, which lasted from 1848 until 1852, was France's only experience with a pure form of separation of powers. It was ended by a presidential *coup d'état*. The Republic became an Empire and the President became Emperor.

[9] Michel Crozier, *The Bureaucratic Phenomenon*, The University of Chicago Press, Chicago, 1964.

CHAPTER FOUR

The Government and Parliament

The Government

THE INCOMPATIBILITY RULE

The Government consists of the Premier and the Ministers. One innovation of the Constitution of the Fifth Republic is the provision (Article 23) which prohibits members of the Government from also being Members of Parliament, official representatives of any national professional organization, or public employees, and which also prohibits them from engaging in any professional activity. Politically, the most important part of this provision is the one which applies to Members of Parliament. Any Member of Parliament who agrees to serve in the Government must give up his seat in Parliament no later than 30 days after his appointment to the Government, and he cannot run for a seat in Parliament again until the next general election.

The 30-day margin, which is provided for in an organic law (see p. 79) implementing the Constitution, suggests that the men who framed it were not convinced that it would always be easier under the Fifth Republic for newly appointed Governments to agree on policies or to win the support of the National Assembly than it had been under the Fourth. The 30-day margin allows the Ministers time to decide whether they can accept the policies of the Government and to assess the Government's chances of duration. The provision was valuable to two MRP Deputies who entered the first Pompidou Government in April, 1962, only to resign just inside the 30-day limit after President de Gaulle held a press conference, about the content of which an MRP Deputy later claimed the MRP Ministers had not been informed in advance, and in which the President opposed the policy of European integration to which the MRP Ministers were strongly attached.

The incompatibility rule, as it is called, contained in Article 23 of the Constitution, was justified by M. Debré on the ground that it would discourage what he called the "race for portfolios," a practice by which Deputies allegedly voted against Governments in the hope of attaining ministerial posts in the next one. Career ambitions probably did contribute to ministerial instability during the Fourth Republic,[1] but they seem to have affected the parliamentary behavior of the Radicals and Conservatives more than that of the MRP, Socialists, and Communists, whose greater parliamentary discipline helped to ensure that their votes were based largely on principle.[2] Fourth Republic Governments may have been threatened less by ambitious Deputies outside the Cabinet than they were by ambitious Ministers within it;[3] M. Mendès-France appears to have thought so in 1953 when he stated that he would ask the members of the Cabinet which he hoped (but was not permitted) to form not to accept posts in the next Cabinet.

Whatever contribution Article 23 may make toward ministerial stability, the separation of the personnel of the Government from the personnel of Parliament would appear to have been a legal necessity. The framers of the Constitution of the Fifth Republic were obliged, by their grant of constituent authority from the last Parliament of the Fourth Republic, to adhere both to the principle of the separation of powers and to the principle that the Government must be responsible to Parliament. The only way in which these two principles can be satisfied simultaneously is to separate the Government from Parliament in terms of their composition.

[1] Philip M. Williams, *Crisis and Compromise; Politics in the Fourth Republic*, Longmans, London, 1964, p. 413.

[2] Duncan MacRae, Jr., "Intraparty Divisions and Cabinet Coalitions in the Fourth French Republic," *Comparative Studies in Society and History* (January, 1963), p. 210.

[3] Philip M. Williams and Martin Harrison, *De Gaulle's Republic*, Longmans, London, 1960, p. 138.

CIVIL SERVANTS AS MINISTERS

When the incompatibility article was written into the 1958 Constitution, Members of Praliament expressed concern that it might signify the intention of the leaders of the Fifth Republic not to appoint Members of Parliament to the Cabinet. This concern was partly justified.

Eight of the 23 members of de Gaulle's transitional Government (not counting de Gaulle himself) were not Members of Parliament, and Premier Debré continued the practice of appointing as Cabinet Ministers high civil servants and other persons who were not Members of Parliament. Between his accession to the premiership in January, 1959, and his resignation in April, 1962, M. Debré appointed 32 men to senior Cabinet posts and many of them had also served in de Gaulle's Cabinet. Of those 32, at the time of their first ministerial appointment either by de Gaulle or Debré, 18 were Members of Parliament (but one of them was defeated at the 1958 legislative election), 11 were high civil servants, 1 was a university professor with governmental administrative experience, 1 was the Secretary-General of the UNR, and 1 was France's greatest living writer, André Malraux. M. Debré himself was a Senator when he was appointed Premier.

Fewer civil servants were appointed to the Cabinet during the Premiership of M. Pompidou. M. Pompidou, however, had never held any elective office at the time of his appointment as Premier, although in 1965 he was elected to the municipal council of a small town in the department of Lot and he was elected to the National Assembly in 1967 from a district in the department of Cantal.

The participation of civil servants in Fifth Republic Governments reflects, in part, the major policy-making role of the President. Foreign policy and defense policy are questions to which the President gives close and continuing attention, with the result that the Ministries of Foreign Affairs and of the Armed Forces are no longer policy-making centers but agencies for the execution of presidential policies, and these two ministries have been occupied exclusively by civil servants since June, 1958. French policy in Algeria was defined by the President, and when negotiations began to be conducted with the Algerian nationalist leaders, the post of Minister of State for Algerian Affairs was created and given to a high civil servant, who worked directly under the President.

Civil servants may have been appointed to Cabinet posts during the early years of the Fifth Republic for other reasons as well. De Gaulle's conception of the Government is that it should be "a team of men united by similar ideas and convictions" rather than an arena of partisan representation. The Government, however, needs the support of the National Assembly in which representatives of the parties sit, and the parties which contribute to the Government's support make claims for posts in the Government. But the party which had the strongest claim on office after the 1958 elections—the UNR—was an uncertain political entity for about 2 years, and it would have been incautious to have accorded it the spoils. Appointing civil servants to the Cabinet was a way of keeping the UNR out of office without giving office to its partisan competitors. The UNR wanted the Ministry of the Interior when the Debré Government was formed in January, 1959, but the UNR was divided at the time between unconditional supporters of de Gaulle and those whose support for him was conditional upon his trying to retain French control over Algeria. The Interior was first given to a Radical and then, for almost 2 years, to a high civil servant. It was not until the spring of 1961, after the January referendum had demonstrated the extent of popular support for the President's policy of self-determination for Algeria and after the second UNR party congress had demonstrated that the party was safely under the control of de Gaulle's unconditional supporters, that a leader of the UNR was appointed Minister of the Interior.

Some ministries were treated as "technical" rather than "political," and these were given for a time to civil servants. But political pressures and UNR complaints about the "technocratic" nature of the régime eventually prevailed, and when the first Pompidou Government was formed some of these posts were turned over to partisans. When the second Pompidou Government was formed after the UNR sweep at the election of 1962, the UNR acquired the lion's share of the Cabinet posts and the number of civil servants in the Cabinet dropped to its lowest point since the beginning of the Fifth Republic.

At the 1967 election, all but two of the Ministers who had never been elected to Parliament ran for seats in the Assembly. All of these Ministers were reappointed to the Government after the election whether they had won or not. As the victorious Ministers

who were reappointed to the Cabinet never really took seats in
Parliament because of the incompatibility rule, and as the defeated
Ministers could not have done so in any case, the Government
formed in April, 1967, after the 1967 elections contained seven
Ministers (including the Premier) who had never served in
Parliament, even though three of them had won seats at the 1967
election (see Table 5).

GOVERNMENT SOLIDARITY

All Governments of the Fifth Republic have been coalitions,
in that Ministers have come from two or more parties and the
Government has required the support of more than one party in
the National Assembly, and there have been conflicts and rivalries
among the parties participating in the coalitions. Early in the
régime the MRP was disgruntled when the composition of the
various presidential committees through which President de Gaulle
operated (see Chapter Three, p. 54) was such that no Minister from the MRP was a member of any of them.[4] A strong current
of opinion in the UNR sought to extend UNR control over
economic and social affairs, but the UNR was given no senior
ministry in those fields until April, 1962, and the Ministry of
Finance was held by a Conservative from 1958 until 1966, except
for two years when it was held by a civil servant. After the 1967
election, at which the Gaullist Conservatives fared proportionally
better than the Gaullist UNR, their leader made it clear that
they expected to have a larger role in shaping the policy of the
majority.

But de Gaulle's hope that the Government could be a homogeneous policy-making body functionally separated from Parliament was realized to a considerable extent between 1962 and 1967.
Ministers were expected either to support the policy of the Government or to resign. All MRP Ministers resigned from the Government in the spring of 1962 over the issue of European integration
(one of them returned to the Government as a Gaullist in 1967),
but most of the Conservative Ministers chose to remain in the
Government when their parliamentary group called on them to
resign at the same time. Some men entered Governments as individuals and not as representatives of parties, and several of them

[4] *Le Monde*, March 15, 1960.

TABLE 5. Composition of Governments After Successive Major Reorganizations, June, 1958–April, 1967 (Senior Ministers Only)

Premier	De Gaulle		Debré			Pompidou I		II	III	IV
	June 9 1958	July 7 1958	Jan. 8 1959	Feb. 5 1960	Aug. 24 1961	April 15 1962	May 16 1962	Dec. 6 1962	Jan. 8 1966	April 8 1967
Parliamentary UNR[a]	2	3	3	4	4	7	8	11	8	8
Nonparliamentary UNR[b]		2	2	1	1	1	1	2	1	6[c]
Conservatives	3	3	3	2	1	3	3	3	1	2
MRP	3	3	3	3	3	5			1	1
Radicals	2	2	1	1	1					2
Socialists	3	3								
Civil Servants[e]	5	7	6	9	9	4	6[c]	3	4	1
Overseas France[f]	1	1	1	1	1	1				1
Diverse[g]	1	1	1	1	1	1	1	1	1	1
	20[h]	23	20	20	20	21	20	21	17	21

[a] UNR (Social Republican in 1958) Ministers who had served as Members of Parliament at any time between 1945 and time of appointment as Minister, but excluding those elected as Deputies in 1958 or later who did not actually serve as Deputies because of application of the incompatibility rule.

[b] UNR leaders who had never served as Members of Parliament prior to appointment as Minister, even though elected as Deputies in 1958 or later.

[c] Includes a civil servant who had been a Socialist Deputy from 1946 to 1951.

[d] All Conservative, MRP, Radical, and Socialist Ministers had served as Members of Parliament prior to appointment as Ministers. Ministers labeled Radical after 1960 and MRP after May 16, 1962, did not represent those parties in the Government but served on an individual basis; they ran as Gaullists at the 1967 election, but not as UNR.

[e] Includes ambassadors and university professors, as well as administrative officials. Civil servant Ministers who ran at the 1967 election are switched to nonparliamentary UNR.

[f] M. Houphouet-Boigny, Deputy from the Ivory Coast who resigned from the French Government upon becoming Premier of the Ivory Coast in May, 1959.

[g] M. André Malraux.

[h] Totals do not include the Premier.

resigned: M. Boulloche in 1959 over the Government's policy concerning subsidies for private schools, M. Sudreau in 1962 over the decision to amend the constitution by referendum to provide for the direct election of the President (MM. Boulloche and Sudreau were elected to the Assembly in 1967 as candidates in opposition to the Government), and M. Pisani in 1967 over the Government's decision to ask Parliament for special powers to legislate by ordinance on economic and social matters (see p. 83).

At the elections of 1962 and 1967, the UNR did not run a candidate against any member of the Government from another party; an official Gaullist electoral organization endorsed and supported the non-UNR Ministers.[5] Such a practice is conducive to Governmental unity, as it reduces incentives for Ministers to criticize one another for electoral reasons.

Parliament

BICAMERALISM

The French Parliament consists of two legislative chambers. There is a National Assembly, consisting of 487 members, and a Senate, consisting of 279 members. (In the early years of the Fifth Republic there were also 71 Deputies and 34 Senators for Algeria and the Sahara, but their seats were abolished in July, 1962, after Algeria became independent of France.)

The National Assembly is directly elected by universal suffrage under an electoral system providing for single-member districts and two ballots (see Chapter Six, pp. 144–145). Unless the National Assembly is dissolved earlier, the powers of the National Assembly expire at the opening of the regular April parliamentary session of the fifth year following its election, and new elections must be held during the 60 days preceding that date.

The Senate is elected indirectly. The department is the electoral district for the 260 Senators from Metropolitan France (the remaining 19 Senators sit for the overseas departments and territories and for the French residing overseas). Senators are elected for each department by departmental electoral colleges consisting

---

[5] In 1958, three of the nine non-UNR Ministers were opposed by candidates running under various Gaullist labels, and two of them lost their seats, one to a candidate who joined the UNR group in the Assembly.

of from about 270 to more than 6000 electors, depending on the population of the department. The electors are the Deputies and departmental councillors for each department, plus delegates elected by the municipal councils of the department.[6] The number of delegates allowed to each municipal council depends upon the size of the town. For towns with 9,000 or more inhabitants, all the municipal councillors are electors, and the councils of towns of more than 30,000 inhabitants elect an additional senatorial elector for each 1,000 inhabitants over 30,000.

In the largest departments, which elect five or more Senators, the electoral colleges choose the Senators on the basis of proportional representation (PR). In the remaining departments, the electoral colleges select the Senators according to a system which provides for two ballots. Senatorial candidates are elected at the first ballot if they receive a majority of the votes, provided that the majority constitute 25 percent of the number of legal electors for that department. For seats not filled at the first ballot, there is a run-off ballot at which pluralities are adequate for election.

Senators serve for 9 years, although one-third of the seats are vacated and an election is held every 3 years. The first Senate of the Fifth Republic was elected in its entirety in 1959, and the Senators elected at that time were divided into three categories based on the alphabetical order of their departments. Lots were drawn to determine which category would serve only for 3 years, which would serve for 6 years, and which would serve the full 9-year term. Accordingly, elections were held for one-third of the seats in 1962 and for another third in 1965. The Senators elected at those elections, as well as those elected at subsequent triennial elections, serve a full 9-year term.

The National Assembly is more representative of France on a population basis than the Senate is. The eight departments of the Paris Region, plus five other departments which each had more than one million inhabitants in 1962, contain one-third of the French population, and while they have 32 percent of the Metropolitan seats in the National Assembly, they have only 26 percent

---

[6] Each department has a council, called the *conseil général*, which consists of from about 20 to 70 members who are elected from subdivisions of the department called *cantons*. Elections of departmental councillors (*conseillers généraux*) are called *élections cantonales*.

Each city and town in France has a municipal council. Elections of municipal councillors are called *élections municipales*.

of such seats in the Senate. Moreover, the composition of the senatorial electoral colleges is such as to favor the representatives of the smaller towns relative to those of the larger ones. In the main, these factors mean that rural France is overrepresented, and urban France underrepresented, in the Senate.

Respective Powers of the Chambers. The respective powers of the National Assembly and the Senate depend upon the wishes of the Government. Unless the Government intervenes, the legislative powers of the two chambers are equal, in that the approval of both houses is required for the adoption of a law. When the two houses disagree, however, the Government may intervene by asking for the creation of a joint-conference committee (*commission mixte paritaire*) to work out an acceptable measure. If the joint-conference committee is unable to reach agreement, or if one or the other of the chambers rejects its conclusions, the Government can ask the National Assembly to make a final decision. The Government, therefore, does not need a majority in the Senate as long as it can count on a majority in the National Assembly. However, if it wishes, it can allow the Senate to have a veto over legislative decisions made by the National Assembly.

Joint-conference committees have been employed for only a small proportion of the bills considered, but these have included the budget and other important and controversial items of legislation. More often than not, the committees are able to reach agreement, even though, for a while in 1964, the UNR and its allies in the National Assembly excluded opposition Deputies from the Assembly delegations to the committees and the Senate excluded Government supporters from the Senate delegations. But even when the committees have agreed, their conclusions have sometimes been unacceptable to the Government or to one or both of the chambers, and the Government has often asked the National Assembly to make the final decision.

The Political Orientations of the Chambers. The need to employ joint-conference committees reflects the different political orientations of the two chambers. While the Government has sometimes had to make concessions to the Deputies in order to maintain its majority, and while it lost that majority completely at the time of the controversy over amending the Constitution by referendum to provide for the direct popular election of the President, the Government is frequently opposed by a majority of the

Senate even when it has the support of a majority in the National Assembly.

In part, this is the result of the different political composition of the two chambers. During the Fifth Republic, the Senate has been the seat of strength of the traditional political parties to which de Gaulle has been opposed and whose strength in the National Assembly has been reduced by the electoral successes of the UNR. In the summer of 1967, the UNR held only 11 percent of the seats in the Senate, while it held more than 40 percent of the seats in the National Assembly.

But the different composition of the two chambers is not the only explanation for their different behavior. Sometimes, particularly before the election of 1962, members of the same party voted differently in the two chambers, the Deputies in favor of the Government's position and the Senators opposing it.[7] This can be, in part, accounted for by the fact that the National Assembly can be dissolved by the President, while the Senate cannot be. Some Deputies may have preferred to support the Government rather than run the risk of a dissolution followed by elections at which they would be cast as opponents of de Gaulle. Senators do not have to take such a consideration into account.

Even if they did, however, they would be under fewer constraints than the Deputies to support the Government. Senators are not elected by the public at large, where de Gaulle's popularity has been great, but by local politicians who are largely refractory to Gaullist political conceptions. The UNR has not been as successful in its efforts to penetrate France's local government councils as it has been in its penetration of the National Assembly (see Chapter Seven, p. 191). Accordingly, most Senators are responsive to the sentiments of a political class which has not been as receptive to Gaullist appeals as the general public has been. This political class continues to elect a Senate whose composition and outlook are not much different from what they were during the Fourth Republic.

There has been considerable discussion in France since 1963 concerning the possibility of reorganizing the Senate. The Senate

[7] This and the following paragraph follow the analysis presented by François Goguel, "Les circonstances du référendum du 8 avril 1962," in François Goguel *et al.*, *Le Référendum du 8 avril 1962*, Armand Colin, Paris, 1963, pp. 23–24.

cannot be dissolved, but its basis and even its existence are subject to constitutional amendment. Before November, 1962, the Senate might have rested secure in the belief that no constitutional amendment affecting it could be adopted without its consent—as the amending article of the Constitution (Article 89) provided. This situation was changed when de Gaulle successfully employed the referendum alone to amend the Constitution to provide for the popular election of the President.

De Gaulle himself has not spoken of reorganizing the Senate, but he has referred several times to the desirability of changing the composition and the role of the Economic and Social Council. This council is a constitutionally established advisory body (Articles 69–71), composed of representatives of labor, business, agricultural, and other economic or social organizations (see Chapter Eight, p. 206). Any reorganization of the Senate, therefore, may well take the form of a merger between the Senate and the Economic and Social Council. In his Bayeux speech of 1946, de Gaulle outlined the prospect of a second chamber consisting both of representatives elected by municipal and departmental councils (much as Senators are now) and of representatives of economic, intellectual, and other groups (much as Economic and Social Councillors are now). Regardless of whether steps are taken to merge the Senate and the Economic and Social Council, or even to have the latter absorb the former, there is strong pressure to alter the Senate's electoral basis in order to bring it more into line with the distribution of population in France.

THE SCOPE OF LEGISLATIVE AUTHORITY

The Constitution of 1958 departs from the traditional French republican principle of unrestricted parliamentary sovereignty by enumerating the legislative powers of Parliament (Article 34). Much as the United States Constitution enumerates the subjects on which Congress may legislate, leaving the remainder to the states, the French Constitution enumerates the subjects on which Parliament may legislate, leaving the remainder to the Government to decide by decree. This arrangement, which might seem like a serious encroachment on the power of Parliament, is not highly restrictive for two reasons. First, no subject of central importance is omitted from the list. Second, the list can be extended by Parliament through the adoption of an organic law (a law implementing provisions of the Constitution). The procedure for the adoption of an organic law is different from that required for ordinary laws, but a determined Parliament could easily extend its legislative jurisdiction. The main difference between organic laws and ordinary laws is that in the absence of agreement between the two chambers after a joint-conference committee has met, the National Assembly must make the final decision by a majority of all its legal members in the case of an organic law, while a majority only of those voting is sufficient for an ordinary law. Organic laws affecting the Senate must be agreed to by the Senate, while the approval of the Senate can be dispensed with for ordinary legislation if the Government can secure the approval of the National Assembly.

More important than the enumeration of the subjects on which Parliament may legislate is a further division made by Article 34 of the Constitution between those subjects on which Parliament determines "the fundamental principles" and those on which it fixes "the rules." This distinction was badly drafted and it has been a source of confusion, but its main purpose was to distinguish between those subjects on which Parliament may legislate only in a general fashion and those subjects on which it may legislate in detail. In the first category, the rule-making powers of the Government are larger than they are in the second, but they never disappear altogether because Parliament cannot legislate in such a detailed fashion that it can cover every possible application of the law. In fact, the Constitutional Council (see below) has distinguished between rules which Parliament may legitimately fix and those which should be left to the Government to fix even in the case of a subject on which Parliament is constitutionally authorized to fix the rules.[8]

It is possible for the Government to permit (or to ask) Parliament to legislate in detail on subjects on which it is not constitutionally authorized so to legislate, and this has happened (although the Senate has also refused to legislate on a matter which it believed the Government should have decided on its own).[9] In this

---

[8] Jean-Marie Cotteret, *Le Pouvoir législatif en France*, R. Pichon & R. Durand-Auzias, Paris, 1962, pp. 108–109.

[9] Charles Roig, "L'Évolution du Parlement en 1959," in Eliane Guichard-Avoub, Charles Roig, and Jean Grangé, *Études sur le Parlement de la Ve République*, Presses Universitaires de France, Paris, 1965, p. 80.

case, however, the Government retains the power to amend by decree any part of the law passed by Parliament which falls within its own decree-making jurisdiction.

The Constitutional Council. Disputes arise over the question of what is the domain of Parliament and what is the domain of the Government in specific cases. These disputes are decided by the Constitutional Council, a body established by the Constitution (Articles 56–63) which umpires certain conflicts between the political authorities pertaining to their respective constitutional powers.

The Constitutional Council has several important functions. It rules on the regularity of presidential elections, legislative elections, and referendum operations. It must approve the constitutionality of the rules of the two legislative chambers and of all organic laws before they can go into effect. When requested by the President, the Premier, or the President of either legislative chamber, it may decide upon the constitutionality of any law or international commitment. And, in the context of the enumeration of Parliament's legislative jurisdiction and the division of this jurisdiction into two categories, in one of which Parliament may legislate in more detailed fashion than in the other, the Constitutional Council decides whether the Government may modify by decree legislative measures adopted by Parliament after the Constitution of 1958 went into effect. It also decides, in cases of disagreement between the Government and the President of either legislative chamber, and at the request of either party, whether a bill or an amendment to a bill is within the legislative jurisdiction of Parliament. Decisions of the Constitutional Council are final; there is no appeal.

By the end of 1963, the Constitutional Council had decided 31 disputes over the respective rule-making powers of the Parliament and the Government. In 22 cases it decided that the rule-making power in question was properly the Government's; in four it decided that the proper jurisdiction was parliamentary; and in the others, there was either no decision or a decision dividing the rule-making power between the Government and Parliament.

The Constitutional Council consists of nine appointed members plus former Presidents of the Republic. The appointed members serve 9-year terms, although like the members of the first Senate of the Fifth Republic, the first nine members appointed were divided into three equal groups, one to serve only 3 years, another to serve 6 years, and the third to serve 9 years. All replacements of the original Constitutional Councillors serve full 9-year terms.

One-third of the appointed Constitutional Councillors are appointed by the President, who also names the President of the Constitutional Council, one-third are appointed by the President of the National Assembly, and one-third are appointed by the President of the Senate. In 1959, each of these officials appointed one person in each of the three groups mentioned above.

The first President of the National Assembly under the Fifth Republic was a supporter of de Gaulle; the first President of the Senate was an opponent. The breakdown of votes taken within the Constitutional Council is not made public, but it was reported unofficially that when the Council declared itself to be without jurisdiction over the constitutionality of the President's and Government's decision to use the referendum alone to amend the constitutional provisions for the election of the President (see Chapter Three, p. 57), it did so by a vote of 6 to 4.[10] Earlier, the Government had asked the Council for an advisory opinion on the form of the proposal, and the Council rendered an unfavorable opinion, but this opinion was not binding.[11]

Former President Auriol expressed his displeasure with what he felt to be the excessively limited competence of the Council by announcing in 1960 that he would not attend any more of its meetings. He returned to attend the meeting in 1962 which decided that the Council was without jurisdiction in the matter of the referendum to amend the Constitution, and then announced again that he would no longer sit with the Council.[12] Former President Coty, who died late in 1962, was reported to have been "in the minority of the Council which had contested the legality of the referendum of October 28."[13]

Delegation of Legislative Power. According to Article 38 of the Constitution, Parliament may delegate its own legislative powers to the Government for a given period of time. During that period, the Government may legislate by ordinances, which take effect immediately, on matters covered by the delegation of power. Before the expiration of the period, the Government is required to present to

[10] *L'Année Politique 1962,* Presses Universitaires de France, Paris, 1963, p. 122.
[11] *Ibid.,* p. 107.
[12] *Ibid.,* pp. 121–122.
[13] *Ibid.,* p. 135.

Parliament a bill for the ratification of the ordinances it has issued. If the Government does not do so, or if it does and Parliament rejects the bill, the ordinances become null and void. If Parliament ratifies the ordinances, they become standing legislation.

Article 38 was invoked for the first time in February, 1960, following the "revolt of the barricades"—the first revolt by French settlers in Algeria against de Gaulle's Algerian policy. At that time, Parliament adopted a law authorizing the Government to take the measures normally within the jurisdiction of Parliament "necessary to ensure the maintenance of order, the protection of the State and of the Constitution, the pacification and the administration of Algeria." The law restricted the delegation of powers to "the Government presently in office," required that the measures taken be subject to signature by President de Gaulle, provided that the delegation of powers would cease if the National Assembly were dissolved, and made the delegation of powers valid for one year. Thirty ordinances were enacted by the Government (and de Gaulle) under this special delegation of powers.

Article 38 requires the Government to consult the Council of State about such ordinances. The Council of State is both the Government's principal legal adviser and France's highest administrative court. In the first capacity, it advises the Government about the legal validity of its acts; in the second capacity, it decides cases brought by the public against the administration. The Government is under no obligation to heed the advice of the Council of State, but it is often wise for it to do so, as the Council of State may, in its judicial capacity, decide a case against the administration and in favor of a plaintiff on the ground that the administration has exceeded its legal authority. The administration, of course, receives its instructions from the Government, so the Council of State is in a position to nullify Governmental decisions on legal grounds.

The Council of State rendered unfavorable advisory opinions on some of the ordinances enacted by the Government pursuant to the delegated powers it received in 1960, but the Government put them into effect anyhow.[14]

Between 1960 and 1967, Article 38 was employed another half-dozen times, and the Government was given the authority to

[14] L'Année Politique 1961, Presses Universitaires de France, Paris, 1962, p. 19.

legislate by ordinance on a variety of matters, including distilling at home; prostitution; the relocation in Metropolitan France of French citizens who had left North Africa; economic, fiscal and legal matters required by France's participation in the European Economic Community; and the evacuation of French Somaliland if the local voters decided, at the referendum held there in March, 1967, to become independent of France (they did not).[15]

Article 38 was employed for the eighth time in May, 1967. The legislative elections of March had returned a narrow Gaullist majority to the National Assembly, and the first major act of the Government which was formed after the election was an unexpected request for a broad delegation of legislative power in economic and social affairs. This request was notable because of the wide range of matters which it covered and because it suggested concern on the part of the Government that it might not be able to secure the adoption of each of its measures on those matters if it followed the normal legislative process. The Government argued that it needed special powers because it was essential to act quickly, but it was believed that the Government also feared that Parliament would amend its proposals if they were presented as regular legislation. The Government obtained the delegation of powers which it requested, but the episode strained relations between the Government and some of its supporters in the National Assembly.

PARLIAMENTARY SESSIONS

The Constitution provides for two regular parliamentary sessions each year (Article 28): a fall session of approximately 11 weeks and a spring session of approximately 12 weeks. The original dates set by the Constitution for these two regular sessions were amended in December, 1963, by the formal amending procedure prescribed by Article 89. The changes were not of political importance. The length of the two regular sessions combined is somewhat shorter than the average annual parliamentary session in England.

Special sessions are provided for and they have been numerous, suggesting that the normal parliamentary sessions are not long enough. The Constitution provides that special sessions may be called by the Premier or by a majority of the members of the

15 *Le Monde*, April 28, 1967.

National Assembly for specific purposes, although only the Premier can call a special session within one month of the closing of the previous session. When a special session is called at the request of a majority of the Deputies it cannot last longer than 12 days (Article 29). Parliament must also be convened specially to hear a message from the President of the Republic if he chooses to deliver one outside of the regular parliamentary sessions (Article 18). Parliament also meets by right when the President is exercising emergency powers under Article 16.

In the spring of 1960 there was a sharp clash between the Deputies and the President over the calling of a special session. A majority of the Deputies invoked Article 29 and requested a special session of Parliament to consider several bills concerning agriculture. President de Gaulle, however, refused to convene Parliament, relying on Article 30 of the Constitution, which provides that "Except when Parliament meets by right, special sessions are opened and closed by decree of the President of the Republic." For all practical purposes, therefore, despite Article 29, a majority of the Deputies cannot call a special session of Parliament unless the President agrees.

PRIMACY OF THE GOVERNMENT IN THE LEGISLATIVE PROCESS

The Constitution of the Fifth Republic gives the Government much greater control over the conduct of the legislative process than it had during the Fourth Republic. The agenda of each chamber must give priority to Government bills (bills introduced by the Government and called *projets de loi*) and to parliamentary bills (bills introduced by Members of Parliament and called *propositions de loi*) which the Government has accepted, in the order established by the Government (Article 48). This means, in effect, that no legislative measures may be discussed without the approval of the Government. During the Fourth Republic, by contrast, the National Assembly had complete control over its agenda, and majorities in the Assembly could block the Government by refusing to consider legislative matters in which the Government was interested. There are still some matters, however, which the chambers may place on their agenda by right. Article 48 of the Constitution provides for a question period and questions are outside Government control; the chambers may conduct internal business such as the election of officers and the establishment of their rules (although the rules of the chambers must be approved by the Constitutional Council); the chambers may consider and vote on requests for the suspension of the detention or prosecution of any of their members (the requests, if voted, must be honored, according to Article 26); and the National Assembly may vote on a motion of censure against the Government (see below, pp. 93–94).[16]

Debate on Government bills in the chamber in which they are first introduced must take place on the text of the bills as they were presented by the Government (Article 42). This has ended the former practice of holding the initial parliamentary debate on a Government bill not on the text as presented by the Government but on the text as revised by the parliamentary committee to which the bill had been sent for study.

If the Government wishes, it may require the chambers to make their decisions by a single vote on all or part of a bill, including only those amendments which were proposed or accepted by the Government (Article 44). This procedure, which is referred to as the "blocked vote" or the "single vote," is used frequently by the Government, as it protects the Government against having its measures trimmed by successive amendments to fit the desires of the Deputies. The procedure can protect the Deputies from having to vote on demagogic amendments, but it also prevents them from reshaping Government measures. Of all the new procedures incorporated into the legislative process of the Fifth Republic, this is the one which Members of Parliament objected to the most.[17]

Even under the Fourth Republic, Parliament relied on the leadership of the Government in the legislative process. Although the right to initiate legislation was held then, as now, by Members of Parliament as well as by the Government, most of the bills enacted into law originated with the Government. More than 75 percent of all the bills introduced into Parliament during the

[16] For a thorough study of the French parliamentary agenda, see Jean Grangé, "La Fixation de l'ordre du jour des Assemblées parlementaires," in Guichard-Ayoub, Roig, and Grangé, op. cit., pp. 167–287.

[17] Nicolas Denis, "L'application des nouvelles règles de procédure parlementaire établies par la Constitution de 1958," Revue Française de Science Politique, X (December, 1960), 910.

Fourth Republic were parliamentary bills, but more than 70 percent of the bills passed were Government bills.[18]

Under the Fifth Republic, the legislative leadership of the Government became more marked. Members of Parliament introduce fewer bills than they did during the Fourth Republic, although they still introduce more than the Government does. During the first 6 years of the Fifth Republic, from 1959 to 1965, more than 90 percent of the bills passed originated with the Government.[19]

A study of all the Government bills and parliamentary bills which were reported out of committee (although not necessarily discussed on the floor of the chambers) between January 15, 1959, and July 27, 1962, shows that the subjects on which the Government took the initiative included the national budget and taxation, international agreements, military organization, the national economy, and general rules concerning legal matters and social welfare. The bills introduced by the Deputies were mainly in behalf of particular economic and social groups, such as farmers, wage earners, civil servants (including school teachers), tenants, and so forth. Most of the parliamentary bills which the Government allowed on the agenda during the period concerned rents, leases, and other conditions of tenancy.[20]

FINANCIAL LEGISLATION

The Government is given exclusive power to initiate legislation authorizing the appropriation of public funds by Article 40 of the Constitution, which reads that: "Bills and amendments formulated by Members of Parliament are not admissible when the result of their adoption would be either a decrease in public resources or the creation or increase of public expenditure." Decisions concerning the admissibility of bills are made first by the officers of the chamber; decisions concerning the admissibility of amendments to bills are made by the Finance Committee.[21] In cases of disagreement between these bodies and the Government, the question is settled by the Constitutional Council, but few cases go that far. As of December, 1963, the Constitutional Council had

[18] Grangé, op. cit., p. 245.
[19] Le Monde, November 25, 1965.
[20] Grangé, op. cit., pp. 263–265.
[21] François Goguel and Alfred Grosser, La Politique en France, Armand Colin, Paris, 1964, p. 181.

ruled on only two cases directly concerning Article 40; in one case it ruled in favor of the Government, in the other it ruled that part of a measure adopted by Parliament was acceptable but another part not.

Budgetary Procedure. Parliament must act on the finance bill within 70 days after its introduction; if it does not, the Government may put the bill's provisions into effect by decree (Article 47). The National Assembly cannot unduly limit the time available to the Senate for its consideration of the finance bill. If the Assembly does not complete its initial deliberations on the bill within 40 days, the Government may send the bill to the Senate, which must act on it within 15 days, after which the normal legislative process is resumed, subject to the provision that the 70-day limit, counting from the initial introduction of the bill in the National Assembly, not be exceeded.

ORGANIZATION OF THE CHAMBERS

The Group. The basic unit of political organization in the two houses of Parliament is the parliamentary group. Sometimes the group consists only of the members of a single national party and bears the same name as the party. Sometimes members of different parties join the same group. Members of loosely organized parties often divide up into two or more groups. Some members do not join a group but simply affiliate with one; others attach themselves to a group only for administrative purposes; still others do not join any group at all.

The number of groups in each chamber varies. At the beginning of 1966, there were seven groups in the Senate and six in the National Assembly. After the election of 1967, only five groups were formed in the National Assembly. Table 6 indicates the names and the sizes of the groups formed in the Assembly after the election of March, 1967, as well as the parties with which their members were affiliated at the time of the election.

The number of members required to form a group is set by the rules of the chambers. At the start of the Fourth Republic, only 14 Deputies were required for a group; the figure was raised to 28 at the end of 1957. The rules of the National Assembly under the Fifth Republic require 30 Deputies. This provision prevented the Communist Party from forming a separate group during the First

Legislature of the Fifth Republic, as the Communists then had only 10 seats in the Assembly.

Group meetings are important in the parliamentary decision-making process, and they are important also for the maintenance of communication between the parties of the majority and the Ministers. A large group like the one formed by the UNR is

TABLE 6.   Parliamentary Groups in the National Assembly, April 3, 1967

Group	Size[a]	Party Affiliations
Union démocratique pour la Ve République Affiliates	180 20	UNR-UDT; some Deputies from other parties elected as Gaullist candidates
Républicains Indépendants Affiliates	39 3	Independent Republicans (Gaullist Conservatives)
Progrès et Démocratie moderne Affiliates	38 3	MRP; non-Gaullist Conservatives; Deputies without major-party affiliation
Fédération de la gauche démocrate et socialiste Affiliates	116 5	Socialist Party; Radical Party; Convention; PSU
Communiste Affiliates	71 2	Communist Party
No group	9	

[a] The total is only 486, as one Deputy from an Overseas Territory had not yet been elected.

SOURCE: Le Monde, March 18, April 5, and April 14, 1967.

organized into a number of working groups which specialize in various subjects, often corresponding to the jurisdiction of ministries. Groups are also important for administrative purposes, such as appointments to parliamentary committees, the election of officers of the chamber, and representation on the Conference of Presidents, which sets the agenda (subject to the prior rights of the Government) and allocates debating time to the various parliamentary groups.

Officers.   Each chamber elects its own officers, collectively called the *bureau*. The National Assembly elects its President for the duration of the legislature, and all its other officers annually, at the start of the regular spring session. The Senate elects its *bureau* after each triennial election of one-third of its members. Since the beginning of the Fifth Republic, the President of the National Assembly has been Jacques Chaban-Delmas, a member of the UNR who has been a Deputy since November, 1946, and Mayor of Bordeaux since 1947. He has the delicate task of trying to satisfy the demands for greater authority of the members of the Assembly over which he presides and at the same time protect the conception of legislative-executive relationships which is held by the President of the Republic.

Since 1947, the President of the Senate has been Gaston Monner-ville, who has been a Senator since 1946, for 2 years from the overseas department of Guiana (for which he had been a Deputy from 1936 to 1940 and from 1945 to 1946) and, since 1948, from the metropolitan department of Lot. M. Monnerville has been a vigorous opponent of de Gaulle, and his strongly critical remarks about the President led the Government to establish a sort of boycott of the Senate after the election of November, 1962. Senior Ministers appear in the Senate infrequently; only junior Ministers normally represent the Government in that chamber.

The *bureau* of the National Assembly consists of the President, six Vice-Presidents, three Questors, and twelve Secretaries. The rules of the Assembly state that an effort should be made to have the *bureau* reflect the political configuration of the Assembly. Until 1962 the posts were allocated among groups roughly proportionately to their size, but after the 1962 election, Communists were again excluded from the *bureau*, even though they then had enough Deputies to form a separate group. After the 1967 election, Communists were elected to one vice-presidency and three secretaryships.

Parliamentary Committees. The Constitution permits each legislative chamber to have no more than six standing committees, a considerable reduction from the Fourth Republic, when the Assembly usually had 19. The Assembly committees had 44 members each during the Fourth Republic, but now they are larger and more unwieldy, as they range in size from 60 to more than 120 members. They could be made more manageable only by circulating or limiting their membership, but the first alternative would operate against the specialization which French Deputies, like United States Congressmen, believe is valuable, and the second alternative would, by excluding some Deputies from committee membership, create inequalities among the Deputies. Two Deputies actually were without committee assignments in the Assembly which was elected in 1962, as there were then 482 Deputies but only 480 committee posts. The number of Deputies was increased to 487 for the election of March, 1967, but in April the Assembly increased the number of committee posts so that no Deputy would be without one.[22]

The six committees of each chamber have broad, but specific, jurisdictions. Informal "work groups" or "study groups" have been created within the committees; those of the Senate tend to parallel the ministries, those of the Assembly tend to parallel types of legislative problems.[23] To some extent, these smaller groups enable the chambers to circumvent the limit on the number of committees, but while they do permit specialized deliberation, the smaller groups cannot make final decisions; these must be made by the full committee.

The Constitution authorizes the Government or the chambers to send bills to special committees rather than to the standing committees. It appears that when the Constitution was drafted, it was believed that special committees would be used regularly. This has not turned out to be the case. The Government rarely asks for a special committee to be formed, although on one occasion, a small number of Deputies succeeded in persuading a near-empty Assembly, over the objections both of the Government and the Assembly's Finance Committee, to send a financial measure to a special committee which was packed with Deputies from rural areas interested in defending a particular interest. The Government was forced to withdraw its measure.[24]

Each standing committee elects its own chairman, and there is considerable continuity in office. Committee chairmanships are not

---

[22] Le Monde, April 28, 1967.

[23] Charles Roig, "L'Évolution du Parlement en 1959," in Guichard-Ayoub, Roig, and Grangé, op. cit., p. 96.

[24] Jean-Luc Parodi, Les Rapports entre le législatif et l'exécutif sous la Ve République, Fondation Nationale des Sciences Politiques, February, 1962, p. 11.

springboards to ministerial office. Few committee chairmen during the Fifth Republic have been appointed to the Government.

The Government and the Assembly

The central principle governing the relations between the Government and Parliament under the Fifth Republic is that the chambers may not take any vote expressing their attitude toward the Government or its policies unless they are asked to do so by the Government itself, except that the National Assembly may vote on a motion of censure against the Government in the conditions prescribed by the Constitution. A motion of censure cannot be voted on in the Senate. If a motion of censure is adopted by the National Assembly, the Government must resign.

The reason for the establishment of this principle (and it has been applied strictly) is that the framers of the Constitution of the Fifth Republic wanted to maintain the ultimate control of the National Assembly over the Government without permitting either the National Assembly or the Senate to become policy-making agencies. Accordingly, while the National Assembly may withdraw its confidence completely from the Government, it may not pass resolutions or otherwise express its views on policy unless the Government asks it to do so. The practice of interpellation which was characteristic of the Third and Fourth Republics is not permitted under the Fifth. An interpellation consisted of one or more questions put to the Government by the Deputies, a debate on the subject of the questions, and a vote on one or more motions in order to express the chamber's views of Government policy on that subject. Votes of that kind can no longer be taken without the Government's consent. Just as the chambers may be required by the Government to decide on legislative questions by a single vote, which permits them to reject what the Government wants but prevents them from qualifying their position by voting on a sequence of amendments (see p. 85), the Constitution (and its strict interpretation) permits the Assembly to reject Government policy and vote a Government out of office but does not permit it to qualify its views on Government policy by means of resolutions. Parliament may ask questions and it may debate the answers which the Government gives, but unless it is asked to do so by the Government, it cannot express its view of Government policy except through a vote on a formal motion of censure in the Assembly.

PARLIAMENTARY QUESTIONS

Both oral and written questions are used as a means of eliciting information from the Government. The framers of the Constitution hoped that the oral question would occupy the same importance in French parliamentary activity that it is alleged to occupy in the House of Commons. However, question time in the National Assembly was originally set for Friday afternoons and attendance was poor, as many Deputies leave Paris by Friday evening to visit their constituencies during the weekend. Toward the end of 1963 the average attendance on Friday afternoon was 20, and at one session Minister of State for Cultural Affairs André Malraux answered questions before an audience which dwindled to three. In December, question time in the Assembly was shifted to Thursday morning.

There are two types of parliamentary questions, those which are followed by debate and those which are not. An analysis of the questions placed on the agenda between January, 1959, and July, 1962, shows that virtually all questions without debate were answered by the Government, and while not all questions designed for debate actually were debated, the number of questions which were debated and which originated with opposition groups was disproportionately large relative to the size of those groups.[25] The opposition, in other words, was favored in this opportunity to discuss matters which might be embarrassing to the Government.

If a Member of Parliament simply wants information from a Minister, and is unconcerned with publicity or the possibility of a debate over the answer, he simply writes the Minister. This is done frequently. Premier Debré circularized his Ministers, reminding them of the necessity for prompt replies to requests from Members of Parliament, especially those who supported the Government.[26] In May, 1964, the Secretary of State for Parliamentary Relations stated that between December 15, 1962, and

[25] Grangé, op. cit., pp. 267–269.
[26] Le Monde, November 4, 1961.

December 15, 1963, the Minister of Finance had addressed 13,400 letters to Members of Parliament.[27]

CONFIDENCE AND CENSURE

The Government is constitutionally responsible to Parliament (Article 20), but this responsibility comes into play only before the National Assembly, according to procedures prescribed in Articles 49 and 50 of the Constitution.

The term "question of confidence" does not appear in the Constitution but its substance remains in these two provisions. Article 49 states that "the Premier, after deliberation by the Council of Ministers, engages the responsibility of the Government before the National Assembly on its program or, possibly, on a declaration of general policy" and that "the Premier may, after deliberation by the Council of Ministers, engage the responsibility of the Government before the National Assembly on the vote of a text." When the Government engages its responsibility—which is another way of saying when it asks for a vote of confidence—on its program or on a statement of general policy, it must resign if it is defeated, regardless of the number of votes cast against it. When the Government engages its responsibility on a text—some specific measure—the procedure is more complex.

In the latter case, once the Government has engaged its responsibility, the Deputies have 24 hours within which to introduce a motion of censure against the Government, if they wish to do so. A motion of censure must be signed by at least one-tenth of the members of the National Assembly. No sooner than 48 hours after a motion of censure is introduced, a vote is taken on it, but only those Deputies voting in favor of the motion, that is, voting against the Government, cast ballots. If these total a majority of the members of the National Assembly—what in French parliamentary terms is called an absolute majority, as opposed to a relative majority, which is a majority of those actually voting—the Government must resign. If the number of votes adds up to less than an absolute majority, the Government is regarded as upheld and the particular measure on which the Government engaged its responsibility is adopted. The Government is similarly upheld and the measure adopted if no motion of censure is introduced (which

[27] *Ibid.*, May 24–25, 1964.

can produce the odd situation of a measure being adopted without a vote and possibly even without debate).

This procedure, which M. Debré acknowledged as unusual, was included in the Constitution of 1958 mainly at the urging, not of Gaullists, but of political leaders of the Fourth Republic, who felt that the advantage which this system gives to the Government would be necessary to maintain Government authority.[28] The requirement of an absolute majority for censure gives an advantage to the Government, and the requirement that only votes cast against the Government be tallied prevents the disclosure of situations where the Government might be supported by fewer Deputies than opposed it, but where, because of abstentions or absences, the opponents of the Government could not muster an absolute majority of the Deputies.

One-tenth of the Deputies may move a motion of censure against the Government even if the Government has not engaged its responsibility before the Assembly. In this case, the same basic rule applies: unless the Government is defeated by a majority of all the Deputies, with only those votes cast against the Government being counted, the Government is upheld. When the Deputies introduce a motion of censure without the Government's having first engaged its responsibility, and the motion fails to pass, the Deputies who signed the motion cannot sign another motion of censure during the same session of Parliament. Futile motions of censure designed simply to harass the Government (and take up parliamentary time) cannot, therefore, be multiplied. This limitation does not apply to the signing of motions of censure in reply to the Government when it has engaged its responsibility before the Assembly; the same Deputies can file censure motions repeatedly if the Government engages its responsibility repeatedly.

It is evident that the Government runs a greater risk of being forced to resign (other things being equal) when it engages its responsibility on its program or on a statement of general policy than when it does so on a particular measure. In the former case it can be reversed by a relative majority and in the latter case only by an absolute majority. Premier Debré, however, engaged the responsibility of his Government on its program shortly after it was

[28] François Goguel, "L'élaboration des institutions de la République dans la Constitution du 4 Octobre 1958," *Revue Française de Science Politique*, IX (March, 1959), 76 and 79.

formed in 1959, and Premier Pompidou did so also, both in April and in December of 1962, after the formation of his first and second Governments. What had appeared to be a precedent in this regard was broken in 1966, however, when Premier Pompidou failed to engage the responsibility of his third Government on its program. As there was not much probability that he would have been defeated had he done so, his failure to do so may be interpreted as a gesture designed to demonstrate that the Government emanates from the President, and that while it may be reversed by the Assembly, it does not require the prior approval of the Assembly.

Between the beginning of the Fifth Republic and the winter of 1967, 15 motions of censure were introduced against the Government (see Table 7). On eight occasions the Deputies replied to the Government's engagement of responsibility: once over the budgetary item for veterans' pensions, four times over the question of France's independent nuclear striking force, and three times over the Government's request for a delegation of legislative power in economic and social affairs (see p. 83).[29]

On the other occasions Deputies filed motions of censure without the Government first having engaged its responsibility on a measure. On several of these occasions the object of the censure motions was not so much the Government as the President. In May, 1960, a motion of censure was introduced by Deputies who were angry over the President's failure to convene the special parliamentary session to discuss agricultural bills which a majority of the Deputies had wanted to hold (see p. 84). The motion of censure introduced in October, 1962, stated that its signers believed that the President had violated the Constitution by deciding to bypass Parliament in amending the Constitution. The motion of censure introduced in April, 1966, stated that "the President of the Republic decided to withdraw the French forces from NATO without consulting the French Government or the French Parliament. . . ."

One motion of censure was adopted during the First Legislature of the Fifth Republic. This was the motion which censured the Government in connection with its role in amending the Constitution by referendum. After the Government's defeat, Premier

---

[29] On one occasion, the Government engaged its responsibility but no censure motion was filed in reply.

TABLE 7. Votes on Censure Motions, 1959–1967

Date[a]	Type[b]	Issue	Votes for Censure[c]	Remarks
1. 27/11/59	C	Budget item for veterans	109	The motion disapproved of Government's economic policy, but approved of President's policy of self-determination for Algeria, to discourage *Algérie française* Deputies from voting for it.
2. 5/5/60	P	President's refusal to convene a special session of Parliament at the request of a majority of the Deputies	122	
3. 24/10/60	C	Nuclear striking force	207	
4. 22/11/60	C	Nuclear striking force	214	
5. 6/12/60	C	Nuclear striking force	215	
6. 15/12/61	P	Unmotivated	199	If the purpose of not citing particulars in the motion of censure was to cumulate the votes of Deputies who opposed the Government for conflicting reasons, the tactic failed.
7. 5/6/62	P	Algeria	113	Motion supported only by opponents of the President's Algerian policy; not supported by the Communists, Socialists, or Radicals, normally in the opposition.

No.[a]	Date	Type[b]	Subject	Votes[c]	Remarks
8.	16/7/62	C	Nuclear striking force	206	After motion failed to pass, Government engaged its responsibility once again, but no new motion of censure was introduced.
9.	5/10/62	P	Decision to submit only to referendum the proposal to amend the Constitution to provide for direct popular election of the President	280	Motion of censure adopted.
10.	28/10/64	P	Agriculture	209	
11.	21/4/66	P	Foreign and defense policy	137	Motion not supported by Communists.
12.	20/5/67	C	Government request for delegation of legislative power in economic and social affairs	236	
13.	9/6/67	C	Government request for delegation of legislative power in economic and social affairs	236	
14.	16/6/67	C	Government request for delegation of legislative power in economic and social affairs	237	
15.	10/10/67	P	Economic and social policy	207	

a Motions 1 through 6 filed against Debré Government; 7 through 9 against First Pompidou Government (formed after election of November, 1962); 11 against Second Pompidou Government (formed after presidential election of 1965); 12 through 15 against Third Pompidou Government (formed after election of March, 1967).

b C means motion was filed after Government engaged its responsibility on a measure; P that Deputies took the initiative.

c For motions 1 through 7, 277 votes were normally required for adoption of a motion of censure; for 8 through 11, 242, for 12 through 15, 244.

Pompidou submitted his Government's resignation to the President of the Republic, but the President asked the Government to remain in office and dissolved the National Assembly. After the elections, which were held in November, 1962, the President accepted the resignation of the Government which had been submitted earlier and reappointed M. Pompidou as Premier. The new Government contained only two senior Ministers and one junior Minister who had not served in the Government at the time of the dissolution, and only two Ministers who had served in the previous Government were not included in the new one.

Motions of Censure and Presidential Emergency Powers. While the president is exercising emergency powers under Article 16, he cannot dissolve the National Assembly and Parliament sits by right. In August, 1961, while Article 16 was in force, the *bureaux* of the two legislative chambers decided to convene a special session, in order to take action on agricultural problems. The Premier was opposed to the special session, and the President indicated that he saw no good purpose for it, but under the terms of the Constitution Parliament meets by right while Article 16 is in force and the President did not try to prevent the special session from being held, although he did state that no legislative decision should be made during the special session. When the chambers met in September, the Government refused to permit the discussion of any bills, although it did permit oral questions with debate. Angry at this limitation of what they regarded as their legitimate powers, all the Deputies except those belonging to the UNR boycotted the sittings of the National Assembly, and the Government was left alone with a minority of supporters.

At this time, the question was also raised whether the Deputies could vote on a motion of censure while Article 16 was in force. The Constitutional Council decided that it was not competent to decide the question, and it was left to M. Chaban-Delmas, the President of the National Assembly, to rule on it. The question was a delicate one. If Parliament could not exercise ultimate control over the Government while Article 16 was in force, it would be difficult to explain why the Constitution permitted Parliament to meet by right at that time, except to permit it to accuse the President of high treason, an eventuality prescribed for in Article 68 of the Constitution. On the other hand, if the Deputies were permitted to censure the Government while Article 16 was in force, the President could not dissolve the National Assembly in return, as he is not permitted to dissolve while Article 16 is in force.

M. Chaban-Delmas settled the problem ingeniously. Relying on the message that the President had sent to Parliament when he invoked Article 16 and in which he said that while Article 16 was in force Parliament retained its power of legislation and control, and on the President's letter to the Premier in which he said that there should be no legislative decisions made by Parliament in a special session while Article 16 was in force, M. Chaban-Delmas ruled that the Assembly could not vote on a motion of censure during a *special* session while Article 16 was in force. His reasoning was that if Parliament could not legislate during a special session the Government could not engage its responsibility on a text during that special session, and that the balance of powers required that the Assembly not be able to censure the Government when the Government could not engage its responsibility.

The implication of the ruling was that the Assembly could vote on a motion of censure while Article 16 was in force only during a *regular* session of Parliament. When M. Chaban-Delmas made his ruling, the next regular session of Parliament was only 2 weeks away. Before the regular session began, however, the President ended the application of Article 16, thereby regaining his right to dissolve Parliament.

M. Chaban-Delmas's ruling, by raising the possibility of a motion of censure being passed at a time when the President could not dissolve the Assembly, had certainly placed pressure on the President to end the application of Article 16. But by relying on the President's own rulings in making his decision, M. Chaban-Delmas had also tended to affirm the authority of the President to decide what the powers of Parliament should be while Article 16 is in force. The decision solved the immediate problem, but it provided no assurance that the same problem would be decided similarly in the future, as future presidential rulings concerning the role of Parliament under Article 16 might be different from those of President de Gaulle in 1961.

CHAPTER FIVE

The Political Parties

The French Communist Party

The French Communist Party (PCF, for *Parti communiste fran-çais*) prides itself on not being "a party like the others," and there is justification for this claim. In its goals, activity, and organization, it differs from the other French parties; at the same time, it forms an important element of the political system which must be taken into account by the other parties.

The PCF was formed in 1920 by those members of the Socialist Party who chose to accept the conditions established by Lenin for membership in the Third International. These conditions included, among others, the same attention to discipline and close organization which the Russian Bolsheviks had exploited so successfully, and the first years of the life of the French party were devoted to organizational efforts both in agricultural and industrial areas. The party was not an important electoral force until 1936, and until that year it remained an isolated and opposition party. In 1936, however, it joined with the Socialists and many of the Radicals in an electoral alliance and, for a short while, supported (but did not participate in) the Popular Front government of Léon Blum.

This shift in policy reflected the overriding purpose of the party, which is to support policies favorable to the Soviet Union. (Léon Blum was later to describe the Communists as a "foreign nationalist party"; de Gaulle referred to them as "separatists" during the days of the RPF; and Socialist leader Guy Mollet has said that the Communists were not of the Left but of the East.) The Popular Front venture was in accord with the policy of opposing the growth of fascism which was being pursued at the time by the Soviet Union and the Third International.

Giving unqualified support to the Soviet Union, however, has sometimes caused severe strains within the party, particularly when it requires sharp reversals of policy which go against the instinctive sentiments of many of its members. When the Russian-German nonaggression pact was signed in August, 1939, 21 of the 72 Communist Deputies resigned from the party. The party leadership supported the pact, but on September 2, the remaining Communist Deputies and Senators voted in favor of a special military appropriation, and the party raised no objections to the announcement by France and Britain the next day that they would engage in hostilities. By October, however, the party was working closer to the Russian line and shortly thereafter it adopted what it called "the only just policy, intransigent and courageous struggle against the imperialist war."[1] The Communists, therefore, did not participate in the Resistance as a party until Germany invaded the Soviet Union in June, 1941.

Participation in the Resistance and the wartime alliance between Russia and the Western allies earned the PCF a leading role in the political system at the Liberation. From the Liberation until May, 1947, Communists participated in French Governments for the first and only time in their history. They sought the key ministries of Foreign Affairs, Defense, and the Interior, but de Gaulle gave them responsibility only for economic development, and there were no industrial strikes in France until 1947. But with the development of the Cold War, strains within French Governments increased, and the Communists moved into the opposition in 1947. They had packed the nationalized coal industry with their supporters while they were in the Government; now that they were out of it they launched near-insurrectionary strikes in the northern coal fields in 1947 and 1948. The strikes were broken by Socialist Minister of the Interior Jules Moch, and the Communists settled down to a period of isolation from which they departed only occasionally during the Fourth Republic.

On rare occasions, the Communist Deputies cast their votes in favor of a Government, which always promptly repudiated them, and sometimes they voted in favor of a bill, but they almost always voted in the opposition. The presence in the Assembly of from 100 to 180 Communists reduced the range of Deputies from which

[1] Jacques Fauvet, *Histoire du parti communiste français*, Fayard, Paris, 1965, vol. II, p. 19.

majorities could be drawn and therefore made government under the Fourth Republic even more difficult that it would have been in any case. And by drawing the support of up to 25 percent of the French voters, about one-half of them manual workers, the PCF ensured that France's industrial workers would be without influence in French government proportionate to their numbers.

The party voted unanimously against calling de Gaulle to power in 1958 and was the only major party to urge a "No" vote at the referendum on the new Constitution. But if the party was opposed to the Fifth Republic, it has not opposed all its policies, and on more than one occasion the leadership has had to correct the results of its opposition reflexes. The day after President de Gaulle announced the policy of self-determination for Algeria, Communist leader Jacques Duclos denounced it as a ruse, and the following day the party's Political Bureau claimed that the policy was doomed to fail. Two months later, the Political Bureau "completed and modified" its earlier statement and accepted de Gaulle's policy as a genuinely new departure, although it urged a "No" vote at the 1961 referendum called by de Gaulle to ratify the policy. It did not risk repudiation again at the second referendum on Algeria, however, and recommended a "Yes" vote in April, 1962. Later the party leaders "regretted and corrected" the action of their parliamentary group in voting against an appropriation for aid to Algeria.

The Communists voted in favor of all but two of the first 15 motions of censure against the Government. They did not support the seventh one, which was introduced in June, 1962, by diehard opponents of the Evian agreement with the Algerian FLN, and it did not support the eleventh one, which was introduced in April, 1966. In connection with the latter, the PCF Secretary General said, ". . . We cannot vote for a text whose object is to condemn the withdrawal from NATO of French troops placed under American command and to maintain American bases in France." The foreign policy of the Fifth Republic is not wholly displeasing to the PCF, and while the party opposes the régime, it has not opposed all that the régime has done.[2]

[2] In the spring of 1966, only PCF and a handful of other Deputies joined with most of the UNR in support of the Government's refusal to include the leaders of the 1962 rebellion against the Government's Algerian policy in an amnesty law.

During the postwar years, the PCF has experienced a number of internal crises which have affected its top leadership. High party leaders have occasionally been purged, sometimes for advocating a policy which was later to be adopted by the party, much along the lines of Jean-Paul Sartre's play *Les Mains Sales*. Until 1956 these conflicts had no visible impact on the party's rank and file or its voters; after 1956 the party's difficulties became more serious.

Two major events occurred in 1956 which had an important effect on the PCF. One was the Twentieth Congress of the Russian Communist Party at which Nikita Khrushchev launched his destalinization campaign; the other was the Russian repression of the Hungarian revolt. The PCF leadership supported the repression but was reluctant to support destalinization, and the party suffered on both counts, particularly among its intellectual members and sympathizers. Party statements referred to Stalin's "faults" and "errors," but did not squarely condemn his "crimes" until November, 1961.

The PCF also found it difficult to orient itself in the new conditions of the Communist world. In 1961 it opposed the Italian Communist Party's doctrine of polycentrism—that all Communist parties are equal and should be free to follow such policies as are adapted to national conditions—only to adopt it in 1964. But the new Secretary-General, Waldeck Rochet, who acceded to the post after Maurice Thorez's death in July, 1964, was no more willing than his predecessor to open the doors to the kind of discussion which the Italian party permits. Under both leaders, the party has been in conflict with the students and other intellectuals in its ranks who want to examine those national conditions more fully than the leadership thinks is desirable.

The Communist vote declined under the Fifth Republic compared with the Fourth, but the PCF gained electoral strength successively in 1962 and 1967 (see Figure 1). Like all French parties, its electoral strength is not evenly distributed geographically, but it is the only party which has run candidates in almost every district at each national election. This inflates its total vote relative to that of the parties which are more selective in entering candidates, but in 1962 the party won less than 5 percent of the vote in only seven districts, all of them strongly Catholic.

The discipline of the parliamentary groups is strong, and for all

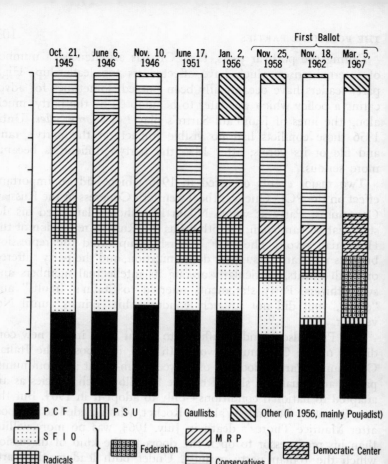

First Ballot

| Oct. 21, 1945 | June 6, 1946 | Nov. 10, 1946 | June 17, 1951 | Jan. 2, 1956 | Nov. 25, 1958 | Nov. 18, 1962 | Mar. 5, 1967 |

PCF PSU Gaullists Other (in 1956, mainly Poujadist)

SFIO ⎫
         ⎬ Federation
Radicals ⎭

MRP
Conservatives
Democratic Center

FIGURE 1.   Results of Elections for the National Assembly, 1945–
1967 (in Percent of Valid Ballots). First Ballot Results
only for 1958, 1962, and 1967.

Based on electoral data from François Goguel and Alfred
Grosser, *La Politique en France*, Armand Colin, Paris, 1964,
pp. 269–272 (for 1945–1951 and 1958); Roy Pierce, "The
French Election of January 1956," *Journal of Politics*, XIX
(August, 1957), 410 (for 1956); François Goguel, "Analyse
des résultats," in François Goguel *et al.*, *Le Référendum
d'octobre et les élections de novembre 1962*, Armand Colin,
Paris, 1965 (Cahiers de la Fondation Nationale des Sciences
Politiques, 142), pp. 306–307 (for 1962); *Le Monde*, March 7,
1967 (for 1967). Figures rounded for graphic purposes.

its internal difficulties the PCF is probably the best organized party in France. The distinctive feature of its organizational structure (as of all Communist parties) is the cell, of which the party claimed to have almost 19,000 in 1966. There are three kinds of cell: the factory cell which meets at the place of work; the local cell which includes party members from a small area, such as a neighborhood, street, apartment house, or even part of an apartment house; and the rural cell which includes party members from one or more small towns. Fewer than 30 percent of the cells are factory cells, although these are the kind which the party prefers in order to develop and maintain class consciousness among its members.

More than three-fourths of the party's federation (departmental) secretaries in 1964 were workers. The party reported in 1959, on the basis of a survey of one-fourth of its cells, that 40 percent of its members were workers. In 1967 the party reported, on the basis of a survey of more than 17,000 cells, that 60 percent of its members were workers.

The age structure of the party's membership in 1966 (as reported in 1967) was as follows: under 25 years of age, 9 percent; 26 to 40, 33 percent; 41 to 60, 40 percent; 61 and over, 17 percent. The party reported at the same time that 13 percent of its members had joined before World War II, 3 percent during the war, 19 percent between the Liberation and 1947, 23 percent between 1948 and 1958, and 42 percent between 1959 and 1966. Seventy-four and one-half percent of the members in 1966 were reported to be men and 25.5 percent women.[3]

The PCF electorate has no doubt always included a large number of malcontents without any fixed political orientation and who have also given their support to other protest groups, such as the Poujadists (see Chapter Six, p. 134); but the PCF may also have attracted the enduring loyalty of more voters than any other single French party. In a survey made in 1952, proportionately more Communist voters indicated that they had complete confidence in their party (and fewer had no confidence in their party) than the voters of any other party, and another survey

[3] This paragraph and the two preceding ones rest on Fauvet, *op. cit.*, Part VI, chaps. 1 and 2, and the report of Georges Marchais, PCF Secretary for Organization, to the XVIIIth PCF Congress, as reported in *Le Monde*, January 7, 1967.

made 10 years later showed that proportionately more people with Communist preferences thought that their preferred party was "the one which best defends people like you" than those with any other party preference.[4] And a survey made in 1962 indicated that 85 percent of the Communist electorate of 1958 also voted Communist in 1962, a higher rate of consistent electoral support than was enjoyed by any other party.[5]

There is a sharp conflict over issues between Communist supporters and the supporters of the other parties. Pierre Fougeyrollas examined the replies given by samples of the French population to 150 questions asked in opinion surveys between 1951 and 1961 for which the replies were tabulated according to the partisan preferences of the respondents.[6] In 104 cases, the replies given by a majority of the respondents with Communist preferences differed from the replies given by a majority of the respondents with non-Communist preferences. One result of this sharp polarization of opinion is that the electorate was often divided on a Communist/non-Communist basis on foreign policy questions (but see above, p. 102), in which the PCF is particularly interested. The French situation in this respect contrasted with that of Great Britain where, on the whole, there was minimal partisan cleavage on foreign policy issues.[7]

The PCF's electoral support comes primarily from industrial workers, seconded by votes from agricultural areas of declining economic and demographic importance. This support is the result of many years of organizational effort, France's retarded economic development during the 1930s, social and economic inequalities which lent confirmation to the notion of class conflict in the minds of French workers, angry antigovernmental attitudes on the part of many rural dwellers, the low levels of political knowledge of many

[4] For 1952, see the figures originally published in *Sondages*, 1952, no. 3, and reprinted in Philip M. Williams, *Crisis and Compromise; Politics in the Fourth Republic*, Longmans, London, 1964, p. 509. For 1962, see *Sondages*, 1963, no. 2, p. 69.

[5] Georges Dupeux, "Le comportement des électeurs français de 1958 à 1962," in François Goguel *et al.*, *Le Référendum d'octobre et les élections de novembre 1962*, Armand Colin, Paris, 1965, p. 183.

[6] Pierre Fougeyrollas, *La Conscience politique dans la France contemporaine*, Editions Denoël, Paris, 1963, pp. 41–42.

[7] M. Davis and S. Verba, "Party Affiliation and International Opinions in Britain and France, 1947–56," *Public Opinion Quarterly*, XXIV (winter, 1960), 590–604.

voters, and the party's anticlericalism. As French society evolves, some of these conditions can be expected to lose their operative effect and the PCF will suffer as a result. But in the absence of convulsive events like war and depression, partisan attachments do not seem to alter easily, and while Communist electoral strength may erode, it is not likely to decline abruptly.

The Socialist Party

The official name of the French Socialist Party, which was formed in 1905, is the *Section française de l'Internationale ouvrière*, SFIO. The party split in 1920 at its Tours Congress, where a majority of the delegates seceded to form the PCF. The schism naturally damaged the Socialists electorally, as the Communists drew votes which would probably otherwise have gone to them.

The SFIO sometimes supported Governments during the Third Republic, although there was a faction in the party which regarded cooperation with bourgeois parties as doomed to failure. The depression and the rise of Nazism in Germany led the party to form the Popular Front alliance with the Communists and Radicals in 1936, however, and in that year the Socialists headed and participated in a Government as a party for the first time.

After World War II, the Socialists had reason to think that they would emerge as France's most powerful party, as much of the planning for France's future which was done during the Resistance reflected socialist principles. This expectation was disappointed, as at the first postwar election the SFIO was outdistanced both by the PCF and the MRP, and the SFIO began an electoral decline which was not halted until 1956. Nevertheless, the SFIO participated in all French Governments from the Liberation until 1951 (except for a few months in 1950), and then from 1956 until the end of the Fourth Republic (except for a few days in 1958).

The SFIO played a leading role in the launching of the Fourth Republic. Vincent Auriol was President of both Constituent Assemblies, and more than anyone else he was the father of the Constitution of the Republic of which he was elected the first President. The SFIO's position was relatively comfortable as long as it was in the central position in the Government and the majority between the PCF and the MRP. However, when the Communists went into the opposition in 1947, it was necessary to replace them with Radicals and Conservatives, and the SFIO's position became more difficult. The balance in the coalition shifted toward economic conservatives, and the SFIO was exposed to demagogic attacks by the PCF. Much of the immediate responsibility for ministerial instability between 1947 and 1951 lies with the Socialists, although ultimate responsibility lies with the situation in which they found themselves. The Socialists were essential to the majority, but with the Communists in the opposition, as well as about 50 Gaullists who rallied to the General when he formed the RPF in July, 1947, so was virtually everybody else. In the effort to gain the concessions from the other groups which they felt were essential, the Socialists resorted to the ultimate weapon available to them—the Cabinet crisis.

Between 1951 and 1956, the SFIO sometimes opposed, sometimes supported, but never participated in the Government. In 1951, the National Assembly passed a law granting indirect state aid to Church schools, and this helped to estrange the SFIO, which voted against it, from the MRP, which voted for it. The two Conservatives who became Premiers during the Fourth Republic did so in 1952 and 1953, and the SFIO opposed their Governments. But when Pierre Mendès-France formed a Government in 1954, the SFIO supported him, and the Mendesist Radicals and SFIO formed an electoral alliance, called the Republican Front, for the elections of 1956.

The SFIO's spell out of office helped it electorally. Its overall gain was not large—it won 15 percent of the votes compared with 14 percent in 1951. But this was its first national electoral gain since October, 1945, and it was particularly encouraging to the SFIO because it resulted from significant increases in strength in northern industrial regions which more than offset losses in southern rural areas. Once again the SFIO was indispensable to any majority, and Guy Mollet became Premier.

The first Socialist-led Government since 1947 paved the way for France's entry into the Common Market, raised pensions, lengthened vacations with pay, put France's Black African colonies and Madagascar on the road to genuine self-government, invaded Suez, and failed to settle the Algerian problem. When Mollet's Government fell as a result of the refusal of the Conservatives to

TABLE 8. Distribution of Metropolitan Seats in the National Assembly, 1945–1967[a]

	Oct. 1945	June 1946	Nov. 1946	June 1951	Jan. 1956	Nov. 1958	Nov. 1962	March 1967
Communists	148	146	166	97	145	10	41	72
Socialists	134	115	90	94	92	44	65	76
Radicals and similar groups	23	39	55	77	77	23	42	40[b]
Christian Democrats	141	160	158	82	72	57	36	} 40[c]
Conservatives	62	62	70	80	96	133	28	
Gaullist Conservatives	—	—	—	—	—	—	20	40
Gaullists[d]	—	—	5	107	16	198	229	190
Poujadists	—	—	—	—	42	—	—	—
Miscellaneous	14	—	—	7	4	—	4	12
	522	522	544	544	544	465	465	470

[a] The party affiliation of some Deputies is not always clear and sometimes shifts, so these figures are approximate.

[b] Includes 24 Radicals and 16 Deputies nominated by the Convention (see pp. 163–166).

[c] Includes Christian Democrats, Conservatives, and Deputies without major-party affiliation in about equal proportions.

[d] Gaullist Union in 1946, RPF in 1951, Social Republicans in 1956, UNR in 1958, UNR-UDT in 1962, Union Démocratique group in 1967 (see p. 167).

SOURCES: For 1945 and 1946, Raoul Husson, *Élections et référendums des 21 october 1945, 5 mai et 2 juin 1946*, Le Monde, Paris, 1946, pp. xiv–xvii and xxix–xxx; and Husson, *Élections et référendums des 13 oct., 10 et 24 nov., et 8 déc. 1946*, Le Monde, Paris, 1947, pp. xxvi and xxx. For 1951, République Française, Ministère de l'Intérieur, *Les Élections législatives du 17 juin 1951*, La Documentation Française, Paris, 1953, p. 43. For 1956, Roy Pierce, "The French Election of January 1956," *Journal of Politics*, XIX (August, 1957), 419. For 1958, Mattei Dogan, "Changement de régime et changement de personnel," in Jean Touchard et al., *Le Référendum de septembre et les élections de novembre 1958*, Armand Colin, Paris, 1960 (Cahiers de la Fondation Nationale des Sciences Politiques, 109), p. 244. For 1962, *L'Année Politique 1962*, Presses Universitaires de France, Paris, 1963, p. 129. For 1967, Le Monde, March 18, April 5, and April 14, 1967.

raise taxes to pay for the Algerian war, which they favored more than the SFIO did, it was the beginning of the end of the Fourth Republic.

The SFIO has traditionally been a disciplined party in Parliament, although it has occasionally divided on important issues. SFIO Deputies divided during the Fourth Republic over the ratification of the European Defense Community treaty. They divided over whether to vote in favor of bringing Charles de Gaulle back to power in June, 1958, and over whether to support the new Constitution at the 1958 referendum. The party's Secretary-General, Guy Mollet, favored supporting de Gaulle, but more than half of the Socialist Deputies voted against him. A Socialist Party Congress voted 70 percent in favor of the new Constitution, but several Deputies then left the party to form a small independent socialist party called at first the *Parti socialiste autonome* (PSA). In 1959, M. Mendès-France and some other Radicals joined this small party, which later merged with other small groups to form the *Parti socialiste unifié* (PSU). The PSU is rich in talent and internal conflicts, but it polls few votes. In 1962, it elected two Deputies; in 1967, it elected four.

The Socialists supported de Gaulle's Algerian policy, but they opposed the Governments of M. Debré and M. Pompidou. They objected to the economic and social policies which were followed and they opposed the growth of presidential power. They voted in favor of all of the first 15 motions of censure introduced against the Government except the seventh one, which criticized the Government's Algerian policy. The SFIO advocated a "Yes" vote at the two referendums on Algeria but, like all the other parties except the UNR and some of the Conservatives, urged a "No" vote at the referendum to provide for the direct popular election of the President.

At the 1958 election, the SFIO improved its electoral showing slightly relative to 1956, but it lost half its seats in the Assembly (see Table 8) because of the play of the electoral system which was used (see Chapter Six). The electoral law which has been used during the Fifth Republic makes electoral agreements among the parties particularly important, and a critical choice which faces each party is what kind of alliances to form. The Socialists are in a delicate position in this regard. Socialist voters are anti-clerical, but they are also anti-Communist. The safest kind of electoral alliances for the SFIO are with Radicals, most of whom are also anticlerical and anti-Communist. But the Radicals are a weak party, and they and the SFIO together can win a majority in only a limited number of districts. Allied only with Radicals, the SFIO may hold its vote but it risks losing seats. When the party turns elsewhere for allies, however, it may gain seats but it risks losing votes. If it allies with the MRP, it risks losing the support of its anticlerical voters; if it allies with the PCF, it risks losing the support of its anti-Communist voters. The Socialists opted principally for alliances with the Radicals and MRP in 1958, but the parliamentary results were disappointing, and in 1962 it allied not only with Radicals but also with the PCF in many districts. The SFIO lost votes in 1962 compared with 1958, but the alliance with the PCF paid off in parliamentary seats, and the SFIO and Radicals formed a national alliance with the PCF for the election of 1967.

The Radicals

The Radical Party (also properly called the Radical-Socialist Party) is formally titled the *Parti républicain radical et radical-socialiste*. It was founded in 1901, but it never has been a highly organized party like the PCF or the SFIO. It was and is based on local political machines scattered throughout the country, and its Deputies and Senators do not regularly maintain parliamentary discipline.

The Radicals' distinctive characteristic during the Third Republic was their anticlericalism. Their strength lay in provincial France, outside the big cities, and while some early Radicals were economically progressive, in the sense of advocating such measures as an income tax, none of them was socialist and most of them were conservative. In this respect, the party's label is a complete misnomer.

The Radicals were the dominant French party during the Third Republic, even after World War I, when the SFIO began to out-vote them. They were indispensable to almost every Government, and they were highly skilled in the kind of political bargaining which is essential to building coalition majorities in Parliament under a multiparty system.

The Radicals' identification with the Third Republic cost them heavily after World War II, when the population repudiated the prewar régime. The Radicals were reduced to a splinter group, compared to the big three of the immediate postwar years—the PCF, the MRP, and the SFIO. Despite all their efforts, they have not been able to win more than 14 percent of the votes since the end of the war, and in 1962 the Radicals, taken in a loose and inclusive sense, won less than 10 percent of the votes.

The Radicals did not improve their electoral strength much as the Fourth Republic progressed, but they gained greatly in influence after 1947, when the Communists moved from the majority to the opposition and Radical support became indispensable to any majority, as it had been during the Third Republic. The Radicals participated in every Government during the Fourth Republic and furnished more Premiers than any other party did. Between January, 1947, and June, 1958, 14 men served as Premier for longer than one month. Of these, seven were Radicals and one was René Pleven, a Deputy from a small group called the *Union démocratique et socialiste de la Résistance* (UDSR) which resembles the Radicals in many respects, not least its role as a source of Ministers, and which is often—as it is in this book—counted with the Radicals when electoral statistics are compiled. The SFIO, the MRP, and the Conservatives each contributed only two Premiers who served for longer than a month. To put these figures another way, the French Government was headed by a Radical or UDSR leader for about one-half the life of the Fourth Republic.[8]

Radical leaders were influential, but the party itself was undisciplined, and Radicals often opposed Governments in which members of their own party served. Pierre Mendès-France won control of the party temporarily in 1955 and tried to turn it into a disciplined group, but he was not successful. The party was sharply divided over Algerian policy and was the seat of strong personal rivalries. Even when rival leaders agreed on major policy matters, they differed over which parties to ally with in order to carry out those policies. The result was that instead of becoming disciplined, the party split into fragments in 1956. New groups were formed and older ones were revived as Radicals who were expelled from the party or who resigned from it sought new bases of organizational

[8] Serge Arné, *Le Président du Conseil des Ministres sous la IVe République*, R. Pichon and R. Durand-Auzias, Paris, 1962, p. 300.

support. There was even a court case over which group was entitled to use the party's official name. In 1958, the party crumbled even further, as M. Mendès-France left it to join the opposition to the Fifth Republic, while other Radicals joined the Gaullists.

Some of the Radicals who left the party to join other groups returned to it during the Fifth Republic, but there were still several groups in that part of the political spectrum which can loosely be called Radical. The Radical Party was the largest of these groups, but there was also the UDSR, which mirrored the dissensions of the Radicals on a smaller scale, and the *Centre républicain*, which was formed during the Fourth Republic by conservative Radicals (whose votes some political analysts think it appropriate to count with those of the Conservatives).

These three groups were linked together in 1962 in a loose organization called the *Rassemblement démocratique*. The *Rassemblement démocratique* was not a separate political party, but a vehicle for maintaining communication among its constituent groups. Other groups of this kind have existed in France before, for similar purposes. One was the *Rassemblement des gauches républicaines* (RGR), which was formed in 1954 to serve as an electoral clearing house for the Radicals, the UDSR, and some smaller groups. The RGR was transformed into a party by some of the Radicals who left the Radical Party in 1956, and it ran some candidates at the 1958 election, but with the return to the Radical Party of some of the leaders who had left it in 1956, the RGR became inactive.

The Radicals are full of paradoxes. During the Fourth Republic they included both elder statesmen of the Third Republic and bright hopes of the rising generation. The Premier who symbolized Governmental immobility, Henri Queuille, and the Premier who symbolized Governmental decisiveness, Pierre Mendès-France, were both Radicals. The Radicals have a long heritage of anticlericalism, yet Radicals with Catholic or indifferent electoral clienteles, particularly in the Paris area, departed from their anticlerical tradition when the school question came before Parliament in 1951. Some of the Gaullist leaders—such as Michel Debré and Jacques Chaban-Delmas—were once Radicals, yet certain Radicals, along with the PCF, campaigned actively against ratification of the Constitution of 1958.

The variety of outlooks within and the indiscipline of the Radical Party make it impossible to speak of it as a bloc, but in the main, the Radicals moved increasingly into opposition to the Fifth Republic and its Governments after 1959. The party officially endorsed the Constitution of the Fifth Republic, but some Radicals opposed it, and because of their historic ties to the Third Republic, Radicals (especially the older ones) probably are more opposed to the presidential character of the Fifth Republic than any other non-Communist group. Many and perhaps most Radicals opposed de Gaulle's Algerian policy; the party's Executive Committee recommended a "No" vote at the first referendum on Algeria, although different departmental party organizations campaigned different ways. The Executive Committee recommended a "Yes" vote at the second referendum, however, and no Radical Deputy voted in favor of the seventh motion of censure, although Radicals voted in favor of all the others through October 1967. Few Radicals have served in the Government during the Fifth Republic. Jean Berthoin, a Radical Senator, was Minister of the Interior for a few months in 1959; Edgard Pisani, a member of the Prefectoral Corps who became a Senator on the RGR ticket in 1954, entered the Government in 1961; and Edgar Faure, who had been Premier and often a Minister during the Fourth Republic, entered the Third Pompidou Government in January, 1966.

Like the SFIO, the Radicals are divided over the alliances they should make in their efforts to gain strength under the Fifth Republic. Most of the Radicals, particularly those from the southwest, are strongly anticlerical and prefer to emphasize their links with the SFIO. Others believe that the clerical question is outmoded, and prefer to take their stand against the Gaullist régime on the issue of foreign policy, in combination not only with the SFIO but also with the MRP. In 1967, however, the Radical Party turned leftward and joined the Socialists in a national electoral alliance with the PCF.

The Christian Democrats

The *Mouvement républicain populaire* (MRP), which is also often referred to as the Christian Democratic Party, was formed during the Resistance, although its roots go back to the liberal Catholic movement of the mid-nineteenth century. This movement never had wide support, however. At first it was censured by the Church and later, when the Church recognized the legitimacy of the Third Republic toward the close of the nineteenth century, the movement was not able to win a large electoral base among French Catholics and it was looked on with suspicion by the anticlerical Republicans.

The fundamental aim of the men who created the MRP was to end the traditional political division in France between clericals and anticlericals. Catholics had demonstrated during the Resistance that they were among the staunchest defenders of French liberal values. The men who formed the MRP were politically democratic and socially progressive. They accepted the principle of the separation of Church and state, but they believed that this principle was compatible with measures such as state aid to Catholic schools. The Third Republic had identified democracy with anticlericalism and Catholicism with social reaction. The leaders of the MRP wanted to break down those traditional reflexes and fully integrate Catholics into the French political system.

Immediately after World War II, the MRP attracted a remarkable wave of electoral support, and for a few months, after the election of June, 1946, it enjoyed the distinction of being the strongest party in France. But this electoral success did not reflect blanket endorsement of its objectives by its voters. The MRP probably profited from a belief that it was the party closest to de Gaulle, and it probably also received the votes of a great many people who did not share the leaders' progressive social outlook, but who regarded the MRP as the most likely obstacle to communism or socialism.

The notion that the MRP was the party of de Gaulle was weakened in 1946 and destroyed in 1947. In January, 1946, de Gaulle resigned as head of the Government, but the MRP did not follow him out of office; instead, it voted in favor of his successor and continued to participate in the Government. Later that year, at the referendum of October, de Gaulle opposed, while the MRP supported, the draft which became the Constitution of the Fourth Republic. And in 1947, de Gaulle created the *Rassemblement du Peuple Français* (RPF), which became a political party and competed with the MRP.

Several MRP Deputies and Senators joined the RPF, including

such leading figures as Edmond Michelet, who became the first Minister of Justice of the Fifth Republic; Louis Terrenoire, who became Secretary-General of the RPF in 1951, Secretary-General of the UNR in 1962, and a Minister of the Fifth Republic; and Roger Dusseaulx, who was Secretary-General of the UNR from March, 1961, to May, 1962, and who also became a Minister under the Fifth Republic. The electoral impact of the RPF on the MRP was severe. In 1951, the MRP vote was cut by half; it won only 13 percent of the votes and it has not succeeded in winning a larger percentage of the vote at any subsequent election.

The reduction in the party's support helped to make it a more homogeneous group, but the MRP was beset by conflicts arising from the difference in outlook between its progressive leadership and its more conservative voters. The leadership felt doctrinally comfortable when the party was allied in a parliamentary coalition with the SFIO, as the two parties tended to agree on economic and social matters, and association with the SFIO helped to demonstrate the "republican" aspect of the MRP. However, a parliamentary coalition with Conservatives often seemed more prudent, as the MRP competes for the electorate of the Conservatives and not for that of the SFIO.

This tension was all the more acute for the MRP during the Fourth Republic as it rivaled the Radicals in its record of holding ministerial office. The MRP was in the Government almost continually from the Liberation until 1954, and from 1947 until 1951 it often had to mediate conflicts between the SFIO and the Conservatives. After 1951 it moved into closer association with the Conservatives than with the SFIO. The latter split with the MRP over the issue of state aid for Church schools and went into the opposition while the MRP remained in the Government until 1954. In 1955 Socialist leader Guy Mollet described the MRP as a "party which should not exist," and the SFIO avoided any compromising alliances with it at the 1956 election. After that election, the MRP and SFIO often voted the same way in Parliament, but they did not appear together in the same Government until the last months of the régime.

Despite these difficulties, the MRP remained one of the more disciplined parliamentary parties during the Fourth Republic. Moreover, it developed a distinctive position on European affairs after 1950 which helped it to build bridges across the religious question, which separated it from the SFIO, and economic and social questions, which separated it from the Conservatives. This position was support for a policy of European integration. Of all the French parties, the MRP was the least divided in its support for the European Coal and Steel Community (which is generally referred to as the Schuman plan, after Robert Schuman, the MRP Minister of Foreign Affairs at the time of its adoption), the European Atomic Energy Community, and the European Economic Community, and it was the most disappointed at the failure of the National Assembly to ratify the treaty for the establishment of a European Defense Community in 1954.

It was on the issue of European integration that the MRP chose to base its attitude toward the Gaullist régime. Fifty of the 57 MRP Deputies voted to censure the Government on the issue of amending the Constitution by referendum to provide for popular election of the President, but the MRP is more likely than the other non-Gaullist parties to accommodate itself to the new constitutional system. Unlike those parties, which have their roots in the Third Republic, the MRP is not attached to the principle of legislative supremacy over the executive. When the Constitution of the Fourth Republic was drafted, the MRP was the only major party in favor of strengthening the executive, although it did not press overly hard to accomplish it. The MRP, like all the parties except the UNR and the Gaullist Conservatives, objects to the "personal" nature of the Fifth Republic, but it objects more to the nationalistic quality of the President's policies. The MRP participated in the Governments of the Fifth Republic until May, 1962. At that time, its Ministers resigned because of their opposition to the President's foreign policy.

The MRP was reduced to the dimensions of a splinter party in 1962, when it received less than 10 percent of the votes, although it polled well in certain areas of the country. The party's localized successes and its national weakness testified to the strength of the traditional division between clerical and anticlerical France which it was the purpose of the MRP to surmount. The MRP was strong where Catholicism was strong (and mainly in rural areas); elsewhere it either met the barrier of anticlericalism or gave way before the Gaullist surge.

By 1964, the MRP was prepared to disappear as a party if it could combine with some other group on acceptable terms. At the presidential election of 1965, Jean Lecanuet, who had resigned as President of the MRP to become a candidate for the presidency with the support of the MRP and anti-Gaullist Conservatives, drew 16 percent of the votes in Metropolitan France (see Chapter Six, pp. 152–153). However, the same MRP/Conservative alliance—organized as the *Centre démocrate* (see Chapter Six, p. 166)—fared poorly at the legislative election of 1967. In the summer of 1967, it was an open question whether the MRP would continue to have a separate existence or whether it would merge itself completely into the *Centre démocrate*.

The Conservatives

There has never been a single united French conservative party, and the conservative groups which exist do not call themselves conservative. The last political group which voluntarily accepted the label *conservateur* consisted of monarchists, who adopted it late in the nineteenth century. French conservatives are generally referred to as "moderates," although there is no political group which bears such a name, or as "independents," a term which has a closer link with the formal nomenclature of this sector of political opinion.

The principal conservative groups during the Third Republic were the *Alliance démocratique*, which was formed in 1901, and the *Fédération républicaine*, which was formed in 1903. These were loose umbrella organizations whose adherents divided into several undisciplined parliamentary groups.

At the outset of the Fourth Republic it appeared that the same tradition of division among conservatives would prevail, as conservative candidates ran for office under a variety of labels and three small, separate conservative groups were formed in the Assembly: the *Parti républicain de la Liberté* (PRL), the Independent Republicans, and a Peasant group. In 1951, however, a national organization called the *Centre national des indépendants et paysans* (CNIP) was formed, and the CNIP succeeded in bringing more order into French conservative ranks than had ever been achieved before. The PRL disappeared, and while conservative Deputies divided into Independent Republicans and Peasant groups in the Assembly after the 1951 election, they merged to form a large group of *Indépendants et paysans d'action sociale* (IPAS) after the 1956 election (although a small group of Peasants tried to maintain a separate identity). After the 1958 election, a single IPAS group was formed again (this time without any separate Peasant representation at all). The unification of the Conservative parliamentary group did not ensure disciplined voting by its members, however, and Conservative unification itself did not survive the First Legislature of the Fifth Republic.

In their lack of parliamentary discipline the Conservatives resemble the Radicals. Also like the Radicals, their electoral strength has generally been based on the local prominence of the Deputy and his sensitivity to constituency interests rather than on the generalized appeal of a party label. The Conservatives have attracted some business support, but their electoral base is predominantly rural and coincides generally, but not exclusively, with strongly Catholic areas. Some of the divisions among the Conservatives are due to rivalries among the leaders, but there are also differences within Conservative ranks which reflect divergent political outlooks. Some Conservatives, usually from modern and prosperous regions, are able to approach the problems of their districts in general, national terms. Others, usually from the poorer southern areas, have acted as though they represented various agricultural pressure groups rather than a national party. Even within the business-oriented wing of the party, there have been differences of outlook which reflect the divergent orientations of small business and big business.

Conservative electoral strength during the Fourth and Fifth Republics never reached its prewar level; voters from traditionally Conservative areas often preferred to vote for the MRP and, later, the Gaullists. But while Conservative electoral strength did not increase until 1956, when it improved slightly, Conservative political influence began to increase as early as the middle of 1947. This was because the Communist shift from the majority to the opposition made some Conservative support indispensable to any parliamentary majority. Two Conservatives served as Premier during the Fourth Republic—Antoine Pinay and Joseph Laniel—and the second (and last) President of the Fourth Republic—René Coty—was also a Conservative. The Conservative Pinay and, later, the Radical Pierre Mendès-France were probably the only two Premiers of the Fourth Republic to enjoy genuine national popularity, although Mendès-France was a reformer and Pinay, in good Conservative fashion, a stabilizer.

Conservatives used their influence at first to prevent economic and social policy from continuing in the direction it had taken in the first postwar years, when several major industries were nationalized and the social security system was expanded, and later to prevent a liberal settlement of the Algerian problem. The Conservatives were unable to undo the early nationalization and social security measures—as they would have liked—but their parliamentary importance enabled them to win concessions on other economic and social matters. Some Conservatives were sympathetic to a liberal solution in Algeria, but most of them were not. Conservatives helped to stir up the wave of nationalism which made it impossible for the Fourth Republic to settle the Algerian problem and paved the way for the return of Charles de Gaulle.

The Conservatives in the last Assembly of the Fourth Republic voted virtually unanimously to bring Charles de Gaulle back to power in 1958, and the CNIP advocated a "Yes" vote at the 1958 referendum on the new Constitution. At the 1958 election, Conservatives did better than at any time since the end of the war. CNIP candidates won 3 million votes, other Conservative candidates won another million, and together the Conservatives outpolled the PCF, as well as the Gaullists. But while the Conservatives, who had the second largest group of Deputies in the Assembly, were the principal beneficiaries after the Gaullists of the new régime, opposition to de Gaulle's policies grew within Conservative ranks. The main issue was Algerian policy, as there was a large block of Conservatives who were opposed to allowing Algeria to become independent. But that was not the only issue, as there were Conservatives who supported de Gaulle's Algerian policy but objected to his foreign policy and/or the presidential character which the political system quickly acquired. There was also a small group of Conservatives who supported the new régime and its policies completely.

These divisions resulted in a variety of maneuvers and half-measures characteristic of a party whose members cannot agree but who want to avoid a party split. The CNIP was the only major group which did not make a formal recommendation to its followers on how to vote at the two referendums on Algeria, in 1961 and 1962. On both occasions their official pronouncements clearly implied opposition to de Gaulle's Algerian policy, but they fell short of recommending a "No" vote and acknowledged the right of the voters to make their own choices.

At the 1961 referendum, 66 per cent of the voters voted "Yes" to the principle of self-determination for Algeria, and some Conservative Deputies sought to dissociate the CNIP from identification with the *Algérie française* cause, but even after the 1962 referendum, at which more than 90 percent of the voters approved the Evian accords by which Algeria received its independence, the Conservative opposition kept up the pressure. In May, when the MRP Ministers resigned from the Government because of de Gaulle's declaration on foreign policy, 57 Conservative Deputies called on the Conservative Ministers to resign also, on grounds of the President's foreign policy *and* his position on Algeria, but the Conservative Ministers refused to resign. In June, almost half of the Conservative Deputies voted in favor of the seventh motion of censure against the Government which so clearly implied disapproval of the President's Algerian policy that only the *Algérie française* Deputies in the Assembly voted for it. The usual opposition groups—the PCF, the SFIO, and the Radicals—had all urged a "Yes" vote at the 1962 referendum on Algeria, and although they opposed other policies of the President, they refused to support this particular motion of censure.

When President de Gaulle announced his intention of holding a referendum for the purpose of amending the constitutional provisions for the election of the President, the Conservatives closed ranks almost completely. The CNIP executive committee declared that it would not endorse as a candidate any Deputy who did not vote the motion of censure which was introduced against the Government for its role in calling the referendum. One hundred and nine of the 121 Conservative Deputies voted in favor of censure. The motion passed, the Pompidou Government was reversed, and President de Gaulle dissolved the National Assembly.

Despite the near unanimity of the Conservatives in voting censure, the Conservatives began to split almost immediately. The CNIP officially recommended a "No" vote at the October referendum to amend the Constitution, but some Conservatives advocated a "Yes" vote and, even before the referendum was held, two dozen Conservative Deputies announced that they would not accept the CNIP label at the forthcoming election. For the election itself, the UNR or other official Gaullist groups endorsed some of those Conservative Deputies, as well as certain other Conservative candidates, and did not run candidates of their own against them. Between the two ballots of the election (see Chapter Six, pp. 146–147), the Conservative Ministers and Gaullist-supported Conservatives announced that they were splitting from the CNIP to form a new group, the *Républicains indépendants* (Independent Republicans). French Conservatives were divided once again, this time between Gaullists and non-Gaullists.

The 1962 election was as disastrous for the Conservatives as the 1958 election had been fortunate for them. The CNIP and Gaullist Conservatives together received only 2½ million votes at the first ballot, compared with 4½ million in 1958. The Conservatives had held more than 120 seats at the close of the previous Legislature; they returned with fewer than 50 Deputies at the start of the new one. In the Assembly, most of the Conservatives joined the Independent Republican group which, along with the UNR, provided the governing majority between 1962 and 1967. As it requires 30 Deputies to form a separate parliamentary group, no other Conservative group could be formed. The IPAS disappeared, and the non-Gaullist Conservatives dispersed into groups with the MRP and Radicals.

The Independent Republicans supported President de Gaulle at the presidential election of 1965 and the non-Gaullist Conservatives supported M. Jean Lecanuet. For the 1967 legislation election, the Independent Republicans and the UNR formed a common electoral front, while the non-Gaullist Conservatives and the MRP also worked together as a common electoral bloc. The non-Gaullist Conservatives fared poorly, but the Independent Republicans did very well; they gained seats while the UNR lost some, and the proportionate contribution of the Independent Republicans to the Gaullist forces in the Assembly was enlarged.

The Gaullists

There have been several Gaullist parties. After de Gaulle made his Bayeux speech in 1946, a Gaullist Union was organized by some of the General's supporters, but de Gaulle did not endorse it and the movement was a failure electorally. In the spring of 1947, de

Gaulle organized the *Rassemblement du Peuple Français* (RPF) of which he became president. The RPF was relatively successful electorally, but it was not successful enough to accomplish de Gaulle's primary objective, which was to force the other parties to capitulate to his constitutional ideas. Impatience among some of the RPF Deputies led them to split away from the RPF in order to support the Pinay Government when it was formed in 1952, and a year later the remainder of the RPF Deputies were also participating in the parliamentary game which de Gaulle despised. In May, 1953, de Gaulle requested that the RPF label not be used for parliamentary or electoral purposes. Gaullists in and out of Parliament continued to keep the Gaullist current alive by organizing under the name Social Republicans. Without the active backing of de Gaulle, however, they were unable to repeat the RPF's electoral success of 1951. In 1956, the Social Republicans won less than one-fourth as many votes as the RPF had won in 1951, and they won only 15 percent as many seats in the Assembly.

On October 1, 1958, the Social Republicans, led by Jacques Chaban-Delmas, Roger Frey, and Edmond Michelet, combined with several other organizations to form a new party, the Union for the New Republic (*Union pour la nouvelle République*—UNR).[9] The other groups were more or less ephemeral organizations which had been hastily formed by veteran Gaullists during the summer to build support for the new régime. The most important of them were the *Union pour le renouveau français*, led by Jacques Soustelle, and the *Convention républicaine*, led by Léon Delbecque. M. Soustelle was a prominent Gaullist of long standing who had been Secretary-General of the RPF, but the origin of his group, which was an offshoot of another organization which he had headed and which was dedicated to the cause of keeping Algeria French, foreshadowed the struggle which was shortly to rend the party and result in his expulsion from it. Léon Delbecque was a more obscure Gaullist militant, but he had been on the scene in Algiers during the May days and is credited

[9] The leading work on the UNR is Jean Charlot, *L'Union pour la nouvelle République; Étude du pouvoir au sein d'un parti politique*, Armand Colin, Paris, 1967. The first, hectic year of the party is treated in Philip M. Williams and Martin Harrison. *De Gaulle's Republic*, Longmans, London, 1960, chap. 6. Brief biographical sketches of the leading Gaullists appear in Pierre Viansson-Ponté, *The King and His Court*, Elaine P. Halperin (trans.), Houghton Mifflin, Boston, 1965.

with having done more than anyone else to channel the revolt against the Fourth Republic into a Gaullist direction.

There were also Gaullists with impeccable credentials who did not join the new party at its founding. The *Association nationale pour le soutien de l'action du Général de Gaulle*, which had actively supported the new constitution during the referendum campaign, did not merge with the UNR. Instead, it dropped from sight and later reappeared intermittently to support de Gaulle at each of the referendums of 1961 and 1962. Its leaders then ran successfuly for the National Assembly at the 1962 election. There were also liberal and labor-oriented Gaullists who stayed out of the new party and ran separately at the 1958 election, sometimes in opposition to UNR candidates, but everywhere unsuccessfully. Some of these Gaullists formed the *Union démocratique du travail* (UDT) in April, 1959. For the 1962 election, the UNR financed the UDT, allocated it more than 30 seats to contest, and endorsed its candidates.[10] After the election, the UDT merged with the UNR to form the UNR-UDT.

The main tasks confronting the new party, whose first Secretary-General was Roger Frey and whose Treasurer was Albin Chalandon, a young banker and businessman, were to endorse candidates and adopt electoral tactics for the November election. A dispute broke out at once among the founders over the kind of electoral strategy to employ. M. Soustelle wanted to form a common front with the *Algérie française* supporters among the Conservatives, Radicals, and Christian Democrats, but this strategy was rejected by the other leaders. The consquences of following M. Soustelle's strategy would have been to commit the UNR from the start to the *Algérie française* cause—when de Gaulle's own Algerian policy was far from evident—and to identify the UNR with the Conservatives, as they contained the largest number of *Algérie française* supporters among the other parties. By rejecting it, as the UNR did, and simply professing fidelity to de Gaulle, the party remained uncommitted to any specific policy for Algeria and remained free to support whatever policy de Gaulle adopted. Its exact location within the party spectrum was sufficiently uncertain for it to be able to draw votes both from Conservative-minded voters and voters who would not have

[10] David B. Goldey, "The French Referendum and Election of 1962: The National Campaigns," *Political Studies*, XI (October, 1963), 295.

supported the party if it had been too closely associated with the Conservatives. This strategy worked well enough to enable the UNR to emerge as the largest parliamentary group in the new Assembly, although the 18 percent of the votes which the UNR won on the first ballot in 1958 was not as strong an electoral showing as the RPF had made in 1951.

ALGÉRIE FRANÇAISE VERSUS UNCONDITIONAL LOYALTY

Relative electoral success did not end the struggle within the party. The *Algérie française* wing intensified its efforts to commit the UNR to its policy of keeping Algeria French, while the orthodox Gaullists—often called by their opponents the "unconditionals"—were prepared to give virtually unconditional support to de Gaulle, whatever policy he might follow. M. Chalandon, who became Secretary-General of the party when M. Frey was appointed to the Government early in 1959, expressed the viewpoint of one orthodox Gaullist in this fashion: "De Gaulle is our clandestine leader. We are somewhat in the position of secret agents who owe total obedience to their military chief, a military chief who does not hesitate to disavow them when things go badly." For almost a year, M. Chalandon was under attack by the *Algérie française* leaders, but when he resigned as Secretary-General in November, 1959, he was succeeded by Jacques Richard, a Senator who was also an orthodox Gaullist.

The orthodox Gaullists never lost control of the various party organs and the parliamentary group in the Assembly. After de Gaulle announced the self-determination policy for Algeria in September, 1959, the UNR group in the Assembly decided that no UNR Deputy should speak during the parliamentary debate on the Government's policy except official group spokesmen, and nine UNR Deputies resigned from the group. Four of them, including M. Delbecque, later asked to be reinstated, but the UNR's political bureau rejected the request and accepted the resignations.

The first UNR party congress (called the assizes in official UNR terminology) was held in M. Chaban-Delmas' stronghold of Bordeaux, in November, 1959. It was a confused and unruly meeting. So far as it is possible to tell, M. Soustelle, the leader of the *Algérie française* wing, received most of the cheers, but the orthodox party leaders controlled a majority of the votes. Any party member could attend the congress, but only Members of Parliament and of the Economic and Social Council, certain party officials, and the accredited delegations from the party's departmental federations (called *unions* by the party) could vote. The orthodox Gaullists controlled the large delegations from Gironde and the Paris region, cast the votes of the Seine delegation as a block, and enlarged their majority on the new central committee.[11] Then, the delegates unanimously adopted a motion on Algeria which probably conceded more to the *Algérie française* group than de Gaulle preferred (it contained the words "against any form of [Algerian] secession"), but it contained none of the group's favorite slogans and affirmed total confidence in de Gaulle, "chief of the State, guide of the Nation."

The Bordeaux congress was the *Algérie française* wing's last chance to gain control of the party. In February, 1960, M. Soustelle was dropped from the Government for having opposed taking action against the insurgents who launched the "revolt of the barricades"; under the new Constitution he could not return to his seat in the Assembly and under the rules of the UNR (later changed) he automatically ceased to be a member of the party's central committee. He continued to advocate a French Algeria and in April, 1960, he was expelled from the party. A handful of Deputies left the party with him. Altogether, the struggle over Algeria cost the party some 30 Deputies and about a year's effort rebuilding the federations where they had been strong. The great majority of the Deputies remained loyal to the orthodox party leadership; in 1962, the UNR renominated 161 of its incumbent Deputies.

MINISTERS AND DEPUTIES

There had been disappointment in the UNR when de Gaulle did not make a clean sweep of the personnel of the old system after his accession to power. The Government was kept small, civil servants were appointed to many important Cabinet posts, and a coalition Government was formed. All this reduced the opportunities for the UNR's personnel to achieve high office in the new régime. Furthermore, Premier Debré's insistence on exploiting

[11] Reports that the membership of the Seine federation had inflated just before the congress do not appear to be accurate. See Charlot, *op. cit.*, pp. 221–222.

the new constitutional provisions designed to strengthen the Government against Parliament operated against the UNR Deputies as much as against those of other parties. The influence of the UNR Deputies in policy-making was much reduced by a President and a Premier who meant what they said about separating powers and curtailing the role of parties. The 1962 election, by returning a near-majority for the UNR alone, relieved the pressure in a superficial sense and aggravated it in a more fundamental one. The UNR by then had fewer political rivals with which it had to share Cabinet posts and it took almost complete possession of the leading positions on the Assembly's six standing committees. But the UNR remained a near-majority party without the influence on policy-making to which its numbers might lead one to think it would be entitled.

Given the dominant position of the President and his enduring concern with foreign affairs and defense policy, the only fields in which the UNR had any scope for independent initiative were domestic social and economic policy. Yet a member of the UNR-UDT was not appointed to a senior ministry in these areas until April, 1962, when Maurice-Bokanowski was appointed Minister of Industry and Commerce. M. Grandval was appointed Minister of Labor in December, 1962. A member of the UNR did not hold the Ministry of Finance until January, 1966, when M. Debré was appointed to the post.

Government-UNR relations have often been strained, but there are frequent consultations between the Government and the UNR Deputies. Ministers report to the UNR group about the activity of their departments, discuss proposals with it, and even participate in the work of the parliamentary group's committees. UNR parliamentary criticism of the Government is sometimes severe, but the Government makes concessions on electorally sensitive issues like local projects, taxes on farmers, and veterans' benefits; and compromises are sometimes hammered out on difficult, major problems. In the fall of 1963, M. Chaban-Delmas said that "in spite of undeniable progress, it is still the case that a better balance must be found between governmental initiative and parliamentary initiative." Yet from 1962 to 1967, the UNR group remained disciplined and solidly in support of the Government. Although the UNR did not have a majority in the Assembly by itself, and the Government also required the support of the Gaullist Conservatives, the French system of legislative-executive relations operated in much the same way as the English one.

The Electorates of the Parties

GEOGRAPHICAL DISTRIBUTION

Regional variation in the electoral strength of political parties is characteristic of all democratic countries, but the regional diversity of the electorates of the various French parties is striking. Map 3 shows which party ran ahead of the others in each electoral district at the first ballot of the 1962 election. In some cases, the party which ran first did so by a slim margin, but the map permits us to view at a glance the regional seats of strength of the various parties.

The Communist Party is strongest in the industrial suburbs which surround the city of Paris; in a number of port cities such as Le Havre, Rouen, and parts of Marseille; in the industrial regions of northern France; along the Mediterranean coast; and in several departments of west-central France. The party's strength in the cities and industrial areas reflects its strong working-class support. Its strength in certain southern, rural areas reflects a tradition of extremist voting which cannot be explained by economic factors but which is part of the political culture of those areas.

The centers of Socialist strength tend to be similar to those of the Communists, except that they do not include the industrial areas around Paris and do include a larger portion of the northern industrial regions and a still larger portion of the southern part of the country. The Socialists were strong in the Paris suburbs earlier in this century, but they were displaced by the Communists. Today, the Socialists compete directly with the Communists for working-class votes mainly in northern France.

The zone of Socialist strength in southern France touches directly on the seats of Radical strength in the southwest. Much as the Communists displaced the Socialists in the Paris suburbs, the Socialists have been encroaching on the main bastion of Radical strength in the southwest. Here, except for the Basque country in the extreme southwestern corner, anticlericalism has a powerful electoral appeal, just as it does a little further north, where Communists, Socialists, and Radicals share the preferences of the voters.

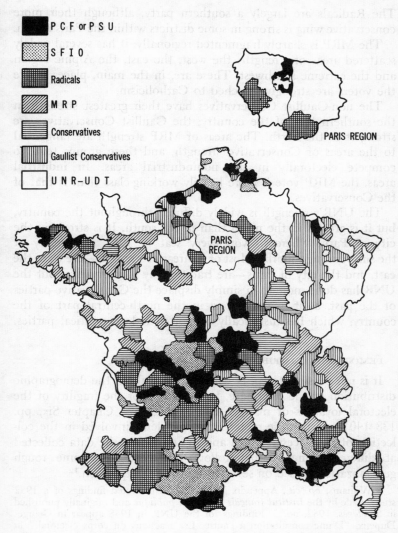

Legend:
- PCF or PSU
- SFIO
- Radicals
- MRP
- Conservatives
- Gaulist Conservatives
- UNR-UDT

PARIS REGION

PARIS REGION

MAP 3. Geographical Distribution of Party Strength (Parties Receiving the Most Votes at the First Ballot at the Legislative Election of November, 1962, by Electoral District).

Electoral data from République Française, Ministère de l'Intérieur, *Les Élections Législatives de 1962*, Imprimerie Nationale and Direction de la Documentation, Paris, 1963.

The Radicals are largely a southern party, although their more conservative wing is strong in some districts within the Paris region.

The MRP is sharply fragmented regionally; it has several widely scattered areas of strength: the west, the east, the Alpine region and the extreme southwest. These are, in the main, places where the voters are strongly attached to Catholicism.

The non-Gaullist Conservatives have their greatest strength in the southern half of the country; the Gaullist Conservatives are strongest in the north. The areas of MRP strength are tangential to the areas of Conservative strength, and these groups tend to compete electorally in the nonindustrial areas. In industrial areas, the MRP vote is more heavily working-class than is that of the Conservatives.

The UNR's strength is widely diffused throughout the country, but it is greater in the north than in the south. It is strong in the city of Paris, where it won every seat in 1962, and many of the surrounding suburbs. Most of its areas of strength—the west, the east, and the city of Paris—are traditionally Conservative, but the UNR has done more than simply displace the Conservative parties of the past, as it is also strong in the north-central part of the country, which has historically supported radical political parties.

DEMOGRAPHIC DISTRIBUTION

It is not possible to speak with certainty about the demographic distribution of the electorate, both because of the fragility of the electoral loyalties of many French voters (see Chapter Six, pp. 138–140) and because of technical problems involved in the collection of the necessary data and in comparing the data collected at different times. What follows, therefore, are some rough generalizations based on several studies of the question.[12]

[12] Williams, *op. cit.*, Appendix 7, reports the corrected findings of a 1952 study made by the *Institut français d'opinion publique* and originally published in *Sondages*, 1952, no. 3. Findings for the UNR in 1958 appear in Georges Dupeux, "D'une consultation à l'autre. Les réactions du corps électoral," in Jean Touchard *et al.*, *Le Référendum de septembre et les élections de novembre 1958*, Armand Colin, Paris, 1965, pp. 144–146, 158. Findings for 1962 appear in Guy Michelat, "Attitudes et comportements politiques à l'automne 1962," in François Goguel *et al.*, *Le Référendum d'octobre et les élections de novembre 1962*, Armand Colin, Paris, 1965. The detailed results of a study made in 1965 by the *Institut français d'opinion publique* appear in *Sondages*, 1966, no. 2, pp. 12–14, and are commented on by Alain Duhamel in *ibid.*, pp. 3–9, and in *Le Monde*, November 20 and November 21–22, 1965.

Sex. The French electorate contains a somewhat larger percentage of women than men. Women abstain from voting more than men, but women who vote constitute a disproportionately large percentage of the electorates of the Gaullist parties (RPF, UNR), the MRP, and the Conservatives. Men, on the other hand, constitute a disproportionately large percentage of the Communist, Radical, and Socialist electorates. This partisan differentiation of the electorate by sex is no doubt closely related to the religious factor, as a larger proportion of French women than men are practicing Catholics, while a larger proportion of men than women are nonpracticing Catholics or nonbelievers.[13]

Age. Voters under 35 years of age appear to give disproportionately large support to the Communist Party and, according to surveys made at different times, this youngest age group has also favored the UNR and the MRP. Voters between 35 and 50 years of age appear to favor the PCF, MRP, Socialists and, to a lesser extent, the Conservatives. Voters over 50 years of age tend to favor the Radicals, the UNR, the Socialists, and the Conservatives.

Education. The electorate of the Communist Party contains disproportionately large numbers of people with no education, a primary school education, or technical or commercial education. People with a primary school education also vote in disproportionately large numbers for the Radicals, Socialists, and MRP. Secondary school graduates tend to favor the UNR, the Conservatives, and the Radicals. Voters with university educations prefer the Conservatives and, to a lesser extent, the UNR or the Radicals.

Occupation. All French parties draw votes from each broad occupational segment of the population, although some parties draw a disproportionately large percentage of their votes from some groups as opposed to others. The Communist electorate regularly contains a disproportionately large number of manual workers, and so, on occasion and to a far lesser extent, does the electorate of the Socialist Party. Farmers vote in disproportionately large numbers for the Conservatives and Radicals and, to a lesser extent, for the MRP and the Socialists. Business people tend to prefer the Radicals and Conservatives, as well as the UNR. Professional and upper managerial groups show a marked preference for the Con-

[13] *Sondages,* 1962, no. 1, p. 31.

servatives. White-collar and lower managerial groups appear to prefer the Socialists and the UNR.

Income. The data on this dimension are limited, but the findings indicate that people with an income of less than about $165 per month vote in disproportionately large numbers for the Radicals, the Communists, the MRP, and the Socialists, while those whose income is higher prefer the Conservatives and the UNR.

CHAPTER SIX

Elections and Electoral Behavior

FRENCH VOTERS ELECTED a National Assembly eight times between the Liberation and the end of March, 1967. The first two elections were for Constituent Assemblies; the first Constituent Assembly prepared a constitutional draft which was rejected by the voters at the referendum of May, 1946; the second Constituent Assembly prepared a constitutional draft which was adopted by the voters at the referendum of October, 1946, and which became the Constitution of the Fourth Republic. Three elections were held during the Fourth Republic and another three during the Fifth Republic. The electoral record of the 23-year period was characterized by large and sometimes dramatic fluctuations in the relative strength of the political parties.

Fluctuations in Electoral Outcome

Figure 1 (see p. 104) shows the electoral strengths of the main French political parties (or groups of parties) from 1945 to March, 1967.

The parties which competed regularly at each election sometimes found their level of electoral support sharply altered from one election to another. The case of the MRP is the clearest in this respect. Founded only in 1944, in 1945 it received 25 percent of the votes. In June, 1946, it received more votes than any other party, yet in 1951 its electoral strength was halved and it began to be reduced almost to the dimensions of a splinter group.

Other parties have experienced very large and usually quite abrupt declines in electoral strength. The PCF's share of the vote dropped by more than 25 percent between 1956 and 1958, and that of the Conservatives decreased by around 50 percent between 1958 and 1962. SFIO strength eroded constantly from 1945 until 1951, and its drop in the share of the vote between November, 1946, and 1951 was about 20 percent. The Radicals' share of the vote declined by almost 50 percent between 1956 and 1958.

These changes in the electoral strengths of the "old" parties—those which competed regularly—were all downward between 1945 and 1962, and they are related to the appearance of new parties, which drew voter support which might otherwise have gone to the old parties. The sharp decline of the MRP in 1951, for example, is no doubt accounted for by the appearance of the RPF. But the fluctuations in strength of the old parties were not all downward. The Radicals increased their share of the vote by more than 25 percent between 1951 and 1956, and the Conservatives gained in 1958 relative to 1956.

Moreover, the electoral strength of the new parties which appeared during the period was by no means constant. The party called the *Union démocratique des commerçants et artisans* (UDCA), more familiarly known as the *Poujadistes* after their leader Pierre Poujade, arose almost from nowhere to win 12 percent of the votes in 1956, but it virtually disappeared electorally in 1958 and actually disappeared electorally in 1962.

The Poujadists were originally a protest group on behalf of small merchants and businessmen who argued that they would be ruined if they paid their taxes. Later, the group picked up substantial support among farmers. The center of Poujadist political strength was in the southern departments where competitive pressures were weighing heavily on marginal farmers, whose economic difficulties naturally extended to the shopkeepers and businessmen of the small towns which were commercial centers for the farm areas. The economic difficulties of many people who voted for the Poujadists were no doubt real, and payment of taxes may well have meant the difference between solvency and bankruptcy for them. Poujadist demagogy attracted their support, but the Poujadist movement did not endure, although rural and small-town grievances remained (see Chapter Eight, pp. 196 and 210).

The successive Gaullist parties had a different, although still checkered, record. The first Gaullist party, the Gaullist Union, was not encouraged by de Gaulle, ran only a few candidates, and won only a small fraction of the votes in 1946. De Gaulle himself created the RPF in 1947, and under his leadership it won 22 percent of the votes in 1951. The RPF was dissolved in 1953, de Gaulle retired temporarily from electoral politics, and the RPF's successor, the Social Republicans, won only 4 percent of the votes in 1956. The UNR, which was formed in October, 1958, in support of de Gaulle and the establishment of the Fifth Republic, won around 18 percent of the first-ballot votes the following month, even though de Gaulle did not endorse the party, and it won almost 32 percent of the first-ballot votes in 1962, when de Gaulle made only one electoral appeal in connection with the legislative election and did not even mention the UNR.

R. D. Masters has devised a method which makes it possible to measure the fluctuations in the strength of political parties combined with the fluctuations in the percentage of abstentions from one election to another.[1] He calls the figure arrived at for each pair of elections the "mobility rate," and it is possible to calculate average mobility rates for any series of elections in a given country as well as to compare the average mobility rates of different countries.

Masters' work indicates that fluctuations in the vote for French parties were even wider in the period between the two world wars than they were between 1945 and 1958, and that for the whole period between, roughly, 1919 and 1958, these fluctuations were wider in France than in the United States or Switzerland (which, like France, has a multiparty system). The average mobility rate for the 11 elections to the popularly elected legislative chamber in France between 1919 and 1958 was 1½ times that for the 19 elections to the United States House of Representatives between 1920 and 1956, almost 4 times that for the elections to the House of Representatives in presidential years between 1920 and 1956, and almost 2½ times that for the 11 legislative elections which were held in Switzerland between 1915 and 1955. Calculations made by the author, employing Masters' method, indicate that for all elections to the French National Assembly, the United Kingdom's House of Commons and West Germany's Bundestag,

[1] R. D. Masters, "Une méthode pour mesurer la mobilité des attitudes politiques," *Revue Française de Science Politique*, X (September, 1960), 658–672.

from 1945 to 1966, the average mobility rate for France was almost 2½ times that for the United Kingdom and more than 1½ times that for West Germany. In terms of variation in party strength plus variations in abstentions, France was less stable in the postwar years than either the United Kingdom or West Germany.

GROSS CHANGES IN PARTISAN CHOICE

There is evidence which indicates that, in recent years, French voters have been more likely to alter their partisan choices from one election to another than English or American voters. This is not a necessary corollary of the wide fluctuations in the outcome of successive French elections, even though it may seem so. Fluctuations in the vote for the parties from one election to another do not provide a direct measure of the amount of consistency of partisan voting. The outcome of an election depends not only upon whether voters switch from one party to another, but also upon switches between abstention and voting (in both directions), upon the choices of voters who are entering the electorate because they have become of voting age, and upon the effects of the absence from the electorate of people who have left it because of death or infirmity. It is conceivable that the outcome of an election can be sharply different from the outcome of the previous election without large numbers of voters switching parties. It would be enough that a large number of former abstainers decided to vote or that a large number of former voters decided to abstain, or that the choices of the new voters were different from those which had been made at the previous election by voters who had since died or become infirm. Similarly, it is conceivable that the outcome of an election can be very similar to the outcome of the previous election even though large numbers of voters switched parties. Such a result could be produced if the switches away from each party were roughly equal to the switches toward each party. The outcome of the two successive elections would give the appearance of consistency among the voters, but it would in fact conceal large numbers of individual alterations in partisan choice.

Recent research suggests that proportionately more French than American or English voters have been switching parties in recent years.

V. O. Key, Jr., estimated, on the basis of a 1960 postelection poll in the United States, that of the voters who voted in the two presidential elections of 1956 and 1960, about 22 percent switched parties while about 78 percent voted for the same party both times.[2] To use Key's terminology, about one-fifth of the Americans who voted both in 1956 and 1960 were switchers and about four-fifths were standpatters.

Georges Dupeux has reported his findings from surveys made of national samples of the French electorate shortly after the elections of 1958 and 1962 in a way which enables us to compare his findings for France with those of Key for the United States.[3] According to data presented by Dupeux, of the voters who voted in the two legislative elections of 1958 and 1962, about 31 percent switched parties while about 69 percent voted for the same party both times. Of the voters who voted in the two legislative elections of 1956 and 1958, an even larger percentage were switchers and a smaller percentage standpatters.

Mark Abrams has reported on the basis of national survey data that almost 90 percent of the English voters who voted for the Conservative and Labor parties in 1959, and who were old enough to vote in 1955, had also voted for the same party in 1955.[4] The data presented by Dupeux indicate that between 1958 and 1962 in France, the greatest degree of consistency of partisan choice was displayed by Communist voters, although not more than about 75 percent of the Communist voters of 1962 probably had also voted for the Communist Party in 1958.[5] The partisan choices of the remainder of the electorate were less consistent. For each of the other parties the proportion of 1962 voters who had voted for the same party in 1958 ranged from about 65 percent to less than 50 percent. The UNR ranks lowest on this particular scale, for the simple reason that the UNR almost doubled its percentage

[2] V. O. Key, Jr., with the Assistance of Milton C. Cummings, Jr., *The Responsible Electorate: Rationality in Presidential Voting 1936–1960*, Harvard, Cambridge, Mass., 1966, pp. 19, 25, and 115.

[3] Georges Dupeux, "Le comportement des électeurs français de 1958 à 1962," in François Goguel *et al.*, *Le Référendum d'octobre et les élections de novembre 1962*, Armand Colin, Paris, 1965, pp. 181–182.

[4] Mark Abrams, "Social Trends and Electoral Behaviour," *British Journal of Sociology*, XIII (1962), 230.

[5] Calculated by the author on the basis of data presented by Dupeux, *op. cit.*, pp. 180–183.

of the vote in 1962 as compared to 1958, which means that a large fraction of its 1962 voters *had* to be people who had not voted for it in 1958.

These comparative data are limited in their time range, and it is possible that for other periods different relations would appear among France, England, and the United States with respect to the gross number of changes in partisan choice made by the voters. Further studies may alter the picture, but on the basis of the data presently available, French voters appear to be less consistent in their partisan choices than English or American voters.

PARTY IDENTIFICATION

Philip E. Converse and Georges Dupeux have related the comparative instability of the French electorate to a more fundamental phenomenon: the comparatively large number of French voters who do not feel any psychological attachment to a political party.[6] Surveys of the American electorate regularly show that about 75 percent of the respondents identify to some extent with a political party;[7] surveys made in England indicate that an even larger percentage of the population identifies with a party;[8] and a 1957 survey made in Norway (which has a multi-party system) indicated that more than 65 percent of the respondents identified with a party.[9] Converse and Dupeux found, in a survey made in France shortly before the 1958 election, that of those people who responded to the question "Which political party do you feel closest to?" less than 45 percent designated a specific political party, while another 10 to 15 percent designated a general category like

[6] Philip E. Converse and Georges Dupeux, "Politicization of the Electorate in France and the United States," in Angus Campbell, Philip E. Converse, Warren E. Miller, and Donald E. Stokes, *Elections and the Political Order*, Wiley, New York, 1966, chap. 14. The chapter appeared originally in *Public Opinion Quarterly*, XXVI (spring, 1962), 1–23. Converse and Dupeux discuss only what they call the "flash party"—a new party which quickly gathers electoral support that can just as quickly disappear—but their argument applies to any large fluctuation in the partisan vote.

[7] Angus Campbell, Philip E. Converse, Warren E. Miller, and Donald E. Stokes, *The American Voter*, Wiley, New York, 1960, pp. 120–128.

[8] Richard Rose, *Politics in England*, Little, Brown, Boston, 1964, p. 86.

[9] Angus Campbell and Henry Valen, "Party Identification in Norway and the United States," in Campbell, Converse, Miller, and Stokes, *Elections and the Political Order, op. cit.*, chap. 13. The chapter appeared originally in *Public Opinion Quarterly*, XXV (winter, 1961), 505–525.

"Left," "Right," or even the labor union to which they belonged.[10]

Some of the crossnational differences in extent of partisan attachments indicated by these surveys may be due to differences in the wording of the questions asked, but the magnitude of the differences and other evidence support Converse's and Dupeux's conclusion that the large number of people without party attachments is a distinctive characteristic of the French electorate.

The relatively low level of partisan identification is related to the relatively large number of French party switchers to the extent that party identification is a major determinant of how people vote. Research on voting behavior in the United States shows that the nature and the strength of a person's party identification is the single most important factor governing his behavior at presidential elections. In the United States, the more strongly a person identifies with a given political party, the more likely he is to vote for the presidential candidate of that party. We have discussed in this section only the *extent* of party identification in France; little has been published concerning the *strength* of party identification in France. But the evidence indicates that the same type of relationship between party identification and electoral choice exists in France as in the United States.[11]

The comparatively wide fluctuations in the outcome of successive French elections and the comparatively large number of party switchers in the French electorate become intelligible in the light of the comparatively small number of French party identifiers. There is a comparatively large pool of French voters without fixed party allegiances. The extent to which the "old" parties can count on widespread and continuing voter loyalty is limited. New parties do not meet the resistance that such voter loyalty represents and, within limits, the old parties themselves may be able to make inroads in one another's electoral support. The stabilizing effect on the outcome of elections which widespread party identification can create appears to be reduced in France, as a large proportion

[10] Converse and Dupeux, *op. cit.*, p. 277.

[11] The United States findings appear in Campbell, Converse, Miller, and Stokes, *The American Voter, op. cit.*, pp. 142–143. The relationship between party identification and partisan choice at the 1962 French legislative elections appears in Guy Michelat, "Attitudes et comportements politiques à l'automne 1962," in François Goguel *et al.*, *Le Référendum d'octobre et les élections de novembre 1962, op. cit.*, pp. 218–220. For the relationship between party preference and electoral choice at the French presidential election of 1965, see this text, Table 10 and p. 161.

of the electorate is potentially responsive at each election to the stimuli of other, and possibly temporary, influences.

Electoral Systems

The eight postwar elections to the National Assembly were held under three different kinds of electoral system. The first three elections were held under a system of proportional representation. The next two were held under a hybrid system which contained majority rule elements but which provided for proportional representation in the cases where majority rule did not apply. The elections of 1958, 1962, and 1967 were held under a system which the French refer to as the *scrutin uninominal à deux tours* (single member district system with two ballots).

PROPORTIONAL REPRESENTATION: 1945 AND 1946

The system of proportional representation (PR) employed in 1945 and 1946 operated as follows: the competing parties presented lists of candidates in multimember districts (the departments, except for a few large ones which were divided into more than one district); the voters cast their ballots for party lists; seats were allocated to the lists in each district roughly proportionately to the percentage of votes won by each list in that district; for the lists entitled to one or more seats, candidates were declared elected according to the order of their names on their parties' lists.

One must say that the allocation of seats was "roughly" in proportion to the percentage of votes received by each party, because the system employed did not aim at perfect proportionality. Once a perfectly proportional system is ruled out, the choice that remains is between mechanisms for allocating seats which produce different kinds of deviation from mathematical perfection. In postwar French experience, the deviations have been of two kinds: one which gives an advantage in the distribution of seats to the parties which win large numbers of votes, and one which gives an advantage to parties which win smaller numbers of votes.

The PR system which was used in 1945 and 1946 operated to the advantage of the large parties. Called "PR based on the highest average," it satisfied the three large parties of the immediate postwar period, the PCF, SFIO, and MRP. By 1951, however, the PCF was in the opposition, de Gaulle's new party, the RPF, was competing in a national election for the first time, and France was governed by what were called Third Force coalitions (to distinguish them from both the PCF and the RPF) based on the SFIO, the MRP, the Radicals, and the Conservatives. The PCF was electorally strong in the industrial suburbs of Paris, which are often referred to as the "Red Belt," and there was reason to believe that the RPF would be electorally strong in Paris proper, as it had won a majority of the seats on the Paris City Council at the municipal election of 1947. Paris and most of its suburbs are located in the two former departments of Seine and Seine-et-Oise. (The department is the principal French administrative subdivision. According to a law passed in July, 1964, in 1968 the two departments of Seine, which included the city of Paris and its inner suburbs, and Seine-et-Oise, which included much of Paris' outer suburbs, were abolished and replaced by six new departments plus Paris, which has a special status as both a commune and a department. See Map 2.)

In order to handicap their Communist and Gaullist opponents, the Third Force parties amended the electoral law in 1951 to require the application of a different PR system in the departments of Seine and Seine-et-Oise. This system is called "PR based on the largest remainder," and works to the advantage of the smaller parties. PR based on the highest average applied in the rest of the country. Accordingly, two different kinds of PR were used in different parts of the country for the elections of 1951 and 1956 (but see the discussion below of alliance provisions in 1951 and 1956). See Appendix 3, which contains an illustration of how PR based on the highest average differs from PR based on the largest remainder.

PR allows each party to run independently of the others and gives the voters an opportunity to indulge their varied preferences. It is advantageous to parties which want to maintain their distinctiveness or which cannot improve their fortunes by pooling their strength with that of other parties. It is disadvantageous to parties which can improve their position by pooling their strength with other parties. Under unqualified PR there are only two ways in which parties can pool their strength. One is by forming coalition lists within districts. The other is by reciprocally refraining from running any candidates at all in certain districts, in the hope that the voters who would normally support the absent party will throw their support to the party which is running. In 1951, the Third Force parties devised a method for permitting parties to benefit by pooling their strength without requiring either coalitions or reciprocal withdrawals of candidates, and without wholly abandoning PR.

PROPORTIONAL REPRESENTATION WITH ALLIANCES: 1951 AND 1956

It has been pointed out that the Third Force parties were concerned enough about the PCF and the RPF to alter the method of allocating seats by PR in two populous departments. An even more important new provision which they wrote into the electoral law permitted the formation of electoral alliances (called, in this particular case, *apparentements*). This provision was designed to prevent the PCF and the RPF from enjoying the benefits of PR in those electoral districts where some or all of the other parties together could command a majority of the votes.

Parties could ally with one another simply by announcing their alliance officially by a given date before the election, provided they entered candidates in at least 30 departments. Alliances were on a district basis and could be made everywhere except Seine and Seine-et-Oise. Allied parties presented separate lists of candidates, but the votes of all allied parties were added together before seats were distributed, and if any group of allied parties (or any single party) won a majority of the votes in the district, those allied parties together (or that single party) were allocated all the seats for the district. Seats were then allocated among the allied parties on a PR basis according to the number of votes each party contributed to the total vote received by the allied parties together. If no single party or group of allied parties won a majority in the district, the seats for that district were distributed among the parties which had competed in the district on the basis of PR.

The electoral system operated in 1951 much as its framers had expected it would. The Communists made no alliances and the RPF made alliances in only about 10 percent of the electoral districts. All four of the Third Force parties joined in alliances in about 40 percent of the districts and many other alliances were formed among various combinations of two or three of those parties. Thirty-eight groups of allied parties won majorities and, therefore, all the seats in the districts in which they were formed. The four Third Force parties together won some 50 percent of the votes and almost 60 percent of the seats for Metropolitan France in the National Assembly.

The same electoral system was used in 1956, but this time the circumstances and the results were quite different from those of 1951. The 1951 election was, in the main, a triangular contest among Communists, the RPF, and the Third Force parties. By 1956, the competitive configuration had changed.

The Communists were still present in strength, but the RPF had been dissolved in 1953 and Charles de Gaulle did not come forth as the electoral leader of its successor, the Social Republicans. A new group, Pierre Poujade's UDCA, entered candidates in almost every district. And the Third Force parties, which had been largely united in 1951, were now badly divided. The Socialists believed that their alliances with the MRP and Conservatives in 1951 had cost them votes among their anticlerical supporters. The MRP and those Radicals who were followers of Pierre Mendès-France were sharply opposed to each other over foreign policy questions. The old Third Force parties, therefore, divided into two opposing groups: the Republican Front, led by M. Mendès-France and M. Guy Mollet, and built around the Mendesist Radicals and the SFIO, and another group which bore no label but which embraced the MRP, the Conservatives, and the non-Mendesist Radicals (whose organizational base was the *Rassemblement des gauches républicaines*).

There were more alliances in 1956 than there had been in 1951, but they were less extensive because of the split in the ranks of the old Third Force parties, which meant that their chances of winning majorities were reduced right from the start. Moreover, the Poujadists did better electorally than anyone expected they would, and they drew votes from the other parties. The result was that only 11 alliances won majorities and received all the seats in their districts. Most of the seats, therefore, were distributed by PR.

The 1956 election produced the last legislature of the Fourth Republic, which failed to find an effective way of ending the Algerian war and which, when faced with the revolt of the French settlers in Algiers in May, 1958, called Charles de Gaulle back to power and gave his Government a grant of special powers, including authority to prepare a constitutional draft for submission to a popular referendum. The grant of special powers specifically excluded authority to alter the electoral system, but the constitutional draft which de Gaulle's Government prepared contained a provision which gave the Government temporary authority to alter the electoral law. The draft constitution was, of course, adopted at the referendum and became the Constitution of the Fifth Republic. Acting under the temporary authority conferred by the new Constitution, de Gaulle's Government adopted a new system for the election of the National Assembly in 1958, and this system was also employed in 1962 and in 1967.

THE SINGLE MEMBER DISTRICT SYSTEM WITH TWO BALLOTS: 1958, 1962, AND 1967

The electoral system used in 1958, 1962, and 1967 marks a departure from the systems used earlier in the postwar period and a return to the type of electoral system which was employed for most national legislative elections during the Third Republic. PR was abandoned, and so was the multimember electoral district.

Under the present system, Metropolitan France is divided into 470 districts (465 for 1958 and 1962; 5 more were added for the 1967 election), each of which returns a single Deputy to the National Assembly. There are 17 additional Deputies for the overseas departments and territories. Each department has at least two Deputies, and this means that a handful of departments with small populations are comparatively overrepresented, but the allocation of Assembly seats to the departments is, on the whole, proportional to population. The populous departments of northern France and the Paris region, for example, are properly represented on a population basis.

The demarcation of electoral districts within the departments produced greater inequalities than the allocation of seats to each department. In 1958, the largest district had about 3½ times as many voters as the smallest, but the great majority of districts contained between 45,000 and 70,000 voters.[12] Population move-

[12] Maurice Duverger, "Paradoxes d'une réforme électorale," in Jean Touchard et al., Le Référendum de septembre et les élections de novembre 1958, Armand Colin, Paris, 1960, p. 228.

ments after 1958 tended to promote the overrepresentation of certain rural areas and the underrepresentation of certain urban areas but, in 1962, the great majority of districts contained between 45,000 and 75,000 registered voters.

The electoral system provides for two successive ballots. At the first ballot, any candidate who wins a majority of the votes in his district, provided his total vote amounts to at least 25 percent of the number of registered voters in the district, wins the seat. If no candidate wins such a majority, there is a second ballot (called *ballottage*) one week later, at which the candidate who wins a plurality of the votes cast wins the seat. No one may run at the second ballot who was not a candidate at the first ballot (this is the most important difference between the system used during the Fifth Republic and that used during the Third Republic, when new candidates could enter the race at the second ballot) and who did not receive the votes of at least 10 percent of the registered voters at the first ballot. (The latter provision was added in 1967; for the elections of 1958 and 1962, a candidate needed to win only 5 percent of the votes cast at the first ballot to qualify for the second.) A candidate who receives the votes of less than 10 percent of the registered voters may run at the second ballot, however, if only one other candidate polled more than 10 percent of the registered voters at the first ballot, in order to ensure a contest at the second. Candidates who fail to receive 5 percent of the votes cast suffer two penalties. Each candidate must pay a deposit of 1000 francs (about $200) which is returned only if the candidate wins 5 percent of the votes cast, and candidates are reimbursed out of public funds for the cost of their legally authorized posters, circulars, and ballot papers only if they win 5 percent of the votes cast.

Most of the electoral contests are decided at the second ballot. Before World War I, more seats were won at the first ballot than at the second, but this relationship was reversed later, and more than 60 percent of the seats were won at the second ballot at the elections of 1928, 1932, and 1936.[13] In 1958, only 39 of the 465 metropolitan seats were won at the first ballot; in 1962, 96 of them were. In 1967, the figure was only 72 of 470 metropolitan seats.

[13] Peter Campbell, *French Electoral Systems and Elections Since 1789*, Faber, London, 1965, pp. 34–37.

SECOND BALLOT ELECTORAL STRATEGIES

Not all parties run candidates in every district even at the first ballot, but at the first ballot there is a wide range of choice and most voters can express their particular partisan preferences. At the second ballot, however, the choice is narrowed, as about half the candidates are either eliminated for failing to receive the required minimum of votes at the first ballot or withdraw from the race. In 1958, the average number of candidates per seat contested at the first ballot was 5.9; at the second ballot it was 3.1. In 1962, the comparable averages were 4.7 and 2.4; in 1967, 4.7 and 2.2.

Candidates withdraw from the race between the two ballots in order to help another candidate win the seat, to prevent another candidate from winning the seat, or both. When a candidate withdraws, he naturally abandons all possibility of winning the seat himself, but he frees voters who may vote for another candidate whom he prefers to still another one. Sometimes withdrawing candidates explicitly endorse the candidate of another party (this is called *désistement*); sometimes candidates withdraw without making any recommendations to their first-ballot supporters (this is called *retrait*).

Parties are able to form alliances with one another under the two-ballot system by mutually withdrawing in one another's favor at the second ballot in different districts. Sometimes parties make formal national alliances by agreeing to withdraw everywhere in favor of the candidate of the allied parties who placed highest in each district at the first ballot or who seems most likely to defeat other candidates to which the allied parties are particularly strongly opposed. The Popular Front electoral alliance of 1936 was an alliance of this sort, and the Communists, Socialists, Radicals, and PSU formed a similar alliance for the election of March, 1967. More often, parties simply make tacit electoral alliances, without formally committing themselves to reciprocal withdrawals. Parties often make limited bargains for the reciprocal withdrawal of candidates in neighboring districts in one or two departments.

Even in the absence of alliances, the parties usually establish national strategic guidelines for withdrawals which they expect all their candidates to follow, although there are almost always some districts where the national policy is not adhered to. These guidelines may be more or less narrowly defined; in some cases they are so broadly defined that the parties' candidates have wide freedom for maneuvering, and the second-ballot tactics of candidates of the same party may vary widely from district to district.

Second-ballot strategies are motivated by both positive and negative considerations. The considerations are positive whenever there is an alliance, as its aim is to win as many seats as possible for the allied parties. They are also positive even in the absence of an alliance if the principal aim of a withdrawing candidate is to help to elect some other candidate. But the parties' second-ballot withdrawals often rest on negative considerations in that they are designed not so much to help elect a given candidate as to prevent the election of another one. The slogan "block the way" (*barrer la route*) is widely used in second-ballot campaign polemics, although whose way is to be blocked varies with the outlook of the parties and candidates. The two most prominent negative strategies are anticommunism and antigaullism.

MAIN LINES OF ELECTORAL CLEAVAGE

When a candidate withdraws in favor of another, it does not automatically follow that the second candidate will receive at the second ballot the sum of the votes which were cast at the first ballot both for him and for the candidate who withdraws in his favor. This is because some of the people who voted at the first ballot for the candidate who withdraws may have a different view than he does of whose way should be blocked. For example, a Socialist may withdraw in favor of a Communist in order to prevent a Gaullist from being elected, but some of the first-ballot Socialist voters may prefer to vote for the Gaullist in order to prevent the Communist from being elected. In calculating second-ballot strategies, therefore, it is not enough for the parties simply to add up the first-ballot votes of different combinations of parties in order to determine which one is likely to win the most votes at the second ballot. At the second ballot, each voter who voted at the first ballot for a candidate who has withdrawn must, unless he abstains, select a candidate who is his second choice or even his third choice, as his second choice may have withdrawn also. The second or third choices of all the first-ballot supporters of a given party are not necessarily the same. The parties, therefore, must estimate what fraction of the first-ballot vote for each candidate who withdraws is likely to go to the remaining candidates.

There are three main lines of cleavage through the French electorate which are basic to the analysis of second-ballot electoral politics. One is the division between Communists and anti-Communists. The Communist Party regularly enjoys the support of a minority of the electorate, but it is opposed by a larger number of voters, including not only those who have clear preferences for other parties but also many who have no partisan preferences at all.[14] In 1962, at a national survey made after the November election, more respondents (51 percent) cited the Communist Party than any other as the party for which they would not have voted in any case.[15] The intensity of anti-Communism probably declined after 1962 (see below, pp. 168–170), but more French voters want to block the way of the Communists than want to block any other party. In straight fights at the second ballot between a Communist and a candidate of any other party, the anti-Communist candidate can be expected to win in the majority of electoral districts.

The Communist/anti-Communist cleavage, however, is crossed by another main line of cleavage: the religious issue. We saw in Chapter One both how important this cleavage is politically and that the clerical/anticlerical dimension is the only one which can provide an unqualified definition of the difference between "Left" and "Right" in French politics. This dimension sets another limit to the response of the voters to different second-ballot electoral strategies. Clerical voters may refuse to support an anticlerical candidate (and vice versa) at the second ballot even if they are urged to do so by the candidate for whom they voted at the first ballot.

The third cleavage of major significance is the division between people who are economically conservative and those who are economically radical or who identify themselves with labor.[16] Voters of either category may refuse to support a candidate whom they perceive as identified with the other category.

These three main lines of cleavage twist their ways through the electorate in a fashion which vitally affects the second-ballot strategies of the candidates in each district. The second ballot

[14] Converse and Dupeux, *op. cit.*, p. 279.
[15] *Sondages*, 1963, no. 2, pp. 59–60.
[16] Converse and Dupeux, *op. cit.*, p. 289.

forces the voters whose preferred candidate has withdrawn to establish priorities along each of these (and possibly other) dimensions, and the candidates must try to anticipate the priorities which the voters will establish. For example, will the Socialist voter who can no longer vote for a Socialist now vote for the Communist who is appealing for working-class votes and is anticlerical, or for the Radical who is economically conservative and anticlerical, or for the MRP candidate who is economically progressive and clerical? The answer varies from district to district, because the saliency of each of the main lines of cleavage varies regionally,[17] and the geographical distribution of partisan antagonisms accounts in part for the variety of electoral strategies which the candidates of a single party may follow at the same election. The strategy which succeeds in one district may be a disaster in another, where the distribution of voter preferences and antagonisms calls for a different electoral combination.

FREE-FOR-ALL: THE ELECTION OF 1958

Only 39 seats were won at the first ballot in 1958: 426 were decided at the second ballot. In addition to the candidates who were eliminated because the election had been decided in their districts on the first ballot or because they had failed to receive 5 percent of the vote, almost 900 candidates withdrew from the race at the second ballot. Still, this left an average of more than three candidates per seat contested, and the pattern of competition varied throughout the districts.

The national policy of the PCF was to withdraw in favor only of candidates who had favored a "No" vote at the September 28 referendum on the ratification of the Constitution of 1958; the policy of the UNR was to remain in the race everywhere there would be no risk of electing a Communist by doing so; the policy of the SFIO was to withdraw in favor only of reliable democrats, economic progressives, and Algerian liberals, which meant, in most cases, for the Radicals or the MRP.[18] None of these national poli-

---

[17] Philip M. Williams, *Crisis and Compromise; Politics in the Fourth Republic*, Longmans, London, 1964, pp. 69 and 317.

[18] Philip M. Williams and Martin Harrison, "France 1958," in D. Butler, ed., *Elections Abroad*, Macmillan, London, 1959, p. 77; *L'Année Politique 1958*, Presses Universitaires de France, Paris, 1959, pp. 143–144; and Maurice Duverger, *op. cit.*, pp. 235–240.

cies was adhered to without exception. The other parties followed no particular rules, although they were sensitive to the possibility of being accused of aiding the Communists by unnecessarily remaining in the race and thereby splitting the anti-Communist vote. Except in a handful of districts, where the Communists' chances were enhanced by the withdrawal (or continued presence) of certain candidates, the PCF was isolated, as it had been both in 1951 and 1956.

The result was a limited, but impressive, UNR victory. The UNR won only seven seats at the first ballot, but it placed first or second in more than 200 districts and built solidly on this foundation. At the second ballot, it won forty percent of all the seats contested, and 70 percent of the seats which it contested. In part, this victory was due to the dispersal of its opponents, but it was due more to the support of the voters, as the UNR's vote increased sharply in the districts where it remained in the race. Although the UNR won more than three times as many seats in districts where it was opposed by two or more candidates than it did where it was opposed by only one, it won two-thirds of its seats by majorities and not by pluralities.

The UNR profited from its position as an anti-Communist party and appears also to have profited from not being too clearly marked on either the religious or economic dimensions of political cleavage. Clerical and anticlerical, economically progressive and economically conservative voters appear to have preferred to vote for the UNR rather than for the candidates of their traditional opponents. Like the Radicals of the Third Republic, who drew votes at the second ballot from Catholics who opposed Socialists and from Socialists who opposed Catholics, the UNR seems to have drawn votes from non-Communist voters of all kinds who preferred it to their historic enemies.[19]

STRAIGHT FIGHTS: THE ELECTION OF 1962

The most striking feature of the 1962 election was the polarization of the second-ballot competition between the UNR and representatives of an informally revived Popular Front type alliance among Communists, Socialists, and Radicals.[20] The UNR

[19] Williams and Harrison, *op. cit.*, p. 81.
[20] François Goguel, "Analyse des résultats," in François Goguel *et al.*, *Le Référendum d'octobre et les élections de novembre 1962, op. cit.*, p. 315.

placed first or second in about 275 of the districts where a second ballot was necessary, so it was well placed to stay in the race. The Communists, Socialists, and Radicals did not make any formal national agreement of the kind which had been made for the 1936 election, but Communists and Socialists reciprocally withdrew candidates in many districts, and both parties also withdrew candidates in order to help Radicals defeat Gaullists. In some districts, the Communists even withdrew their candidates in favor of anti-Gaullist candidates who had received fewer votes on the first ballot than their own candidates, something that they had never before done at a national legislative election.

The polarization between the UNR and the representatives of the informal Popular Front type alliance was reflected in a sharp increase in the number of two-party contests at the second ballot and in an altered distribution of competing candidates compared with 1958. In 1958, there had been only 84 two-party contests at the second ballot (20 percent); in 1962, there were 218 of them (59 percent). In 1958, the UNR had faced a Communist alone in only 36 districts; in 1962, it did so in 87. In 1958, the UNR had faced a Socialist alone in only 7 districts; in 1962, it did so in 57. In 1958, the UNR had nowhere faced a Radical alone; in 1962, it faced a Radical alone in 21 districts.

By pooling their forces, the parties of the Popular Front type alliance gained seats compared with 1958, but so did the UNR. The main losers in 1962 were Conservatives. The Popular Front type alliance seems to have aroused a strong current of anti-Communism. Large numbers of voters (including many who had voted Socialist or Radical at the first ballot) seem to have voted for the UNR at the second ballot as the party most likely to "block the way" to Communism.[21] In the straight fights between the Popular Front parties and the UNR, the former won 40 percent of the contests and the latter won 60 percent. The UNR won 40 percent of the votes cast at the second ballot, and for the first time in French Republican history a single party came close to winning a majority of the seats in the Assembly.

The 1962 election produced a remarkable UNR electoral victory but it also produced the beginning of a strong anti-Gaullist electoral alliance among Communists, Socialists, and Radicals. The Popular Front type of alliance which was informally created

[21] *Ibid.*, pp. 315–316.

in 1962 brought the PCF out of the electoral isolation in which it had remained since the spring of 1947 and established a pattern which was to be followed at the presidential election of December, 1965, and the legislative election of March, 1967.

The Presidential Election of 1965

President de Gaulle ran for re-election under the new system of direct popular election in December, 1965. He ran less well than anyone had predicted he would before the campaign started; he received less than a majority of the votes on the first ballot, when he competed against a field of five other candidates. On the second ballot, when he ran against only one other candidate, he won a decisive, but far from landslide, victory (see Table 9).

De Gaulle's principal opponent was François Mitterrand, a member of the small *Union démocratique et socialiste de la Résistance* (UDSR). M. Mitterrand was officially supported by the PCF, the SFIO, and the Radical Party (although not all Radicals supported him), none of which entered a candidate of its own. This

TABLE 9.   Results of the Presidential Election of December 5 and 19, 1965 (Metropolitan France)

	December 5		December 19	
Registered Voters	28,233,167		28,223,198	
Voting	24,001,961		23,862,653	
Abstentions	4,231,206		4,360,545	
	(15.0%)		(15.5%)	
Invalid Ballots	244,292		665,141	
Charles de Gaulle	10,386,734	(43.7%)	12,643,527	(54.5%)
François Mitterrand	7,658,792	(32.2%)	10,553,985	(45.5%)
Jean Lecanuet	3,767,404	(15.9%)		
Jean-Louis Tixier-Vignancour	1,253,958	(5.3%)		
Pierre Marcilhacy	413,129	(1.7%)		
Marcel Barbu	277,652	(1.2%)		

SOURCE: *Le Monde*, December 30, 1965.

arrangement avoided the difficulties which the main participating parties would probably have had in reaching agreement on the selection of a candidate from the ranks of any one of them. There was also the factor of the uncertainty of the outcome; had de Gaulle won a crushing victory, each of the three parties could have argued that he would have not done so had a candidate from its own party been running against him.

The candidate who did the most damage to de Gaulle's chances of being elected on the first ballot was not M. Mitterrand, as his votes would probably not in any case have gone to de Gaulle, but Jean Lecanuet, a former president of the MRP who ran with the support both of his own party (except for its Gaullist members), the anti-Gaullist Conservatives, and those Radicals who refused to support M. Mitterrand. Although M. Lecanuet received only some 15 percent of the votes on the first ballot, his support came from voters who, in his absence, would most likely have supported de Gaulle, and it was his candidacy which did most to prevent de Gaulle from winning a majority on the first ballot.

The other three candidates together received less than ten percent of the votes, but they each, in their separate ways, symbolized phenomena associated with French political life. Jean-Louis Tixier-Vignancour, a destructive opponent of French Republics, was the candidate of the most bitter opponents of the decision to give Algeria independence. Pierre Marcilhacy, a provincial "notable" who had been a Senator since 1948, was without a national political following. Marcel Barbu had sat for several months as a Deputy in the first Constituent Assembly, but he was without illusions about his chances for election and wanted only to make use of the radio and television time accorded to him to "express his anger and his indignation"; his candidacy recalled the eccentric candidates who frequently appear at French elections, usually in Paris.

On the first ballot, de Gaulle won a majority of the votes in 13 of the 90 metropolitan departments; Mitterrand in only 2. Mitterrand ran ahead of de Gaulle in 20 departments; Lecanuet nowhere outdistanced de Gaulle but he ran ahead of Mitterrand in 10 departments, while Tixier-Vignancour ran better than Lecanuet in 4 departments. De Gaulle ran strongest in the north, northeast and northwest; Mitterrand in the south and in central France; Lecanuet in the west; and Tixier-Vignancour in those places in

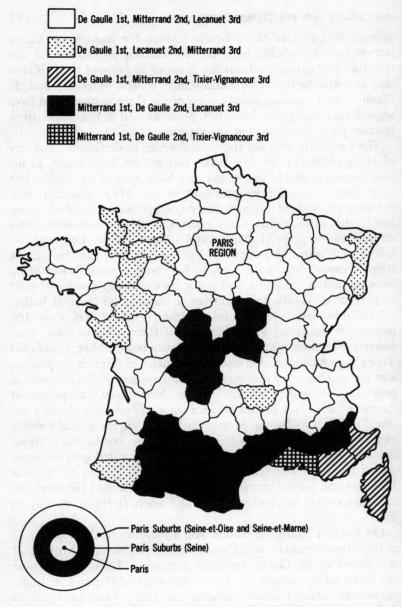

Key:

☐ De Gaulle 1st, Mitterrand 2nd, Lecanuet 3rd

⣿ De Gaulle 1st, Lecanuet 2nd, Mitterrand 3rd

▨ De Gaulle 1st, Mitterrand 2nd, Tixier-Vignancour 3rd

■ Mitterrand 1st, De Gaulle 2nd, Lecanuet 3rd

▦ Mitterrand 1st, De Gaulle 2nd, Tixier-Vignancour 3rd

PARIS
REGION

Paris Suburbs (Seine-et-Oise and Seine-et-Marne)
Paris Suburbs (Seine)
Paris

Map 4. The Presidential Election of 1965 (Distribution of the Candidates' Strength at the First Ballot).
Electoral data from *Le Monde*, December 7, 1965.

the south (and in Corsica) where there were large concentrations of Algerian returnees (see Map 4).

The second ballot was, according to law, a straight fight between the two top contenders, de Gaulle and Mitterrand. De Gaulle won a majority in 66 departments; Mitterrand in 24. The geographical distribution of the votes was similar to that of the first ballot; de Gaulle's greatest strength was in the north and Mitterrand's in the south and center, although de Gaulle polled well in some southern areas and Mitterrand polled well in certain northern urban areas, such as the Paris suburbs, Le Havre, and Le Mans, where he outdistanced de Gaulle.

At the referendum on the ratification of the Constitution of the Fifth Republic, de Gaulle's position in favor of a "Yes" vote was supported by 80 percent of the voters. At the referendum on the adoption of a policy of self-determination for Algeria, de Gaulle was supported by 75 percent of the voters, and at the referendum on the ratification of the agreement between France and the Algerian nationalists settling the Algerian war, he was supported by 90 percent of the voters. At the referendum on amending the Constitution to provide for the direct popular election of the President, de Gaulle was supported by 62 percent of the voters. Yet at the second ballot of the 1965 presidential election, when the voters could choose between only two candidates, de Gaulle received only 55 percent of the votes, a smaller percentage, by way of comparison, than was received by the winning candidate at 8 of the first 17 presidential elections held in the United States during the twentieth century.

Gaullism as a Political Force

It is customary in the study of politics to speak of social, economic, religious, historical, ideological, and political forces. What is meant by this is simply that people's political behavior is affected by such factors as the kind of society in which they live, their level of income, their occupational role, their educational experience, their religious affiliation, the historical traditions which have become part of their memories, the ideas which they accept as true or the goals which they regard as desirable, their attachment to political parties, and so on.

But not all political forces are impersonal. In politics, men are always trying to persuade others to follow them, and the political significance of personal qualities cannot be overlooked. The relative success or failure of political leaders or would-be leaders depends greatly on circumstances and on their judgment, but it also depends upon their personal appeal. The capacity of personality to overcome the tugs of other forces at work in a society is an important political phenomenon. In France, political developments since 1958 have been marked by the capacity of Charles de Gaulle to win the support of large numbers of French men and women. In this respect, it is proper to speak of Gaullism as a political force.

ATTITUDES TOWARD DE GAULLE

Converse and Dupeux found that when people constituting a national sample of the French electorate were asked, in the fall of 1958, what they liked and disliked about General de Gaulle, favorable references outnumbered unfavorable references by four to one. Among the favorable references, almost half referred to personal qualities, less than 20 percent referred to leadership qualities, and less than 20 percent referred to his past activity.[22]

Attitudes toward de Gaulle did not show marked variations relative to the age, educational level, or occupation of the respondents, although women had a somewhat more favorable attitude than men did. In these respects, the Gaullism of 1958 was similar to the Gaullism of the Resistance, when a Vichy police report stated that Gaullism "recruits in all sectors of the population."[23]

The factor which was found to correlate most closely with attitudes toward de Gaulle was the respondents' attachment to a political party. People who identified with parties which were favorable to de Gaulle had more favorable attitudes toward him than did people who identified with parties which were hostile to him.

[22] Philip E. Converse and Georges Dupeux, "De Gaulle and Eisenhower: The Public Image of the Victorious General," in Campbell, Converse, Miller, and Stokes, *Elections and the Political Order, op. cit.,* chap. 15, pp. 298–299. An abridged translation of the chapter appeared under the title "Eisenhower et de Gaulle: Les généraux devant l'opinion," in the *Revue Française de Science Politique,* XII (March, 1962).

[23] Henri Michel, *Les Courants de pensée de la Résistance,* Presses Universitaires de France, Paris, 1962, p. 733.

However, only people who identified with parties which were very hostile to de Gaulle had unfavorable attitudes toward him. People attached to parties which were only rather hostile to de Gaulle had mildly favorable attitudes toward him, and people attached to parties which were neutral to de Gaulle favored him quite strongly, although not so strongly as did the people attached to parties which favored him.

This phenomenon was found to be identical to that involved in General Eisenhower's popularity in the United States in 1952 and 1956. The people who were most opposed to Eisenhower were those who regarded themselves as strong Democrats; the people who were most in favor of him were those who regarded themselves as strong Republicans; and the people occupying intermediate positions on the party dimension held appropriately intermediate attitudes toward Eisenhower.

On the basis of their comparative analysis, Converse and Dupeux concluded, in part, as follows:

The strategy often followed by the general of avoiding or minimizing party commitment is very fruitful for him. But where such strategy is impossible, the victorious general alone among political aspirants appears to have the potential of maximizing the electoral strength of his own party to its very limit while achieving some inroads among parties unequivocally opposed to him and large inroads among parties who hesitate.[24]

This conclusion has remarkable predictive power, and it makes it possible to explain the vicissitudes of de Gaulle's electoral record. When de Gaulle was supported by most of the parties (as he was in 1958) and/or when he could assume a stance "above parties," his popular support was greater than when he was opposed by most of the parties or when he appeared in a partisan role himself.

At each of the referendums since September, 1958, de Gaulle tried to present himself as "above parties," but the extent of the support he received from the parties varied. At the 1958 referendum on the Constitution, his position was officially supported by all the major parties except the PCF and he was supported by 80 percent of the voters. At the first referendum on Algeria, in 1961, he was

[24] Converse and Dupeux, "De Gaulle and Eisenhower: The Public Image of the Victorious General," *op. cit.*, pp. 344–345.

TABLE 10. Presidential Voting Intentions, December 1–2 and December 14–16, 1965 (in Percent of Respondents Who Indicated Their Intended Vote)

| | December 1–2 | | | | | December 14–16 | | |
	Percent of Sample	De Gaulle	Mitterrand	Lecanuet	Others	Percent of Sample	De Gaulle	Mitterrand
Sex:								
Men	47	38.5	32.5	20	9	50	49	51
Women	53	47	23.5	20	9.5	50	61	39
Age:								
20–34	30	35	32.5	21	11.5	29	49	51
35–49	28	37	29	24.5	9.5	30	55	45
50–64	26	47	27	19	7.0	25	55	45
65 & over	16	58.5	19	11	11.5	16	65	35
Occupation of head of family:								
Farmers	15	38	22	28	12	17	59	41
Industrialists & businessmen	11	44	14	24	18	10	67	33
Upper management & free professionals	5	32	23	26.5	18.5	5	63	37

Middle management, technicians & white collar	18	38.5	31.5	21	9	15	55	45
Workers	30	42.5	34	16	7.5	33	45	55
Retired & non-working	21	52	24.5	14	9.5	20	60	40
Region:								
Paris Region	19	46	29	15.5	9.5	17	51	49
North-West	19	42	25	27	6.0	20	61	39
North-East	25	51	24	19	6.0	26	58.5	41.5
South-West	15	39	25	23	13.0	14	47.5	52.5
South-East	22	31.5	33.5	16	19.0	23	52	48
Size of Community:								
Rural	35.5	43.5	25	21	10.5	35	57	43
Less than 20,000	12	43	26	21	10	14	53	47
20,000–100,000	14.5	40	32	15.5	12.5	14	47.5	52.5
Over 100,000	24.5	40.5	30	20.5	9.0	21	57.5	42.5
Paris area	13.5	48.5	23.5	17	11	16	52	48
Political Preference:								
PCF, SFIO, Radicals		73	13	9	5		14	86
MRP, Conservatives		5	27	49.5	18.5		71	29
UNR, Gaullist Cons.		2.5	89.5	4	4		93	7
No Preference		19.5	43	21.5	16		60	40

SOURCE: *Sondages*, 1965, no. 4, pp. 21–38, 75. (By permission of the *Institut Français d'Opinion Publique*.)

supported by the MRP and the SFIO, as well as by the UNR, but the partisan opposition to his position was greater than it had been in 1958 and he was supported by 75 percent of the voters. At the second referendum on Algeria, in 1962, de Gaulle was supported by every major party (including the PCF) except the Conservatives, who took no official position on the issue, and he achieved his greatest electoral strength—90 percent of the voters.

By the time of the referendum of October, 1962, on the question of amending the Constitution to provide for direct popular election of the President, the situation had changed greatly. De Gaulle could no longer appear to be wholly "above parties" because he was engaged in a direct conflict with almost all of them, as only the UNR and a small group of dissident Conservatives supported his position. At the same time, the electoral situation was ambiguous in that the voters were participating in a referendum and not in an election of the kind where partisan loyalties are most likely to come directly into play. The result was that de Gaulle's position still won handily, with 62 percent of the votes, but this was the lowest level of support he had yet received.

At the presidential election of 1965, de Gaulle became engaged in the kind of electoral contest in which partisan loyalties are more likely to be directly operative than they are at a referendum. The credibility of his stance "above parties" had been eroded; in November, 1965, 44 percent of a sample of the adult population indicated that they thought de Gaulle had acted for seven years as "the leader of a majority political formation," while only 31 percent believed that he had acted as "a man outside of political formations."[25] De Gaulle's relatively small share of the vote at the first ballot and his relatively small majority at the second ballot, compared with the magnitude of his referendum victories, reflects the greater capacity of his opponents to draw on traditional party loyalties at an election than at a referendum.

DE GAULLE'S ELECTORATE

The composition of de Gaulle's and his opponents' electorates can be estimated on the basis of sample surveys which were made among the adult population. Table 10 shows the results of pre-

[25] Michel Brulé, "Les Français et le mandat présidentiel," *Sondages*, 1965, no. 4, p. 47.

election surveys of voting intentions just before each of the two ballots, broken down according to various demographic and other categories. Table 11 shows the results of a postelection survey designed to illuminate the relationship between religion and voting at the presidential election.

The most striking aspect of Table 10 is the relationship it shows between political preferences and voting intentions, a relationship which fully confirms the conclusions reached by Converse and Dupeux (see p. 157). The overwhelming majority of people who expressed preferences for the two parties which supported de Gaulle at both ballots, the UNR and the Gaullist Conservatives, expressed the intention to vote for de Gaulle before each ballot. Conversely, the overwhelming majority—but a smaller one—of people who expressed preferences for the parties which jointly supported M. Mitterrand at both ballots, the PCF, the SFIO, and the Radicals, expressed the intention to vote for M. Mitterrand before each ballot.

TABLE 11. Distribution of the Vote at the Presidential Election of December 5, 1965, by Degree of Religious Practice (by percentages)

Claimed to Have Voted on December 5, 1965, for:	Regularly Practicing Catholics[a] (23)	Occasionally Practicing Catholics[b] (36)	Nonpracticing Catholics[c] (27)	No Religion (10)
General de Gaulle	55	37	28	14
Mitterrand	7	23	37	56
Lecanuet	17	11	6	4
Tixier-Vignancour	4	3	2	1
Marcilhacy	1	1	2	1
Barbu	—	—	1	1
No reply	16	25	24	23
	100	100	100	100

[a] Percent of sample consisting of Catholic respondents who attend church weekly.

[b] Percent of sample consisting of Catholic respondents who attend church several times ("quelques fois") a year.

[c] Includes the percent of sample consisting of Catholic respondents who never go to church (20) plus the percent of sample consisting of persons who did not reply to the question: "What is your religion?" (7). Four percent of the sample, consisting of persons with a religion other than Catholic, were omitted from the analysis because of the small number of cases.

SOURCE: Michel Brulé, "L'appartenance religieuse et le vote du 5 décembre 1965," *Sondages*, 1966, no. 2, pp. 15–17. (By permission of the *Institut Français d'Opinion Publique*.)

Before the first ballot, M. Lecanuet polled better in the survey than did any of his opponents among the people who expressed preferences for the two parties which supported him—the MRP and the Conservatives. Although de Gaulle polled better than any of his opponents among people who expressed no political preferences, he did less well among this group than did his opponents combined.

At the survey made before the second ballot, M. Mitterrand gained more, percentagewise, than de Gaulle did among each of the four groups of people classified according to political preference. Both candidates made the greatest gains among people who expressed preferences for the MRP and the Conservatives, as those people provided most of the support for M. Lecanuet and the other candidates before the first ballot. But while M. Mitterrand multiplied his first-ballot supporters among this group by a factor of almost six, and de Gaulle multiplied his first-ballot support among this group by a factor of less than three, de Gaulle started out with more than five times as much strength within this group as M. Mitterrand had and, therefore, his gain in absolute numbers of supporters from this group was greater than that of M. Mitterrand. This gain, along with the smaller gains de Gaulle made within each of the other categories, accounted for his second-ballot majority.

The correlations displayed between electoral choice and religious affiliation and degree of religious practice are also impressive. They were found by the author of the study to be much closer than those between electoral choice and age, sex, or occupation. "In a society where people take pleasure in emphasizing everything which makes it different from its own past," he concludes, "it is worth calling attention to the persistence on the political plane of such a deep and traditional cleavage."[26]

Political Regrouping for the Election of 1967

During the heydays of the RPF, André Malraux once said that there would soon be in France "only the Communists, us, and nothing." The remark may seem curious, as until 1962, the "noth-

[26] Michel Brulé, "L'appartenance religieuse et le vote du 5 décembre 1965," *Sondages*, 1966, no. 2, p. 19. Author's translation.

ing" to which M. Malraux had referred—the Socialists, the Radicals, the MRP, and the Conservatives—always totalled more popular votes at national elections than the Gaullists and Communists combined. While they failed to accomplish this in 1962, they still amassed more popular votes together at the first ballot than either the PCF or the UNR did individually, although they did not poll as well as the UNR and the Gaullist Conservatives taken together. But M. Malraux's remark takes on a clearer meaning when viewed in the light of those parties' electoral rivalries and political differences. Taken together, they represented a large number of voters, but this collective electoral strength did not represent a unified electoral force in support of common policies.

The "old" parties took several steps between 1963 and 1967 to remedy this situation by pooling their strength and reducing the electoral competition among themselves. The electoral success of the UNR in 1962, the parallel decline in the electoral and/or parliamentary strength of the "old" parties, and the new system of direct popular election of the President, all encouraged the notion that the old parties would have to combine into fewer (and presumably larger) groups if they were to survive politically. Accordingly, the non-Communist, non-Gaullist parties regrouped by forming two new organizations, the *Fédération de la gauche démocrate et socialiste* and the *Centre démocrate*. At more or less the same time, the Gaullists also took steps to unify their electoral efforts. The result of this regrouping of political forces was that the election of 1967 took place among a small number of tightly organized electoral blocs.

STAGES IN PARTY REGROUPING[27]

Gaston Defferre's Attempt. In December, 1963, Gaston Defferre, the Socialist Mayor of Marseille, announced that he would be a candidate at the presidential election scheduled to take place in December, 1965. In the spring of 1965, he took the initiative in trying to establish a new political organization, to be called the *Fédération démocrate socialiste*, embracing the SFIO, the Radicals, the MRP, and an organization called the *Convention des institutions républicaines* (which included the representatives

[27] Figure 2 provides a guide to the progressive regrouping of the non-Gaullist parties.

of about 50 political clubs and unofficial representatives from the Socialist and Radical parties), but excluding the Communists. At the outset, M. Defferre received a more enthusiastic response from the MRP than he did from his own Socialist Party, whose Secretary-General, Guy Mollet, preferred to leave the door open to alliances with the Communists and to avoid formal affiliation with the clerical MRP; but M. Defferre's efforts to win the sup-

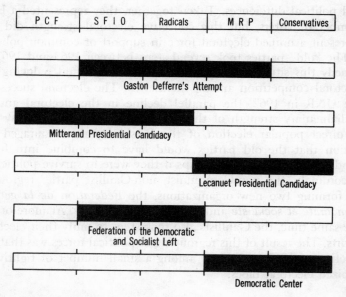

| PCF | SFIO | Radicals | MRP | Conservatives |

Gaston Defferre's Attempt

Mitterand Presidential Candidacy

Lecanuet Presidential Candidacy

Federation of the Democratic
and Socialist Left

Democratic Center

FIGURE 2.   Stages in the Regrouping of Parties.

port of his own party tended to alienate the MRP. When representatives of the three main parties and smaller groups involved met in June, 1965, in order to try to work out the basis for a new federation, it was impossible for them to do so. They differed too widely on a host of issues: whether the proposed federation should support a presidential candidate, whether it should remain a federation or eventually be transformed into a unitary organization, the clerical question, and even whether the word "socialist" should be included in the proposed group's name. It was demonstrated that any new grouping of parties could not include, at least for the time being, both the SFIO and the MRP. Shortly afterward, M. Defferre withdrew his candidacy for the presidency.

The Fédération de la Gauche Démocrate et Socialiste. Less than a month after M. Defferre's withdrawal from the presidential race, there was a meeting of the SFIO's National Council at which M. Mollet proposed the creation of a political federation embracing the Socialists, Radicals, and certain political clubs, but not the MRP. At the same meeting, Jules Moch said that it was much more important to defeat de Gaulle at the forthcoming presidential election than it was to elect a Socialist as President, and that "we must find a man acceptable to our party, to the Radicals and even to the Communist Party." The strategies of MM. Mollet and Moch were both adopted. In September, 1965, the SFIO, the Radical Party, the UDSR, and the *Convention des institutions républicaines* (hereinafter referred to as the Convention) formed the *Fédération de la gauche démocrate et socialiste* (Federation of the Democratic and Socialist Left, sometimes referred to as the FGDS, sometimes as the Federation). In the same month, the "acceptable man" was found when François Mitterrand announced his candidacy for the presidency.

The *Fédération de la gauche démocrate et socialiste* did not play an important role during the presidential election campaign. M. Mitterrand received the formal support of its constituent groups, as well as of the PCF, but some Radicals did not support him and were not happy at being linked to a federation which excluded the MRP and was allied with the PCF through joint support of M. Mitterrand for the presidency.

After the 1965 presidential election, M. Mitterrand became President of the Federation, and in May, 1966, the Federation announced the appointment of a Shadow Cabinet, somewhat along the lines of the English model. Virtually from the start, the Federation became preoccupied with the problem of deciding what electoral tactics it would follow at the next legislative election. The organization displayed the tensions, long familiar to its Socialist and Radical members, of a group divided between members who sought to maintain an opening on the left for an electoral alliance with the PCF and those who sought to maintain an opening on the right for electoral alliances with the MRP and even, for some, the Conservatives. As the election approached, however, the Federation moved leftward and it made a formal and explicit agreement with the PCF for mutual withdrawals at the second ballot of the election of 1967. Moreover, the Federation succeeded in doing in 1967 what Socialists and Radicals had never done before: virtually abolishing electoral competition at the first ballot between candidates of the two parties. The Federation nominated a single candidate (almost always the incumbent Deputy in districts where he was a Radical or a Socialist) in over 400 districts, thereby trying to convert the combined strength of its constituent groups into a single electoral force. After the election, the Socialist, Radical, and Convention Deputies elected under the Federation label formed a single group in the National Assembly with the same name.

The Centre Démocrate. Just as M. Mitterrand became president of a new group after the presidential election, so did Jean Lecanuet, the former President of the MRP who had spoiled de Gaulle's chances of election at the first ballot in 1965. M. Lecanuet became President of the *Centre démocrate* (Democratic Center—CD) at its inaugural meeting in April, 1966. The CD, consisting of the MRP, the non-Gaullist Conservatives, and some middle-of-the-road, Radical-type politicians who opposed the left-leaning strategy of the Federation, was a more faithful reflection of M. Lecanuet's supporters at the 1965 presidential election than the Federation was of M. Mitterrand's supporters, as the Federation did not include the PCF, which supported M. Mitterrand. There was, however, a clear parallelism between the Federation and the CD. Both represented efforts on the part of small parties to pool their efforts under a common electoral banner. Just as the Federation nominated a single candidate in most districts at the election of 1967, so did the CD (in about 375 districts). And just as the Federation was a minority which needed additional electoral support, so was the CD. The Federation found a powerful ally in the PCF, but there was no major party which the CD could ally with. The strategy of the CD appears to have rested on the hope that their candidates would be supported by middle-of-the-road voters opposed both to the Federation, because of its alliance with the PCF, and the Gaullists. This strategy failed, and the CD fared poorly at the 1967 election. After the election, Deputies elected under the CD label formed a group in the new Assembly named "Progress and Modern Democracy."

Gaullist Unification. In the spring of 1966, Premier Pompidou announced the formation of a *Comité d'action pour la Ve République* (Action Committee for the Fifth Republic), consisting of representatives of the UNR-UDT and of the Gaullist Conservatives, and certain other Gaullist leaders. The main functions of the Gaullist Action Committee were to decide on electoral strategy and to nominate candidates. It was agreed from the start that the Action Committee would support only one candidate in each district at the second ballot, but there was some disagreement over first-ballot tactics. At first, Valéry Giscard d'Estaing, the leader of the Gaullist Conservatives (the Independent Republicans—see Chapter Five, pp. 121–122) wanted the Action Committee to permit UNR and Gaullist Conservative candidates to compete with each other at the first ballot, thereby giving Gaullist voters a chance to indicate which type of Gaullist candidate they preferred. The Action Committee decided, however, to nominate only one Gaullist candidate in each district, thereby concentrating the Gaullist vote on a single candidate right at the first ballot. The Action Committee nominated a single candidate in each of France's 470 metropolitan electoral districts, but after the election, the Gaullists divided into two parliamentary groups: a large *Groupe d'Union démocratique pour la Ve République* (Democratic Union for the Fifth Republic), consisting mainly of Deputies from the UNR-UDT, and a smaller group of Independent Republicans, consisting of the Gaullist Conservatives.

The Election of 1967

The legislative election of 1967 was fought among tightly disciplined electoral blocs. The first ballot was mainly a contest among four groups, each of which entered a single candidate in the districts where they competed: the Gaullists, the PCF, the Federation of the Democratic and Socialist Left, and the Democratic Center. Only 15 percent of the Metropolitan seats were won at the first ballot (most of them by Gaullists) and the main competition took place at the second ballot, in almost 400 Metropolitan districts.

The second ballot was primarily a contest between Gaullists and an alliance of the "Left," consisting of the PCF, the Federation, and the smaller *Parti socialiste unifié* (PSU) (see Chapter Five, p. 110). The PCF and the Federation agreed to withdraw in one another's favor at the second ballot in order to ensure the success of their candidate who was best placed to defeat the Gaullist candidate. For most of the districts, "best placed" was interpreted to mean the candidate of the allied parties who received the largest number of votes at the first ballot, but the PCF withdrew about a dozen of its candidates where they ran ahead of the Federation by only a small margin at the first ballot but where it was believed that the Federation candidate stood a better chance than the PCF candidate to win at the second ballot.

The results of the straight fights between the Gaullists and the parties of the Left are shown in Table 12. Both the PCF and the Federation did much better against the Gaullists than the PCF, SFIO, and Radicals had done in 1962. While the Gaullists had won 60 percent of their straight fights with the Left in 1962, they won only 42 percent of them in 1967. The first-ballot supporters of the PCF and the Federation appear to have showed remarkable discipline in transferring their votes at the second ballot to "the single candidate of the left." There is reason to believe that even some people who voted for the Democratic Center at the first ballot cast their votes at the second ballot for the left-wing candidate rather than for the Gaullist,[28] even though the official policy of the CD was to "block the way" of the Communists.

It is not surprising that the PCF's voters transferred their support to the Federation in those districts where the Federation contested the second ballot, as they have generally shown a high degree of electoral discipline. It was unusual for so many Socialist and Radical voters to support a Communist at the second ballot, for many people who prefer the Socialists or Radicals had been strongly anti-Communist in the past (see above, pp. 147–149). Anti-Communist feeling appears to have softened between 1962 and 1967. At a survey made in 1964, more people indicated that they thought that the national role of the PCF since the Liberation had been useful (38 percent) than harmful (27 percent), although 17 percent of the respondents who expressed a preference for the SFIO and almost one half of those who expressed a pref-

[28] Raymond Barrillon in *Le Monde*, March 15, 1967, and Alain Duhamel in *ibid.*, March 16, 1967.

TABLE 12. Straight Fights Between Gaullists[a] and the "Left" at the Second Ballot
1958–1967

| | 1958[b] | | | 1962[c] | | | 1967[d] | | |
| | Number of Contests | Won by Gaullist | | Number of Contests | Won by Gaullist | | Number of Contests | Won by Gaullist | |
		Number	Percent		Number	Percent		Number	Percent
Gaullists vs. PCF	36	34	94	90	76	83	129	73	57
Gaullists vs. SFIO	7	6	85	64	22	34			
Gaullists vs. Radicals				24	7	29			
Gaullists vs. Federation							129	37	27
Gaullists vs. PSU				3	3	100	6	2	33
	43	40	93	181	108	60	264	112	42

[a] Includes UNR for 1958 and all official Gaullist candidates, regardless of party, for 1962 and 1967.
[b] SOURCE: Maurice Duverger, "Paradoxes d'une réforme électorale," in Jean Touchard *et al.*, *Le Référendum de septembre et les élections de novembre 1958*, Armand Colin, Paris, 1960 (Cahiers de la Fondation Nationale des Sciences Politiques, 109), p. 238.
[c] SOURCE: François Goguel, "Analyse des résultats," in François Goguel *et al.*, *Le Référendum d'octobre et les élections de novembre 1962*, Armand Colin, Paris, 1965 (Cahiers de la Fondation Nationale des Sciences Politiques, 142), pp. 314–315.
[d] Calculated from the election results published in *Le Monde*, March 14, 1967.

erence for the Radicals thought that the role of the Communists had been harmful.[29] It appears that by 1967, the anti-Communism of many Socialist and Radical voters played a lesser role in determining their votes than other factors.

The effectiveness of the PCF/Federation alliance at the second ballot in 1967 brought about a considerable change in the distribution of parliamentary seats, even though the distribution of the partisan vote at the first ballot did not differ much from that of 1962. The Gaullists polled a slightly larger share of the first-ballot vote in 1967 than they had polled in 1962, but they lost about 40 seats. (These losses were suffered by the UNR; the Gaullist Conservatives won more seats in 1967 than they had had just before the election.) The Federation and the PSU together won almost exactly the same share of the vote at the first ballot in 1967 as the SFIO, Radicals, and PSU together had won in 1962, but they gained about 15 seats. The PCF increased its share of the first-ballot vote slightly, but it made the largest gain in seats, jumping from 41 to 73. The parties of the Democratic Center lost both votes and seats.[30]

The Future of the Gaullists

Despite the regrouping of parties which took place before the 1967 election, and despite the appearance of two large electoral blocs at the second ballot of that election, the solidarity of each of the main blocs was far from complete. The PCF and the Federation were able to cooperate for electoral purposes, but they were not able to produce a common program before the election. The Federation itself was, as its name implied, a coalition of existing parties rather than a coherent political unit, and if either the SFIO or the Radicals chose to depart from it, that section of the party spectrum would be as fragmented as it had been before. The MRP was probably more willing than any other party to give up its separate existence and merge itself into some new political group, but the Democratic Center was crushed between the left-

[29] *Sondages*, 1964, no. 3, pp. 44–47.
[30] The comparisons of the vote in 1962 and 1967 come from François Goguel, "Les élections législatives des 5 et 12 mars 1967," *Revue Française de Science Politique*, XVII (June, 1967), 438.

wing parties and the Gaullists in 1967, and such an unfavorable result could be expected to lead to a reconsideration of strategies. Even the Gaullists were not a homogeneous political unit. After the 1967 election, the Gaullist Conservatives formed their own parliamentary group, separate from the group containing the Gaullists of the UNR, and they could be expected to try to expand their influence within the governing majority. The Government's resort to Article 38 in May, 1967, to obtain delegated legislative powers in economic and social affairs (see Chapter Four, p. 83) can be interpreted in part as a maneuver to prevent the Gaullist Conservatives from exercising too much influence over the shaping of Government policy in those fields. The parties, in other words, continued to display tactical fluidity and tried to retain as much freedom of action as possible, even as they regrouped to meet the electoral circumstances.

The appearance of the UNR after the collapse of the Fourth Republic had a marked effect on the electoral strength, parliamentary representation, and electoral tactics of the other parties, but it cannot be said that their structure and behavior were transformed in any permanent and fundamental way. The strikingly new phenomena were the electoral success of the UNR, particularly in 1962, the near-majority standing of the UNR in the National Assembly between 1962 and 1967, and the parliamentary discipline displayed by the Gaullists during those years.

The 1967 election, which produced a bare Gaullist majority of some half-dozen votes, posed a parliamentary problem for the Government, which resolved it in the short run by resorting to Article 38 soon after the election. But it also pointed toward a more fundamental question, on the answer to which the future of the French party system may depend. What is the probability of the UNR remaining a strong electoral force, and a large, disciplined parliamentary party, especially after Charles de Gaulle is no longer on the political scene?

The regrouping of the anti-Gaullist parties was not inevitable, but it was intelligible in the light of the obstacle they confronted in a strong UNR. If the UNR were to remain strong, it would be logical (but still not inevitable) for the anti-Gaullist parties to close their ranks further. But if the UNR's electoral strength were to diminish significantly or evaporate altogether, it could reasonably be expected that the anti-Gaullist parties would not only gain in strength but also, without the incentive for regrouping represented by the strong UNR, return to their traditional pattern of fragmentation.

It has been widely assumed since 1958 that the electoral success of the UNR has been a reflection of de Gaulle's popularity, and not of its own intrinsic popularity. M. Terrenoire, a leading Gaullist, said in 1959: "The voters have elected us, not because of us, but because of him." In fact, this is less likely to have been the case in 1958 than it was in 1962. Survey data indicate that less than 15 percent of the voters associated the UNR with de Gaulle *before* the 1958 election, while almost 60 percent did so *after* the election.[31] Shortly before the 1962 election, the percentage of respondents who linked the UNR with de Gaulle ranged from 37 to 65, depending on the specific question asked; after the election, the range was from 56 to 81 percent.

A link between de Gaulle and the UNR seems to have been established clearly enough in many voters' minds, but the question remains whether this will be enough to sustain the electoral strength of the UNR in the future. There are good reasons for thinking that it will not. The electoral fate of the Social Republicans, who won only 4 percent of the votes in 1956, provides an indication of what can happen electorally to a Gaullist party when de Gaulle is not active politically. The presidential election of 1965 indicated how difficult it could be even for de Gaulle to win a partisan election, although the extent of his success was remarkable in view of the fact that he ran against almost all the parties. And the volatility of the French electorate, which was characterized as recently as 1958 by a relatively thin distribution of party identification, suggests that a party which makes a sudden rise may just as easily, in different circumstances, suffer a sudden decline.[32]

There is countervailing evidence, however, which suggests that the UNR may become a permanent feature of French politics. The morale and political interest of its voters have been comparatively high,[33] and it was second only to the PCF in its ability in 1962

[31] Converse and Dupeux, "De Gaulle and Eisenhower: The Public Image of the Victorious General," *op. cit.*, p. 335.

[32] Converse and Dupeux, "Politicization of the Electorate in France and the United States," *op. cit.*, p. 279.

[33] Georges Dupeux, "D'une consultation à l'autre. Les réactions du corps électoral," in Jean Touchard *et al.*, *Le Référendum de septembre et les élections de novembre 1958, op. cit.*, p. 149.

to hold its voters of 1958.[34] Whether it is likely to maintain this record of consistent electoral support in the future, however, depends upon its ability to satisfy its voters enough for them to develop a permanent attachment to it.

The leaders of the UNR try to present their party as modern, forward-looking, pragmatic, and unencumbered by the ideological conflicts of the "old" parties. In 1958 and 1962, the UNR appeared successful in avoiding being clearly located on the religious and economic dimensions of cleavage, although few voters regard it as "Left," about a fourth regard it as "Center," and from about a third to more than half regard it as "Right," with the remainder having no opinion. To the extent that ideological concepts such as socialism and capitalism have declined in importance—to be replaced by the more neutral concept of economic development— the UNR appears to be well placed to profit from the change. At a survey taken after the 1962 election, 29 percent of the respondents indicated that they thought the UNR was the party most concerned with the economic development of the country, while the runners-up (the PCF and SFIO) were each picked by only 9 percent of the respondents.[35] But it is by no means sure that the old ideological concepts are withering away, and religion, in particular, is still a powerful electoral force, as the 1965 presidential election demonstrated.

To the extent that urbanization is modern, much of the UNR's electoral strength comes from modern areas, as it runs well in the cities. Yet Gaullism meets its limits in the cities also. We have seen that there is good reason not to equate a referendum with a partisan election, but the UNR is linked in the public mind with de Gaulle and de Gaulle's own electoral record is relevant to a consideration of the future of the UNR. At the referendum of October, 1962, de Gaulle's "Oui" position did less well in France's 32 cities of more than 100,000 population than it did in France as a whole.[36] While the UNR is strong in the cities, so are the SFIO and the PCF.

Even if the UNR retains its Gaullist inheritance intact, there is no guarantee that it will not squander it by inability to remain

[34] Georges Dupeux, "Le comportement des électeurs français de 1958 à 1962," op. cit., p. 183.

[35] Sondages, 1963, no. 2, p. 71.

[36] François Goguel, "Analyse des résultats," op. cit., pp. 300–301.

united. The UNR might, for example, be unable to agree on a single candidate for the presidency or it might be torn by rivalries for other posts, such as the premiership. It may not, in other words, be immune to the difficulties that other parties have experienced.

Political scientists do not yet know enough about the conditions of a successful breakthrough by a new party into an ongoing party system to be able to make any firm predictions for the future of the UNR. We know that other new French parties have surged briefly and then either declined or disappeared. We know also that new parties have appeared less spectacularly and acquired dedicated, if limited, support. If the UNR retains the support of most of its voters and remains a major party, it will have accomplished something without precedent in modern French history.

CHAPTER SEVEN

Political Participation
and Political Personnel

ON JANUARY 1, 1966, the population of Metropolitan France was estimated to be 49,157,200, including some 1,400,000 *rapatriés* (French citizens now residing in France who, before decolonization, lived in the overseas territories and departments, mainly in Algeria), and about 2,000,000 foreigners. Somewhat more than half of the total population was female, although this is due primarily to the higher age brackets; there were more males than females under age 65. More than 34 percent of the population were under 20 years of age and more than 12 percent of the population were 65 years of age or older.

Political Participation

VOTING

There were 28,233,167 registered voters for the first ballot of the presidential election of 1965. There were undoubtedly more eligible voters than registered voters. The French system of voter registration minimizes the effort required of the citizen. The electoral lists are revised each year by local authorities; there are appeal procedures for people whose names are overlooked; and residence requirements present no obstacles. Still, it is just about impossible to keep the lists up to date, especially in areas affected heavily by internal migration, and many more voters would be registered if they took the initiative. Estimates of the number of

175

eligible but unregistered voters have ranged from 1,000,000 to 4,000,000 in recent years.[1]

Not all registered voters vote at any given election or referendum. Between October, 1945, and March, 1967, abstentions ranged from a low of 14.9 percent of the registered voters (for the first ballot of the 1965 presidential election) to a high of 31.3 percent (for the 1962 legislative election). The abstention rate is generally higher in the southern half of the country than in the northern half. In part, this is because the most rugged mountain ranges are in the southern half of the country. The north-south differential in abstentions is probably also due partly to imperfect registration records. Corsica, for example, always has the highest abstention rate, but many people who are registered there live elsewhere. Several of the southern departments which have high abstention rates, such as Cantal, Creuse, and Gers, are losing population, and the registration lists may not accurately reflect the population loss. Conversely, the higher turnout reported for the north may reflect the failure of many new arrivals to be included on the lists. Close study of electoral patterns has also shown a correlation between high electoral turnout and strongly Catholic communities.[2]

VOTING PLUS

On the basis of a survey of a sample of the French electorate made in December, 1958, Georges Dupeux prepared an index of political participation using the following criteria: (1) High participation—voting plus two of the following activities: attendance at one or more public meetings; reading of electoral posters; efforts at persuasion of other people; (2) Moderate participation: voting plus one of the other activities; (3) Slight participation: voting only; and (4) No participation: neither voting nor any of the

[1] Maurice Duverger, Les Institutions françaises, Presses Universitaires de France, Paris, 1962, pp. 79–80. René Rémond, "Participation électorale et participation organisée," in Georges Vedel, ed., La Dépolitisation, mythe ou réalité?, Armand Colin, Paris, 1962, pp. 74–76. Jean Meynaud and Alain Lancelot, La Participation des Français à la politique, Presses Universitaires de France, Paris, 1965, p. 15.

[2] Alain Lancelot and Jean Ranger, "Analyse des résultats," in François Goguel et al., Le Référendum du 8 janvier 1961, Armand Colin, Paris, 1962, pp. 121–131.

other activities.[3] Dupeux found that 18 percent of the respondents fell into the category of high participation; 36 percent in the category of moderate participation; and 46 percent in the categories of slight and no participation (grouped together and referred to below as low participation). Within each category, men participated in politics more actively than women. (Politics is a man's game in France, as it is elsewhere. Women were not permitted to vote until 1944, although Léon Blum appointed three women as junior Ministers in his Popular Front Government in 1936. Women are less interested in politics than men are,[4] perhaps because the parties place so little confidence in them. Few women are nominated for national office, and even fewer are elected: the Assembly elected in November, 1946, contained the most women—32 out of 544 seats; the Assembly elected in 1958 contained the fewest—6 out of 465 seats. Even on the local level, few women are elected: less than 2½ percent of French municipal councillors are women.[5] Women hold important political responsibilities only in Parisian local government, and even there they are far from proportionate to their numbers.)[6]

Dupeux also found that participation was higher in the rural areas than in the towns and cities, and that people in farm families participated more than people in manual worker families. People in farm families did not participate as much as people in professional and executive families, but this was because of the greater participation of the women in professional and executive families. Taking men only, farmers had the highest participation rate of any broad occupational category.

PARTY MEMBERSHIP

Party membership is an elusive datum. Estimates of party membership made around 1947, and often based on the claims of the parties themselves, indicated that some 3,500,000 people were party members, but this figure is almost certainly exaggerated, although

[3] Georges Dupeux, "France," in "Citizen Participation in Political Life," UNESCO, International Social Science Journal, XII (1960), 40–53.
[4] Georges Dupeux, "L'opinion publique et la dépolitisation," in Georges Vedel, ed., op. cit., pp. 102–103.
[5] Le Monde, September 23, 1965.
[6] Mattei Dogan and Jacques Narbonne, Les Françaises face à la politique, Armand Colin, Paris, 1955, esp. p. 177.

it is impossible to know by how much. The parties have acknowledged much lower membership figures since those years, but it is still difficult to separate the wish from the reality. At a survey in 1958, 2.7 percent of the respondents claimed party membership, 10.6 percent refused to answer the question, and 86.6 percent said that they were not party members.[7] Applied to an electorate of 28,000,000 people, these percentages mean that about 750,000 people were party members and that another 3,000,000 people might have been. A more recent estimate places the figure for party membership in 1962 at no more than 500,000.[8]

Whatever the total party membership may be, the Communist Party has the largest membership, and this is probably larger than that of all the other parties combined.[9] Recent estimates of the PCF membership range from 200,000 to 320,000. The Socialists were reported to have about 90,000 members in 1965, but only about 75,000 were paying dues regularly.[10] The UNR may have as many members as the SFIO. The MRP probably has about 40,000 members, and the other parties fewer still.

DEMONSTRATIONS

Public demonstrations occurred frequently during the early years of the Fifth Republic but have been rare since 1963. It is difficult to estimate the extent of participation in popular demonstrations, as official, impartial, and interested accounts of the number of participants in any given demonstration vary. In February, 1962, after a demonstration (which had been prohibited) in Paris resulted in bloodshed comparable to that of February 6, 1934 (see Chapter Two, p. 30), the Government authorized a funeral procession for the victims in which either 150,000, several hundreds of thousands, or more than 1,000,000 people participated, depending on whether one accepts the estimate of the police, the press, or the people who organized the procession.[11] Urban demonstrators are probably mainly party and union members. It seems

[7] Dupeux, "France," op. cit., p. 44.

[8] François Goguel and Alfred Grosser, La Politique en France, Armand Colin, Paris, 1964, p. 106.

[9] Ibid.; and Rémond, op. cit., p. 90.

[10] Le Monde, June 3, 1965.

[11] L'Année Politique 1962, Presses Universitaires de France, Paris, 1963, pp. 16–17.

reasonable to say that if all the causes for which people have demonstrated in France in recent years were to mobilize their forces simultaneously, the total number of participants would be larger than the number of party members, although smaller than the 18 percent of the population who ranked high on Georges Dupeux's participation index in 1958.

In May, 1958, some 200,000 people demonstrated in Paris on behalf of the parliamentary Republic,[12] and in June, 1960, some 25,000 delegates of the *Comité d'Action laïque* who met outside Paris to oppose state aid to private schools were joined by a crowd estimated at between 200,000 and 400,000 people.[13] Most of the demonstrations between 1958 and 1962 centered on the Algerian war or on farm problems. The insurrectionary activities of the *Organisation de l'Armée Secrète* (OAS)—see Chapter Eight, p. 210 —on behalf of the cause of *Algérie française* encouraged demonstrations by their opponents. Anti-OAS demonstrations and demonstrations in support of a negotiated Algerian peace regularly brought out some 15,000–20,000 people in Paris in 1960 and 1961. The same years were notable also for farm demonstrations (at least one of which was exploited by *Algérie française* sympathizers). In the winter of 1960, there were farm demonstrations in various parts of the country in which, according to the press, almost 100,000 people participated[14] (see also Chapter Eight, p. 210).

LOCAL OFFICEHOLDING

There are about 470,000 locally elected municipal councillors in France's 38,000 cities and towns (all known as *communes*, regardless of size). This is an impressively large number when compared with the figures for several other democratic countries. In France there are about 170 municipal councillors for every 10,000 voters, or about 13 times as many proportionately as there are in England and Wales, about five times as many proportionately as there are in the United States, and more than twice as many proportionately as there are in Norway.[15]

[12] Philip M. Williams, *Crisis and Compromise; Politics in the Fourth Republic*, Longmans, London, 1964, p. 56.

[13] *L'Année Politique 1960*, Presses Universitaires de France, Paris, 1961, p. 66.

[14] *Ibid.*, pp. 3, 19–20.

[15] Stein Rokkan, "Introduction," in "Citizen Participation in Political Life," UNESCO, *International Social Science Journal*, *op. cit.*, p. 11.

By no means all municipal councillors have a clearly defined partisan orientation; almost 10 percent of those elected in 1959 were described in the official statistics as having run on tickets for "local administration" or for the "defense of local interests," and more than 40 percent of those elected in 1965 were described in that fashion in the official statistics, although a large portion of these were probably conservatives. Many municipal councillors are probably not politically active beyond the local level, whether or not they display a national partisan label. Yet it is at this level that the majority of what has been called the French political class—and which has been estimated at not more than 15,000 or 20,000 people[16]—have their roots.

A large number of municipal councillors have a regular, if intermittent, national political role through participation in the senatorial electoral colleges. These consist of more than 100,000 people, of whom about 90,000 are municipal councillors. And it was France's municipal councillors who first elected Charles de Gaulle as President of the Fifth Republic. The presidential electoral college provided for in the original text of the Constitution of 1958 consisted of about 80,000 persons, of whom some 65,000 were municipal councillors.

There are also about 3000 departmental councillors (*conseillers généraux*), many of whom are also municipal councillors. The mayors of important cities, departmental councillors, and the presidents of the departmental councils (*conseils généraux*) often play prominent national political roles as well as local ones (see below, pp. 188–189).

National Political Personnel

CANDIDATES FOR THE NATIONAL ASSEMBLY

Between 1919 and 1936, the average number of candidates for each seat in the popularly elected national legislative chamber— then called the Chamber of Deputies—was between five and six.[17]

[16] François Goguel, "Six Authors in Search of a National Character," in Stanley Hoffmann *et al.*, *In Search of France*, Harvard, Cambridge, Mass., 1963, p. 395.

[17] Mattei Dogan, "Les candidats et les élus," in Maurice Duverger, François Goguel and Jean Touchard, *Les Élections du 2 Janvier 1956*, Armand Colin, Paris, 1957, p. 426.

For the first three postwar elections, the same average prevailed, which meant that there were somewhat fewer than 3,000 candidates for the National Assembly at each election. The electoral law which governed the elections of 1951 and 1956 provided that alliances could be made only among parties which entered candidates in at least 30 departments, and this helped to inflate the number of candidates at those elections, as some groups presented candidates in 30 departments only in order to be eligible to make alliances in a few districts where they were competing seriously. The result was that in 1951 there were almost 4000 candidates, representing an average of more than seven per seat, and in 1956 there were more than 5000 candidates, representing an average of almost ten candidates per seat.

Elections under the Fifth Republic were marked by a reduction in the average number of candidates per seat (5.9 in 1958, 4.7 in 1962, and 4.7 in 1967), but while the number of full-fledged candidates was thus reduced in 1958 to the level of 1945 and 1946, and in 1962 to the lowest level of the postwar period (2172 candidates), there are actually twice as many names on the ballots as there are full-fledged candidates. This is because of the provision which the electoral law used during the Fifth Republic makes for *suppléants*, or alternates.

Alternates. Each candidate for the National Assembly has an alternate whose name appears on the ballot along with that of the candidate. If a Deputy accepts a post in the Government, appointment as a member of the Constitutional Council, or appointment to some temporary post lasting longer than 6 months, or if the Deputy dies in office, his seat is automatically filled by his alternate. Seats vacated for other reasons are filled by by-elections, except that no by-election may be held during the last 12 months of the maximum constitutional duration of each legislature. During the First Legislature of the Fifth Republic, 32 alternates became Deputies, and one of them also became a Minister.[18] During the Second Legislature, 57 alternates became Deputies.

The alternate system applies also to those Senators who are elected by majority vote, and if the seat of any of those Senators is vacated for any of the same reasons described for the Deputies, the seat is automatically filled by the Senator's alternate. The

[18] William Andrews, "The Suppléant System for the French National Assembly," *Parliamentary Affairs*, XVI (summer, 1963), 274–278.

rule for by-elections is similar also, except that there may be no senatorial by-election within the year preceding the next scheduled election of one-third of the Senators.

The alternate system does not apply to those Senators who are elected by PR. If for any reason one of their seats is vacated, it is filled by the candidate who, at the election at which the departed Senator was elected, ranked just after the last candidate elected on the same list as the Senator whose seat is vacated. In other words, if a UNR Senator accepts appointment to the Government, his Senate seat is filled by the UNR candidate for the Senate in the same district who failed to be elected at the last election, but who would have been elected if the UNR list had received enough votes to be entitled to another Senate seat from that district.

The alternate system can be useful electorally. With two people running for each seat, tickets can be balanced and campaign efforts shared. It is also a way for people to acquire electoral experience. More than 70 candidates for the National Assembly in 1962 had been alternates in 1958, although not always in the same district, and more than one-fourth of them were elected. In about 30 cases, people who had been candidates in 1958 became alternates in 1962. In some cases, the incumbent Deputy stepped aside to become the alternate for a younger man or a party leader. (In March, 1967, 35 outgoing Deputies ran as alternates.) In about 50 cases, 1958 alternates became alternates again in 1962, but for different candidates.

If an alternate replaces a Deputy in the Assembly, he may not run against that Deputy at the next election, although he may run against any other Deputy; several Deputies who gained their seats by having been alternates in 1958 successfully ran for the National Assembly in 1962. Some candidates in 1962 chose as their alternates candidates who had opposed them in 1958, while a few chose as alternates the *alternates* of 1958 opponents. In a handful of cases, candidates in 1962 were opposed by their 1958 alternates.

Under the alternate system, when the candidate is likely to become a Minister, the candidate is the main public contender but the alternate is likely to occupy the seat in the Assembly. If a Minister intends to run again in the same district, he may not wish to neglect the interests of his constituents. In this sense, the districts which furnish members of the Government may be said to have two representatives rather than one.

THE DEPUTIES

Turnover in Parliamentary Personnel.   There was a sharp break in continuity of parliamentary personnel between the Third and the Fourth Republics. Most prewar Deputies were made ineligible for public office by legislation adopted at the Liberation (but repealed in 1953), and fewer than 15 percent of the Deputies elected from Metropolitan France from 1945 to 1956, inclusive, had been Deputies during the Third Republic.[19] But while few leaders of the Third Republic returned to parliamentary life after the war (only three Premiers of the Third Republic returned to Parliament after 1945, although a fourth—Léon Blum—was Premier for a month just before the inauguration of the Fourth Republic without being a Member of Parliament), prewar Deputies provided a disproportionately large share of the political leadership of the Fourth Republic. Almost one-fourth of the Ministers from October, 1945, to March, 1957, had been prewar Deputies, and so had half the Premiers and both Presidents of the Republic.[20]

The Fifth Republic enacted no legislation affecting the eligibility for office of Fourth Republic Deputies, but discontinuity between the parliamentary personnel of the Fourth and Fifth Republics was almost as striking as that between the Third and the Fourth Republics. More than 60 percent of the Deputies elected from Metropolitan France in 1958 had not previously been Members of Parliament, although almost all of them had been politically active in some capacity during the Fourth Republic.[21] More than two-thirds of the Metropolitan Deputies elected in 1962 had been elected to the Assembly for the first time either that year or in 1958.[22]

Similar discontinuities are evident at the leadership level. Of

[19] Mattei Dogan and Peter Campbell, "Le personnel ministériel en France et en Grande-Bretagne (1945–1957)," *Revue Française de Science Politique*, VII (October-December, 1957), 802.

[20] *Ibid.*, pp. 802–804.

[21] Mattei Dogan, "Changement de régime et changement de personnel," in Jean Touchard *et al.*, *Le Référendum de septembre et les élections de novembre 1958*, Armand Colin, Paris, 1960, p. 262.

[22] Mattei Dogan, "Le personnel politique et la personnalité charismatique," *Revue Française de Sociologie*, VI (1965), 309.

the 63 people who served in the Government longer than one month between January, 1959, and February, 1966, only 12 had been senior Ministers between January, 1947, and June, 1958, and two of these had served only in the atypical Government of Premier Mendès-France. Only five of the 28 members of the Government formed by Premier Pompidou in January, 1966, had been Members of Parliament before 1958. Three of the five had been senior Ministers and one had been a junior Minister during the Fourth Republic, but only former Premier Edgar Faure can be regarded as a former *ministrable* (see Chapter One, p. 21) of the Fourth Republic.

Wartime Background. France's postwar political leaders, whether of the Fourth or Fifth Republics, came from the ranks of the wartime opponents of Germany and the Vichy régime. Fifty-five percent of the 1112 men and women who were elected as Deputies from Metropolitan France between the Liberation and the end of the Fourth Republic had been active in the Resistance movement, and another 14 percent—many of whom could also be placed in that first category—had been arrested, interned, imprisoned, or deported to concentration camps, had been awarded military decorations for their wartime service, or had—as prewar Members of Parliament—voted against establishing the Vichy régime.[23] The corresponding figures for the Deputies elected in 1958—excluding those who were less than 21 years old in 1940—are 46 percent and 17 percent.[24] Many of the postwar Deputies had been politically active before joining the Resistance, but for some of them, participation in the Resistance was their first major political act. Seventy-seven of the 262 Metropolitan Deputies elected in 1958—including one-fourth of the UNR Deputies—who had begun their political careers before the age of 35 belong in this category.[25]

It was pointed out in Chapter Two that it is possible to regard the Resistance movement as containing two elements: the Gaullist Resistance, directed from overseas, and the Metropolitan Resist-

[23] Adapted with permission of The Macmillan Company from Mattei Dogan, "Political Ascent in a Class Society: French Deputies 1870–1958," in Dwaine Marvick, ed., *Political Decision-Makers*, p. 86. Copyright © 1961, The Free Press, a Corporation, New York.

[24] Mattei Dogan, "Changement de régime et changement de personnel," *op. cit.*, p. 257.

[25] *Ibid.*, p. 255.

ance, based on the groups organized within France itself, sometimes by parties or unions. Mattei Dogan points out that the parliamentary personnel of the Fourth and Fifth Republics may be distinguished on this basis.[26] The Deputies of the parties which dominated the Fourth Republic came principally from the Metropolitan Resistance; the Gaullist Deputies of the UNR, which dominates the Fifth Republic, came principally from the Gaullist Resistance.

Occupational Background. The Deputies from Metropolitan France elected between the Liberation and the end of the Fourth Republic came from a wide range of original occupational backgrounds.[27] The largest single occupational group represented was businessmen (taking into account everyone in business from corporation directors to middle and lower level management personnel, as well as private entrepreneurs, but excluding engineers), who accounted for 16 percent of the Deputies. The next largest group, and perhaps a more homogeneous one in occupational terms, consisted of teachers (mainly primary and secondary school teachers), who accounted for 15 percent. The next largest group represented was the legal profession (13 percent), and farmers and industrial workers each accounted for about 12 percent. The remainder consisted of doctors and pharmacists, journalists, engineers and architects, high civil servants, and a few military officers, priests, and women who had not worked before becoming Deputies. This distribution is, of course, not representative of the occupational distribution of the national work force, which consists of much larger percentages of farmers and industrial workers, and a much smaller percentage of professional people, such as teachers, lawyers, doctors, and so forth.

The occupational experience of the Deputies often varied widely from party to party, as the parties do not recruit their personnel uniformly among occupational groups. The only party whose Deputies were representative of the occupational distribution of all the Deputies elected during the period was the MRP, and the only

[26] *Ibid.*, p. 256.
[27] This discussion of the occupational backgrounds of the Deputies elected between the Liberation and the end of the Fourth Republic is adapted with permission of The Macmillan Company from Mattei Dogan, "Political Ascent in a Class Society: French Deputies 1870–1958," in Dwaine Marvick, ed., *Political Decision-Makers*, p. 67. Copyright © 1961, The Free Press, a Corporation, New York.

occupation represented in comparatively large numbers by Deputies from all the main parties was farming; but even in this case, farmers were overrepresented by the Conservatives and underrepresented by the SFIO relative to their representation among all the Deputies.

The PCF recruited disproportionately heavily (again, relative to the occupational distribution of all the Deputies) among industrial and white-collar workers. No other party recruited its Deputies so largely from these groups (the Radicals, Conservatives, and Gaullists together accounted for only four Deputies from them), with the result that almost three-fourths of the former industrial workers and more than one-half of the former white-collar workers who served as Deputies during the period were Communists, and virtually all the others were MRP or SFIO Deputies. On the other hand, only a small number of PCF Deputies had been lawyers, doctors, or in business. The large number of former industrial and white-collar workers among the PCF Deputies means that they were more representative of the national work force than the Deputies of any other party, but even the PCF diverged from the national distribution, particularly with reference to teachers, among whom it also recruits comparatively heavily, although not as much as the SFIO does.

The SFIO recruited more than one-third of its Deputies among teachers, and more than 40 percent of all the Deputies who had been teachers were Socialists. No other party recruited as large a percentage of its Deputies from a single occupational group as the PCF did among industrial workers or the SFIO among teachers, but the Conservatives recruited disproportionately heavily among farmers and lawyers, the Radicals also among lawyers, and the Gaullists among business people.

The occupational stratification of the first two Assemblies elected during the Fifth Republic was quite different from that of the Assemblies elected during the Fourth as a result of the different recruitment bases of the Gaullists, who gained seats in Parliament, and of those parties which lost the most seats to them.[28]

[28] The discussion of the occupational background of the Deputies elected in 1958 and 1962 rests on the occupational composition of each of the Assemblies elected in those years and appearing in République Française, Ministère de l'Intérieur, Les Élections Législatives, La Documentation Française, Paris, 1960, pp. 96–97; and République Française, Ministère de l'Intérieur, Les Élections Législatives de 1962, Imprimerie Nationale, Paris, 1963, pp. 120–121. I have

The principal losers (of parliamentary seats) in 1958 were the PCF and to a lesser extent the SFIO, and their losses meant a corresponding decline in the representation of the occupational groups among which those two parties recruited most heavily: industrial workers, white-collar workers, and teachers. In 1962, the PCF and SFIO won back some seats, but the Conservatives suffered badly, and their losses helped to reduce the number of farmers and lawyers in the Assembly. The Assembly elected in 1962 contained fewer farmers and lawyers than any previous Assembly elected since the end of World War II.

The decline in the number of former industrial and white-collar workers, teachers, farmers, and lawyers was compensated for by increases in those occupational groups among which the UNR recruited most heavily: business people (particularly from among the middle and lower level managerial groups and technical personnel which the French refer to as *cadres*), people from the medical profession, and former military officers.

National Office and the Grass Roots

It is not unusual in many countries for a politician to serve a political apprenticeship in one or more local or regional offices before gaining national office, and this has been the practice to a large extent in France. More than two-thirds of the Deputies between 1900 and 1940 had held local office before becoming Members of Parliament, and some 40 percent of the Deputies elected between the Liberation and the end of the Fourth Republic had also served in local office before winning their seats in the National

---

compared the composition of those assemblies with that of the earlier ones, not with the figures reported by M. Dogan for the Fourth Republic, as his figures refer to the total number of Deputies elected, not to the composition of each Assembly. The occupational background of the Deputies elected from 1945 through 1956 appears in: Raoul Husson, *Élections et référendums des 21 octobre 1945, 5 mai et 2 juin 1946*, Le Monde, Paris, 1946, pp. xiv-xvii and xxix-xxx; Husson, *Élections et référendums des 13 oct., 10 et 24 nov. et 8 déc. 1946*, Le Monde, Paris, 1947, pp. xxvi and xxx; République Française, Ministère de l'Intérieur, *Les Élections Législatives du 17 Juin 1951*, La Documentation Française, Paris, 1953, pp. 55–56; République Française, *Les Élections Législatives du 2 Janvier 1956*, La Documentation Française, Paris, 1957, pp. 63–64.

Assembly.[29] Almost three-fourths of the Metropolitan Deputies elected in 1958 held local elective office at the time of, or had held local elective office prior to, their election to the Assembly.[30]

MULTIPLE OFFICEHOLDING

It is unusual for members of national parliaments to hold local elective office at the same time, but this is common practice in France. Michel Debré, who was later to serve simultaneously as a Deputy from the overseas department of Réunion (an island in the Indian Ocean) and as a member of the municipal council of Amboise in the metropolitan department of Indre-et-Loire, of whose *conseil général* he was also a member, wrote in 1955 that "it is an almost unbearable mark of inferiority for a Member of Parliament not to hold a local elective office at the same time."[31] Not only do local officeholders who become Members of Parliament retain their local offices, but Deputies and Senators who do not hold local offices often seek to obtain them. About 600 Deputies and Senators were candidates at the municipal elections of March, 1965, and so were 12 of the 26 members of the Government, including the Premier. Most Deputies and Senators are also municipal councillors or departmental councillors (*conseillers généraux*) or both, and many of them are mayors or presidents of departmental councils or both. (The mayor is a municipal councillor elected by the municipal council; the president of the departmental council is a departmental councillor elected by the departmental council.)

Local office confers on a Deputy the obligation (and the opportunity) to serve his constituents on the local level and on the national level at the same time. In the smaller towns, the rate of electoral participation is higher for municipal elections than it is

---

[29] Adapted with permission of The Macmillan Company from "Political Ascent in a Class Society: French Deputies 1870–1958," in Dwaine Marvick, ed., *Political Decision-Makers*, p. 67. Copyright © 1961, The Free Press, a Corporation, New York.

[30] Mattei Dogan, "Changement de régime et changement de personnel," *op. cit.*, p. 260.

[31] Michel Debré, "Trois caractéristiques du régime parlementaire français," *Revue Française de Science Politique*, V (January–March, 1955), 22. Author's translation.

for elections to the National Assembly,[32] which suggests greater interest in local than in national affairs. Frenchmen have more confidence in local elected officials than they do in Deputies or Senators as defenders of their interests.[33] Deputies may be able to build support at national elections on the basis of successful performance of local government functions. What the French call *parachutage*, the practice of running candidates in districts where they are not local citizens, occurs principally in the largest cities where participation (and presumably interest) in local elections is not as great as it is in the smaller towns.

CANTONAL ELECTIONS

There is reason to believe that the importance for a Deputy also to be a departmental councillor has grown since 1958. A glance at Table 13 shows that the percentage of Metropolitan Deputies elected in 1958 and 1962 who were also departmental councillors was higher than it had been previously, and that it approached the proportions customary for the Senate. (The local role of Senators is even more important than that of Deputies, as Senators are elected by departmental electoral colleges consisting primarily of local officeholders.) The reason for this is probably the changeover from multimember districts to single-member districts in 1958. When Deputies were elected from lists of candidates on the basis of the total number of votes received by each list in each large district, a candidate with a strong local base of support might not be elected if his party was weak in the rest of the district. When the electoral districts were made much smaller in 1958, local concentrations of strength within them took on added importance. Each department is divided into a number of *cantons*, and there is one departmental councillor for each canton. Except for the large cities, where the electoral district for the National Assembly may be a single canton or even part of a canton, the electoral districts for the Assembly consist of anywhere from a few to a dozen or more cantons, which are often of very unequal

---

[32] Mark Kesselman, "French Local Politics: A Statistical Examination of Grass Roots Consensus," *American Political Science Review*, LX (December, 1966), 963–973.
[33] *Sondages*, 1963, no. 2, p. 68.

TABLE 13. Number of Departmental Councillors and Presidents of Departmental Councils elected as Deputies and Senators from Metropolitan France, 1946–1962

National Assembly

Year	Deputies Elected	Departmental Councillors NUMBER	Departmental Councillors PERCENT	Presidents of Departmental Councils
1946 (Nov.)	544	151	28	13
1951	544	177	31	28
1956	544	175	32	23
1958	465	221	47	17
1962	465	209	44	16

Senate

Year	Senators[a] Elected	Departmental Councillors NUMBER	Departmental Councillors PERCENT	Presidents of Departmental Councils
1948	246	112	46	22
1952	123	50	40	5
1955	123	81	65	11
1958	123	60	50	8

[a] Councillors of the Republic in 1948.

SOURCE: François Retournard, *Le Rôle et l'influence de l'Assemblée des présidents des Conseils généraux dans la vie publique française depuis 1946*, Fondation Nationale des Sciences Politiques, Paris, 1964. (By permission.)

populations. A candidate for the Assembly with a strong following in one canton, particularly if it is among the large ones in his district, has a good base from which he may be able to carry the district. These considerations, however, apply only to the smaller towns and rural areas. City dwellers are largely indifferent to cantonal elections; in 1964 the national abstention rate at the cantonal elections was over 40 percent, but the percentages were 57 at Nantes, 59 at Marseille, 64 at Bordeaux, and almost 70 at Dijon and Strasbourg.[34] This is because the boundaries of most cantons were established more than a century and a half ago, and there are such gross inequalities of representation among them that

[34] *Le Monde*, March 6, 1964, and March 17, 1964.

people in the heavily populated urban areas can hardly have much confidence in departmental councils which consist of one representative per canton.

THE UNR AND LOCAL OFFICE

Strength at local elections is not, alone, an adequate explanation for the strength of a candidate or a party at national elections. If it were, it would not be possible to account for the remarkable surge of new national parties in France, such as the MRP and later, at intervals, the RPF and the UNR. Similarly, the considerable strength on the local level of Radicals and Conservatives did not prevent serious inroads into their electoral strength at the national level. Yet each new party which has ambitions to remain a permanent political force tries to sink roots into the political community at the local level. The MRP tried to do so, and the UNR has tried to do so also, although the UNR's success locally is not proportionate to its success nationally. After the municipal elections of 1965, the UNR controlled the town halls of only 16 percent of the cities with populations greater than 30,000 (fewer than were controlled by either the PCF or the SFIO) and it controlled the town halls of only 13 percent of the cities with populations between 9,000 and 30,000, compared with almost 25 percent for the SFIO and 15 percent for the PCF.[35]

UNR Deputies without local offices have sought them with as much interest as any Radical of the Third Republic or Socialist of the Fourth. The UNR won broad national electoral support in 1958, 1962, and 1967, but the French electorate is more volatile nationally than it is locally. The UNR is seeking to ensure its survival as a party, and its Deputies are seeking to ensure their political survival individually, by building strength at the grass roots. In France, it is not certain that a party can win elections regularly at the national level if it cannot win them regularly at the local level as well.

[35] *Ibid.*, March 23, 1965, and March 24, 1965.

CHAPTER EIGHT

Interest Groups

Attitudes Toward Groups

Broadly speaking, there are two opposing normative theories of interest groups, and both, in their modern guise, originated with Frenchmen. One theory views interest groups as bulwarks of freedom in that they stand between the isolated individual and the power of the central state. This interpretation appears in Montesquieu's concept of "intermediate powers," although Montesquieu, who marked the transition from late feudal to early modern society, thought of intermediate powers in feudal rather than modern terms: the estates of nobility and clergy, and free cities. (The link between Montesquieu's late feudal conceptions and present-day interest groups appears in the frequent references to interest groups, by their French critics, as *féodalités*). De Tocqueville, who followed in the tradition of Montesquieu, held the same view about the importance of intermediate powers for individual freedom, but he conceived of such powers in the modern form of associations of individuals deliberately created to achieve certain purposes (although he also emphasized local self-government, just as Montesquieu had emphasized free cities). According to both Montesquieu and de Tocqueville, the capacity of intermediate powers to resist encroachments by the central state is a good, as it protects the people affiliated with those intermediate powers from the central state.

The opposing theory of interst groups stems from Rousseau. According to this theory, interest groups are harmful insofar as their particular interests diverge from the common interest. Rousseau argued that good laws would have to be expressions of what he called the general will: what men would want if everyone participated equally in making the decision and if the decision applied equally to everyone. Any smaller body of men would not express the general will, but rather what he called particular wills—those interests peculiar to the smaller group. Particular wills would differ from the general will, and while they might be desirable from the point of view of the group expressing them, they would not be in everyone's interest; only the general will would be in everyone's interest.

Unlike Montesquieu and de Tocqueville, who believed they were describing real, observable situations, Rousseau produced an entirely theoretical proposition. The former were saying, in effect, that interest groups are good because we can see what they in practice do; Rousseau was saying that interest groups would be bad if laws were made the way he thought they ought to be made. National laws have never been made in France (or anywhere else) as Rousseau argued they should, yet official expressions of attitude toward interest groups throughout French Republican history have been much more similar to the view that Rousseau based on his ideal than to the views that Montesquieu and de Tocqueville based on direct observation.

President de Gaulle and other leaders of the Fifth Republic, such as Michel Debré, reflect this particular French tradition in heightened form. They continually emphasize the need to maintain the authority of the "State" against the pressures of *les féodalités* and claim to act in the national interest as opposed to special interests. They do not deny the legitimacy of special interests, but they hold that these must be limited in their influence. In 1945, then Provisional President de Gaulle refused to receive a delegation of trade union leaders who wanted to discuss the electoral law with him, on the ground that the electoral law was not a proper concern of unions.[1] In 1960, when President de Gaulle refused to convene a special session of Parliament to deal with agricultural problems, although a majority of the Deputies had requested one, he justified the position which he took partly on the ground that the Deputies had acted under the pressure of an interest group (as indeed they had) which, "Whatever its representative nature may be with respect to the economic interests which it promotes, is none the less, according to law, devoid of any political qualifications and responsibilities."[2] During

[1] Charles de Gaulle, *Mémoires de Guerre*, vol. III, *Le Salut*, Plon, Paris, 1959, p. 268.
[2] *Le Monde*, March 19, 1960.

the debate on a motion of censure which was introduced at the next opportunity by Deputies who were angry at the President's refusal to call the special session, Premier Debré said that "All interests, those of the workers, of the civil servants and of the peasants, those of the Bretons, of the Lorrainers and of the Provençals, are respectable; but in a democracy the Government and the Parliament must think first of all the nation. No one, I believe, can question that."[3]

National leaders everywhere claim that what they have decided is in the national interest while what their opponents have decided is not, but the repetitive insistence on the need to maintain the authority of the state which is characteristic of the Gaullist leadership of the Fifth Republic is not typical of other Western democracies. In part, it reflects the Gaullists' desire to distinguish the Fifth Republic from the Fourth, which they perceived as a political system that was constantly vulnerable to conflicting pressures (including their own), but more fundamentally it proceeds from de Gaulle's habit of giving primordial consideration to questions of national defense and international relations. For these realms, it is not illogical to think of France as a single actor rather than as an aggregation of social groups with competing interests, although (quite apart from the fact that Frenchmen may hold different views concerning national defense and foreign policy) there inevitably come points at which the purely domestic claims of interest groups touch on the potentialities of defense and foreign policy because resources allocated to one purpose cannot be used for another.

The position of the leaders of the régime may be to subordinate special interests to their conception of the national interest, but interest groups abound in France. It could not be otherwise in a society which permits freedom of organization. It is virtually impossible to take an inventory of interest groups, but there is no reason to believe that they are less numerous or less active under the Fifth Republic than they were under the Fourth.

GROUP MEMBERSHIP

In the fall of 1962, 31 percent of the respondents in a national survey indicated that they belonged to a *syndicat* (a general term

[3] *Ibid.*, May 7, 1960.

designating trade unions and other forms of professional organization, including employers' organizations), which means that one
of every two working French men and women belonged to some
professional organization.[4] On an occupational basis, organizational membership was highest among workers, and among industrialists and top management and professional people; less high
among farmers and small business men (although other surveys
have shown higher rates of organizational membership among
farmers than this particular survey did); and lowest among white-
collar workers.

People with university educations had a higher rate of organizational membership than people with less schooling, although
people only with primary school educations had a higher rate of
membership than did high school graduates. The lowest rates of
organizational membership (except for nonworking people) appeared among the two groups which most need the help that
organizational membership may provide: the poorest people and
the oldest people.[5]

There is evidence that French people have more confidence in
their *syndicats* for the protection of their interests than they do
either in political parties or elected officials. The distribution
of responses from people concerning this point varies with the
specific wording of the question asked, but they agree as to the
higher standing of the *syndicats* in the public mind.[6] Members
of professional organizations have more confidence in them than
do nonmembers.

GROUP GOALS

The claims which French interest groups make, and which often
are in conflict with one another, embrace a vast range of issues.
The Catholic Church and its supporting organizations, such as the
Secrétariat d'études pour la liberté de l'enseignement et la dé-

[4] *Sondages*, 1963, no. 2, pp. 61–62.
[5] The poorest and the oldest (and the nonworkers) are often the same
people. A national survey made in 1961 among a sample of French people 60
years of age and older, representing some 25 percent of the adult population,
indicated that half of these people had a monthly income from all sources of
310 francs ($63) or less, and that half of the persons aged 60 or over who
lived alone had monthly incomes from all sources of 200 francs ($41) or less.
(*Sondages*, 1962, nos. 3 and 4, p. 27.)
[6] *Sondages*, 1963, no. 2, pp. 67–68.

fense de la culture, which won campaigns both in 1951 and 1959 to provide state aid for the education of children in Catholic schools, and organizations determined to prevent the state from financially supporting the educational activity of the Church, such as the *Ligue française de l'enseignement,* engage in a struggle over the socialization of French children for reasons that are fundamentally moral. The *Ligue des droits de l'homme* is interested in protecting civil and political liberties. The various political clubs which sprang up around France between 1958 and 1960, including the prestigious Club Jean Moulin, turned their attention to a whole host of public issues, from the Algerian war to the nuclear striking force. The *Organisation de l'Armée Secrète* (OAS) sought to overthrow the Fifth Republic in its effort to prevent Algeria from becoming independent of France.

But most interest group activity concerns the distribution of income and opportunity in French society. Business, labor, agriculture, and their hundreds of subgroups; veterans' organizations, and organizations of *rapatriés* from North Africa; regional groups such as the *Comité d'étude et de liaison des intérêts bretons* (CELIB) which was founded in 1953 to protect the interests of Brittany, are primarily interested in the welfare of their constituents. France is a dynamic and productive country, but economic growth produces social problems as well as social benefits. Economic efficiency drives out the marginal producer, and many farms, shops, and industries succumb to the pressures of competition. The young leave the marginal farms to their elders as they pursue opportunities in industry, commerce, and the civil service (see Table 14). Cities grow while the rural and small-town population declines (see Table 15). French wealth is growing, but Frenchmen share unevenly in its distribution and in their prospects for the future (see Tables 16 and 17). Interest groups in France, as elsewhere, seek both to gain for their clienteles larger shares in the fruits of economic growth and to protect them from its adverse effects.

Major Interest Groups

AGRICULTURE

Few of France's major social or economic categories are represented by a single interest group. Before World War II, there were

TABLE 14. Distribution of Working Population by Categories of Economic Activity, 1954 and 1962

	1954	1962	Percent of Change
Fishing, agriculture, and forestry	5,218,000	3,898,000	−25
Extractive industries	388,800	311,600	−20
Building and public works	1,384,200	1,657,300	+20
Manufacturing	5,092,100	5,354,900	+ 5
Transportation	777,500	797,000	+ 3
Commerce, banking, and insurance	2,668,400	2,950,600	+11
Services	1,657,100	1,908,900	+15
Public services (gas, electricity, water, communications), public administration, and national defense	1,637,900	2,078,000	+27
	18,824,000	18,956,300	

SOURCE: Institut National de la Statistique et des Études Économiques (INSEE), *Tableaux de l'économie française*, 1963, pp. 128–131.

TABLE 15. Distribution of Population by Size of Commune, 1901–1962

Population of Commune	1901	1946	1954	1962
Less than 1,000	30.5%	27.5%	25.5%	22.2%
1000–5,000	34.0	25.0	24.5	22.6
5,000–100,000, of which:	21.5	31.0	33.0	36.8
5,000–20,000				(17.1)
20,000–100,000				(19.7)
More than 100,000	14.0	16.0	17.0	18.4

SOURCES: Institut National de la Statistique et des Études Économiques (INSEE), *Mouvement économique en France de 1944 à 1957*, Imprimerie Nationale and Presses Universitaires de France, Paris, 1958, p. 31, and Institut National de la Statistique et des Études Économiques (INSEE), *Tableaux de l'économie française*, 1963, p. 96.

TABLE 16. Estimated Distribution of Income, from All Sources, of Nonfarm Families, 1965

Proportion of Families (in percent of total number)	Monthly Income[a]
11% of the families have an income of less than	$88
13% of the families have an income between	$88 and $176
17% of the families have an income between	$176 and $264
20% of the families have an income between	$264 and $353
21% of the families have an income between	$353 and $529
13% of the families have an income between	$529 and $882
5% of the families have an income of more than	$882

[a] French francs converted at 4.9 francs to the dollar and rounded to the nearest dollar.
SOURCE: *Le Monde*, November 7–8, 1965.

TABLE 17. Indicators of Regional Income[a] per Capita in 1958[b]

Paris Region	159.6	Auvergne	82.8
Upper Normandy	102.8	Center	81.9
North	102.6	Burgundy	81.8
Rhône-Alps	101.5	Languedoc	79.6
Lorraine	101.0	Lower Normandy	77.3
France as a Whole	100.0	Acquitaine	75.9
Alsace	99.8	Loire Country	75.4
Champagne	93.8	Pyrenees-South	74.4
Franche-Comté	91.4	Limousin	72.6
Provence-Côte d'Azur	90.1	Poitou-Charentes	69.9
Picardy	89.6	Brittany	68.7

[a] Only includes income from direct work (but excludes certain wages such as the remuneration of household workers and nonprofessional military personnel); excludes all social security payments, pensions, and income from capital.
[b] For location of regions, see Map 5.
SOURCE: Lucienne Cahen, "Évolution régionale des revenus des particuliers de 1955–1956 à 1958," Institut National de la Statistique et des Études Économiques (INSEE), *Études et Conjoncture*, XVI (May, 1961), Presses Universitaires de France, Paris, pp. 375 and 389.

two main farm organizations: one oriented toward the interests of large landowners and associated with conservative Catholic political groups, the other built around the anticlerical Radical Party and associated with the Ministry of Agriculture, which was occupied much of the time by a Radical (see Chapter One, p. 21). During the Vichy régime, a single Peasant Corporation was created, but this did not outlast the Liberation, when an effort was made to organize all agriculture under a single, Socialist-oriented group, the *Confédération générale de l'agriculture* (CGA). This effort to replace a single right-wing agricultural organization with a single left-wing one was short-lived, however, as one of the constituent units of the CGA, the *Fédération nationale des syndicats d'exploitants agricoles* (FNSEA), gradually outstripped it in importance, with the result that after 1954 the FNSEA became the most important, although not the only, agricultural interest group in France.

The FNSEA is a federation embracing over 30 specialized organizations based on major crops or agricultural products, such as wheat, milk, beets, and so forth, and which have considerable autonomy in their efforts to protect the interests of their members. It includes another organization as well, the *Centre national des jeunes agriculteurs* (CNJA). The CNJA seemed for a while in 1959 and the early 1960s to be on the verge of repeating the accomplishment of the FNSEA in becoming predominant over its parent organization, the CGA, by becoming predominant over *its* parent organization, the FNSEA. Discontented with what they believed to be the sterile emphasis of the FNSEA's leaders on price supports as the sole solution to the problems of the farmer, the young leaders of the CNJA, many of whom had risen through a rural Catholic youth organization, the *Jeunesse agricole chrétienne* (JAC), and some of whom had links with the MRP, succeeded in winning key posts in the FNSEA and tried to turn attention toward long-range plans for agriculture, such as investment, education, farm consolidation, and various social security measures.

The pressure from the CNJA was great enough for some people to suggest that the old Third Republic conflict between "left" and "right" in French agriculture had been replaced with a conflict between generations, but the more traditional farm leaders did not lose control of the FNSEA. Governments of the Fifth Republic have responded to FNSEA pressure concerning prices. On the whole, however, Fifth Republic agricultural policy has been based on principles much closer to those expressed by the CNJA than those of the FNSEA.

In addition to the FNSEA and its autonomous subunit, the CNJA, there is the *Assemblée permanente des présidents des chambres d'agriculture* (APPCA). The Chambers of Agriculture are public organizations, supported out of public funds, whose members are elected by three separate electoral colleges: one consisting of more than 3,000,000 farm operators (owners, cash tenants, and share-croppers), another of some 300,000 farm owners who do not operate their own farms, and a third of some 375,000 agricultural wage earners.[7] The Chambers of Agriculture are active in the dissemination of information about agricultural techniques, but their governing body, the APPCA, is also an active agricultural pressure group. There is some overlapping membership between the APPCA and the governing body of the FNSEA, and FNSEA leaders sometimes enter lists of candidates for the Chamber of Agriculture elections.

There are other agricultural organizations in France. The *Confédération nationale de la mutualité, de la coopération, et du crédit agricoles* (CNMCCA), consisting of "technical" groups concerned with cooperatives, mutual-aid associations, and farm credit, also concerns itself with broader farm questions. The CNMCCA is regarded as the successor to the old Radical farm group of the Third Republic. There is a *Confédération française de la coopération agricole* (CFCA), which is regarded as conservative, and there is the *Mouvement de défense des exploitations familiales* (MODEF), whose candidates in the Chamber of Agriculture elections are supported by the Communists. In certain departments, the FNSEA organizations are opposed by rival farm organizations controlled by Communists, Socialists, or Radicals.

One agricultural interest group, the *Comité de Guéret*—named after the prefecture (departmental capital) of Creuse, France's most rural department—operated intermittently but prominently for over a decade.[8] Formed in 1953, the Guéret Committee's influence extended over 19 departments of central France. It

[7] *Le Monde*, February 1, 1964.
[8] Gordon Wright, *Rural Revolution in France: The Peasantry in the Twentieth Century*, Stanford University Press, Stanford, Cal., 1964, p. 123.

specialized in demonstrations and roadblocks and went conspicuously into action in 1953, 1957, and 1961.

Farm group leaders have often spoken of creating a common front, but the various groups have rarely acted in unison. In the summer of 1966, however, farm group leaders decided to create a *Conseil de l'agriculture française* (CAF) to cap the FNSEA, the CNJA, the CNMCCA, and the CFCA, as well as to maintain liaison with the APPCA.[9]

LABOR

The French labor movement has also historically been divided into several groups. Unions developed during the last quarter of the nineteenth century, and in 1895 the *Confédération générale du travail* (CGT) was formed. It was not long, however, before the divisive forces of religion and communism affected the union movement. In 1919, the *Confédération française des travailleurs chrétiens* (CFTC) was formed in an effort to organize the Catholic workers, and in 1921, in an action which paralleled the split in the Socialist Party in 1920 when the PCF was founded, a minority of the CGT seceded from the parent group to form the *Confédération générale du travail unitaire* (CGTU), which came increasingly under Communist control. The CGT and the CGTU merged again in 1936, at the time of the Popular Front, and the reunited CGT emerged at the Liberation as the dominant union confederation, but its unity was broken once again in 1947 as a result of the vicissitudes of politics.

The PCF left the Government and the majority in the spring of 1947, and in the fall of that year the CGT launched a wave of strikes which resulted in widespread disorder throughout France. Some of the non-Communist CGT leaders saw this as an episode in the Cold War rather than as legitimate action on behalf of worker interests, and they formed the *Confédération générale du travail—Force ouvrière* (CGT-FO), usually called simply *Force ouvrière* (FO). Not all the leaders of the CGT are Communists, but its long-time Secretary-General, Benoît Frachon, who acceded to the newly created post of CGT President in June, 1967, was a member of the Political Bureau of the PCF, and so was his

[9] *Le Monde*, June 24, 1966.

successor as Secretary-General, Georges Séguy. The executive board of the CGT consists of the President, the Secretary-General, and 12 Secretaries. In June, 1967, three of the 12 CGT Secretaries were top-ranking Communists and two others were known to belong to the Communist Party.[10] The CGT's activities have generally been in harmony with the position of the PCF, but the non-Communist members became particularly outspoken after 1955, and the CGT leaders were evidently embarrassed after the Russian repression of the Hungarian revolt in 1956.

The CFTC reappeared after the war and in 1964 changed its name to *Confédération française démocratique du travail* (CFDT) in an effort to extend its appeal to anticlerical workers. As a result of these transformations, there are three main union confederations in France today, the CGT, the CGT-FO, and the CFDT, as well as a smaller CFTC consisting of those CFTC unions which refused to drop the Christian reference from their label.

The figures for union membership, like those for party membership, are uncertain. No one seems to doubt, however, that the CGT is by far the largest union, and it may have more than three times as many members as either the FO or the CFDT. The hostility between the CGT and the FO is such that it is more difficult for these two groups to act in concert than it is for the CGT and the CFDT to join forces. Some observers see in the French union movement a shift away from wages and hours types of controversies to controversies over other conditions of employment, especially in the more modern industries which employ highly skilled labor. It is clear from the labor relations record, however, that interest in wage levels and job security are still prominent among the unions' concerns.

French unions bargain not only with private employers and employers' associations, but also with the management of the nationalized industries (railroads, coal mines, electricity and gas, and the Renault automobile firm, in particular), and in this respect they apply pressure to the government in the normal conduct of their economic bargaining activities. But French unions also act as interest groups in a more general fashion. They are particularly interested in social welfare legislation. This is true of unions everywhere, but the interest be more acute in France than elsewhere because French private employers have traditionally

[10] *Ibid.*, June 17, 1967.

been so reluctant to bargain with unions that the unions acquired early the habit of seeking benefits indirectly by trying to persuade the political authorities to adopt legislation providing for social welfare measures financed largely or exclusively by taxes on employers or by general taxation.

BUSINESS

There are several employers' and managerial organizations in France, just as there are several main labor and agricultural organizations. The two main business organizations are the *Conseil national du patronat français* (CNPF) and the *Confédération générale des petites et moyennes entreprises* (CGPME, usually referred to simply as PME). The PME is formally an affiliate of the CNPF, but it is virtually an independent organization, with a distinctive leadership and distinctive interests. The CNPF represents principally big business; the PME represents small business, particularly businesses which are owner-operated and owner-financed. Just as the FNSEA has its "young Turks" in the CNJA, the CNPF has its young Turks in the form of the *Centre des jeunes patrons* (CJP); and just as there has been a separate Catholic union federation, the CFTC, there is also a *Centre français du patronat chrétien* (CFPC).

The CNPF tries to serve and coordinate some 400 national trade associations which, in turn, are linked to more than 5000 other industrial and commercial groups. Such influence on public policy as big business may be able to exercise, either through the CNPF or its constituent associations, no doubt rests on the importance of big business to the economy. There are hundreds of thousands of industrial firms in France, but 1400 of them produce half of the industrial output of the country (measured in terms of value added),[11] and the country's prosperity depends greatly on their continuing operation and growth.

The strength of the PME lies in the hundreds of thousands of business people which it claims to represent. Until recent years, at least, the PME benefited from the politicians' belief that public attitudes favored the little man and were suspicious of big business. It is possible that this balance of opinion is growing less one-sided

[11] *Ibid.*, March 9, 1967.

than it is thought to have been. There are, of course, many more "petits" than "gros" in France, as everywhere else. However, since 1946 French planning authorities have been urging the advantages of industrial growth, wages are about 25 percent higher in large industrial firms than in small ones,[12] and in recent years the Government has encouraged industrial mergers and preached the virtues of bigness in its efforts to enhance France's competitive position vis-à-vis the giant American industrial firms. It is possible that the notion of industrial growth is being incorporated into public values, and a less unfavorable attitude toward big business may also be developing.

In their pressure group activity, the CNPF has usually been discreet, the PME vocal.[13] In 1965, however, the CNPF took the unusual step of publishing a doctrinal statement in favor of such things as profit, private investment, and the authority of management within the firm, and opposing certain forms of state intervention in business affairs and competition by state-owned concerns with private enterprise.[14] On the whole, however, big business seems to have cooperated with the French economic planning program, and while it opposed the creation of the European Coal and Steel Community and expressed concern over rapid reduction of tariffs within the European Economic Community, big business in France is probably less protectionist and more competitive-minded than it has ever been before.

Methods of Operation

NEGOTIATION

Interest groups try to persuade policy-makers of the justice of their particular causes. The most common method they employ is negotiation, and the French political system provides numerous channels by which interest groups can communicate with policy-makers. The Premier and the Ministers receive delegations from interest groups regularly. At the ministerial and administrative

[12] *Ibid.*, August 20, 1959.
[13] Philip M. Williams, *Crisis and Compromise; Politics in the Fourth Republic*, Longmans, London, 1964, p. 361.
[14] *Le Monde*, January 20, 1965.

levels there are thousands of advisory groups whose members include representatives of interest groups. Informal contacts between interest group representatives and administrators provide a constant flow of communication. Big business probably enjoys advantages of access to administrators over most other groups because of common background and training (although the CNJA was also reported to have particularly good relations with the Ministry of Agriculture). High civil servants and top-level management often come from the same schools, and the practice of *"pantouflage"*—high civil servants taking jobs in private business—provides big business with a corps of top managers familiar with the governmental administration and its personnel.

THE PLANNING MACHINERY

The French economic planning system provides other formal channels of representation for interest groups. France has been engaged in national economic planning since 1946, when the first French postwar plan, generally called the Monnet Plan, after Jean Monnet, who devised the French planning system and who was the first French General Planning Commissioner. French plans are essentially investment programs which prescribe the direction, amount, and (more recently) regional distribution of investment funds. A major role in the drafting of these plans is played by some 30 Modernization Committees. Most of these are concerned with particular sectors of the economy, such as steel, electricity, agriculture, etc., and are called vertical committees, but some—called horizontal committees—are concerned with questions which cut across all sectors of the economy: finance, labor, research, productivity, and regional development. Each Modernization Committee consists of from 30 to 50 members which include government officials, technical experts, businessmen, and representatives of business associations and labor unions.

Representatives of the labor unions and farm organizations are greatly outnumbered on the Modernization Committees, however, and from 1948 to 1959 the Communist-influenced CGT was not represented on them at all.[15] (Refusal to participate in advisory committees is sometimes used as an instrument of pressure; in

[15] Pierre Bauchet, *La Planification Française*, Éditions du Seuil, Paris, 1962, pp. 46–48, 66, 128.

the summer of 1965 the farm organizations refused to participate in the work of the Modernization Committee for agriculture because of their discontent with the French position in negotiations with the other countries of the European Economic Community.) The CGT, however, has been more closely integrated into the French decision-making machinery under the Fifth Republic than it was for most of the Fourth. After the severe strikes of 1947 and 1948, CGT officials, who were often Communists, were removed from various administrative posts they had held previously, principally in the nationalized industries, and both the PCF and the CGT were bypassed in many regular consultative processes. In 1958, General de Gaulle invited representatives of the CGT as well as of the other unions to meet with him, but the CGT declined the invitation. Representatives of the CGT were received by the Premier for the first time during the Fifth Republic in September, 1963, and by the President for the first time in the spring of 1965.

For regional planning purposes, France was divided into 21 development regions (*circonscriptions d'action régionale*) in June, 1960 (see Map 5). Each development region has a *Commission de développement économique régional* (CODER), half of whose members are designated by various interest groups, such as employers' organizations, unions, and Chambers of Agriculture. (One-fourth of the members are mayors and departmental councillors from the region; the other fourth are direct appointees of the Premier.) The CODER give advice on matters concerning the economic development of each region. While final decisions on the regional distribution of investments rests with the national authorities, these regional committees provide an opportunity for local interests to be heard. In such circumstances, it would not be surprising to see the multiplication of regional interest groups such as the CELIB (see p. 196). In the fall of 1965 a new group, modeled on the CELIB, was founded on the initiative of the departmental labor unions, to promote the economic interests of the department of Var.

THE ECONOMIC AND SOCIAL COUNCIL

Another arena for the regular representation of interests is the Economic and Social Council. This is an advisory assembly, provided

MAP 5. French Development Regions.

Regional names from Ambassade de France, Service de Presse et d'Information, *France, Town and Country Environment Planning*, New York, December, 1965, p. 9.

for in the Constitution, to which the Government may submit any bill, and must submit all plans and Government bills for long-term economic and social matters (except the budget), for its opinion. The Economic and Social Council consists of 200 members who serve 5-year terms. Of these, 130 are representatives of the main labor, employer, agricultural, and other organizations (designated by the organizations themselves); 64 are appointed by the Government; and 6 are appointed by the governing boards of the nationalized industries. In addition, the Government appoints about 75 other people who serve for 2 years and who participate in the discussions of the Council but have no vote when the body as a whole renders its opinions. A study of the voting in the Economic and Social Council between 1959 and 1962 showed that the labor representatives were frequently isolated, and that the farm delegates were particularly favored in that they were the group with which the others tended most often to agree.[16]

INTEREST GROUPS AND PARLIAMENT

It is sometimes alleged that interest groups pay less attention to the Deputies as pressure points under the Fifth Republic than they did under the Fourth, as a result of the relative strengthening of the executive under the new constitutional (and Gaullist) system. No doubt interest groups have in many instances shifted their focus of persuasion; it would be surprising if they did not seek out the crucial points of decision-making in their efforts to receive satisfaction of their demands. But the French Parliament is not powerless, and interest groups continue to try to persuade Deputies and Senators to support their particular views. Despite the rebuff which the farm organizations (and the Deputies) received when President de Gaulle refused to convene a special session of Parliament during the spring of 1960, the farm organizations continued to court the Deputies and in the fall of 1964 they urged the opposition Deputies to introduce a motion of censure against the Government.[17] But pressure is more likely to be effective if it

[16] R. Goetz-Girey, " 'La distance sociale' et les groupes du Conseil Économique et Social (1959–1962)," *Revue Économique* (Paris), XIV (November, 1963), 801–824.

[17] Yves Tavernier, "Le syndicalisme paysan et la Cinquième République (1962–1965)," *Revue Française de Science Politique*, XVI (October, 1966), 884.

is applied to the majority than to the opposition, and the majority is far from immune. According to Louis Vallon, the Gaullist *rapporteur général* of the National Assembly's Finance Committee, Government legislation sometimes meets "unexpected resistance as much from the opposition as from the majority. It is a matter of induced resistance, which comes from the influence of pressure groups on Parliament."[18]

ESCALATION OF PRESSURE

In the negotiation process, interest groups no doubt confine themselves to arguing their cases on the merits as they see them. They try to win concessions for their causes, and they try to show how their causes benefit not only their own constituents but others as well. But interest group activity carries with it the implied threat of withdrawal of support from those policy-makers who do not respond favorably. Usually, the kind of support involved is political support: propaganda, votes, and perhaps campaign contributions. Not all interest groups participate in electoral campaigns, but some do. At the presidential election of 1965, the CGT and the state primary school teachers' organization, the *Fédération de l'éducation nationale* (FEN), supported M. Mitterrand, and the FNSEA announced indirectly but clearly that it opposed President de Gaulle at the first ballot.

Negotiation does not always succeed in producing the results which a group desires. Sometimes, when negotiation fails to satisfy a group, it alters the level of its activity. Escalation of the persuasion process can take various forms: demonstrations, strikes or other forms of noncooperation, or violence. Demonstrations occur occasionally in France, and we have seen that they were particularly numerous between 1958 and 1962 (see Chapter Seven, pp. 178–179). Strikes are frequent, particularly in the nationalized industries, where the pattern is usually that of massive but brief walkouts (although a coal miners' strike in 1963 lasted for five weeks). Most strikes have purely economic motives, although early in the postwar period, particularly in 1947, 1948, and 1953, the Communists were able to mobilize the unions for political purposes, and some strikes early in the Fifth Republic were designed to express opposition to the *Algérie française* extremists.

[18] *Le Monde*, May 29, 1965.

The most violent group in postwar France emerged from the *Algérie française* extremists—the *Organisation de l'Armée Secrète* (OAS). Formed early in 1961 by civilians and army officers who were to be unrepentant participants in the abortive "revolt of the generals" of April, 1961, the OAS mounted a campaign of death and destruction in its efforts to prevent Algeria from becoming independent and, when that goal appeared unattainable, embarked on a scorched earth policy in Algeria. Most of the OAS's violent activity was confined to Algeria, but it also conducted a terrorist campaign in Metropolitan France and tried several times to assassinate President de Gaulle. More than 3000 people were sentenced for their activities related to Algeria under the Fifth Republic (although not all were members of the OAS or active after the collapse of the revolt of April, 1961). Almost all of these people benefited from presidential or legislative amnesty, however, and as of April, 1966, there were fewer than 90 still serving prison terms.[19]

Apart from the OAS revolutionaries and the *Algérie française* sympathizers among the *rapatriés* from North Africa, France's most discontented citizens during most of the years of the Fifth Republic were probably farmers. While the OAS was engaging in rebellion in Algeria in the summer of 1961, angry farmers in Metropolitan France were engaging in "the most extensive and violent jacquerie that modern France has known."[20] There is no common measure to the murderous activities of the OAS and the damage done by the agitated farmers (although the OAS tried to encourage the rural discontent in order to harness it to its revolutionary purpose),[21] but disorder broke out in Brittany and spread through half of France's departments. Produce was destroyed, roads were blocked, trains were halted, telephone lines and railroad tracks were sabotaged, and people were injured in clashes with riot police. Almost one-third of the farmers in a national sample later claimed to have participated in demonstrations, including 45 percent of those who claimed to have known demonstrations were taking place in their region.[22]

[19] *Ibid.*, April 19, 1966.

[20] Wright, *op. cit.*, p. 167.

[21] Henri Mendras and Yves Tavernier, "Les manifestations de juin 1961," *Revue Française de Science Politique*, XII (September, 1962), 655.

[22] *Sondages*, 1966, nos. 3 and 4, p. 64.

Success and Failure

The violence of the OAS produced only tragedy. The violence of the farmers was followed by the appointment of a new Minister of Agriculture, some immediate concessions, and, perhaps, the more rapid implementation of the Government's overall farm policy, for which the agricultural groups now clamored although they had opposed it when it was first announced. In the constant tug of pressures applied by interest groups, whatever means they employ to impress the political authorities, some groups win and others lose or, and this is probably what happens most frequently, some sort of compromise is reached.

Some groups may be more or less successful than others over a relatively long period of time because of the prevailing balance of political forces. The Catholic groups, for example, have generally been successful throughout the entire postwar period in their efforts to win state financial support for the education of children in Catholic schools, while the opposing secular groups have been unsuccessful in their resistance to those efforts.

The same groups will win on some occasions and lose on others, as the validity of their arguments, the concrete issues, the circumstances, the balance of political forces, and the resources which the groups can bring to bear change from time to time. Faced with a railroad workers' strike in the summer of 1959, the Government offered limited concessions and President de Gaulle added his signature to an antistrike order issued by the Government which threatened to draft enough workers to keep the railroads operating. The unions backed down. In 1963, the coal miners struck, and the President again signed a Governmental antistrike order which drafted all the miners as of a certain date. This time, however, the unions did not back down; the draft order was not enforced, the President's popularity dropped to the lowest point it had reached since the start of the Fifth Republic, and the unions won substantial concessions. The leaders of the Fifth Republic, like those of any régime which rests on universal suffrage, make their decisions within a framework of shifting and diverse group pressures.

CHAPTER NINE

Problems of French Politics

The Fifth Republic and Its Opponents

Charles de Gaulle was returned to power in June, 1958, with the consent of political leaders of the Fourth Republic who feared that, if he were not, there would be an invasion of Metropolitan France by the French army in Algeria. A long-time critic of the political habits, institutions, and policies of the Fourth Republic, de Gaulle sought and received authority to prepare a new Constitution, subject to ratification by the French electorate. A new Constitution was drafted and approved by a large majority of the French voters in the fall of 1958.

The new Constitution was designed to increase the autonomy and powers of the French executive relative to Parliament. Executive powers were divided between a Government responsible to the National Assembly and a President not held politically accountable for his acts. The result was a hybrid system which contained elements of both the presidential and the parliamentary systems. The provisions for direct democracy, in the form of the referendum, were important for strengthening the executive with respect to Parliament, but they were quite compatible with either the presidential or the parliamentary features of the system.

It was widely believed for a short time after the new Constitution was drafted that the parliamentary aspects of the system would normally prevail over its presidential aspects. According to this interpretation, the main policy-making agency and the source of executive leadership would be the Government, while the President would be a kind of umpire of the system, holding his important powers in reserve for situations in which the other constitutional authorities could not operate smoothly. But General de Gaulle, who had been chief policy-maker since June, 1958, as the last Premier of the Fourth Republic, did not relinquish that role when he became the first President of the Fifth Republic in December, 1958. On the contrary, he consolidated his predominance as chief policy-maker in all matters of central concern.

Between 1958 and 1962, the French political situation resembled that of the Fourth Republic in some ways and differed from it in others. The UNR furnished the core of the parliamentary majority which supported de Gaulle and the Government, but the composition of the majority varied, depending upon the particular issues involved. Faced with a large number of *Algérie française* supporters in Parliament and in the army, de Gaulle followed a cautious and tortuous route to independence for Algeria that was similar in some ways to the route that Premier Edgar Faure, in similar circumstances during the Fourth Republic, had followed to independence for Morocco.[1] Yet the possibility of a dissolution of the National Assembly helped to maintain parliamentary support among Deputies who might not have given it otherwise, and on two occasions de Gaulle employed the referendum to demonstrate popular support for his Algerian policy.

There were repeated conflicts between the Government or the President and the non-Gaullist parties during the period, as well as a struggle within the UNR over Algerian policy. Members of Parliament objected strongly to the Government's frequent use of Article 44 of the Constitution, which permitted the Government to require a simple "for" or "against" vote by the Deputies on an entire legislative measure. In the spring of 1960, there was a sharp struggle between the President and a majority of the Deputies over whether the latter could call a special session of Parliament. In the late summer of 1961, there was a conflict between the Deputies and the President over whether Parliament could legislate while sitting by right because of the simultaneous application of presidential emergency powers, as provided for in Article 16 of the Constitution. In the fall of 1962 de Gaulle threw down the gauntlet directly before the non-Gaullist parties by moving to amend the Constitution by means of the referendum alone in order to provide for the direct popular election of the President. Throughout these conflicts, there were two opposing conceptions of political organiza-

[1] Philip M. Williams, *Crisis and Compromise; Politics in the Fourth Republic*, Longmans, London, 1964, p. 443.

tion. On the one hand, the Gaullists sought to anchor the power of political initiative in the executive and to confirm the position of the President as the head of the executive. On the other hand, the anti-Gaullist groups wanted to establish Parliament's right at least to share in, and perhaps to monopolize, the power of political initiative.

Between the legislative elections of 1962 and 1967, the system operated more smoothly. The crisis atmosphere and violence of the Algerian war period disappeared. De Gaulle and the Government had the support of an adequate majority in the National Assembly, consisting of a near-majority bloc from the UNR-UDT alone, plus the Independent Republicans—the Gaullist Conservatives. No further use was made of the referendum. Relations between the Goverment and its parliamentary supporters probably came closer to operating as they do in England than ever before in French Republican history.

Yet as the political system of the Fifth Republic operated more satisfactorily than it had earlier from the point of view of its supporters, the régime and its supporters began to come under stronger attack by their opponents than they had previously. A new version of the Popular Front, which had been formed in 1936 to defend the Third Republic, was now formed thirty years later to attack the Fifth Republic. The presidential election of 1965 demonstrated that by running separately de Gaulle's opponents could accumulate more votes than he could, although they could not concentrate their combined electoral strength on a single opposing candidate. The legislative election of 1967 returned a bare parliamentary majority for the UNR-UDT and the Independent Republicans. In fact, those two parties did not win a majority of the seats from Metropolitan France; they owed their slim parliamentary margin to the fact that they won 13 of the 17 seats from the overseas departments and territories.[2]

Throughout the whole period from 1958 through 1967, the régime's leaders alternated between displays of self-confidence and a defensiveness that matched that of the early leaders of the Third Republic, who coined the slogan "The Republic is in danger" to rally their forces against their opponents at the turn of the century. At each electoral contest, the leaders of the Fifth

[2] François Goguel, "Les élections législatives des 5 et 12 mars 1967," *Revue Française de Science Politique*, XVII (June, 1967), 452.

Republic argued that the very existence of the régime was at stake, that the struggle was between the Fifth Republic and the Fourth, between the new régime and the bad old ways. After almost ten years of existence, the Fifth Republic had failed to acquire legitimacy in the opinion of all the major democratic parties. Not only the Communists, but also the parties of the Federation of the Democratic and Socialist Left and of the Democratic Center included various and more or less specifically stated plans for constitutional revision in their programs for the 1967 legislative election.[3]

The anti-Gaullist parties' constitutional recommendations differed on various points, but they all reflected the desire to increase the role of Parliament in the policy-making process. No party recommended returning to the Constitution of the Fourth Republic, although the changes recommended by the Communist Party surely would have that effect, and those recommended by the Federation of the Democratic and Socialist Left probably would also. The Democratic Center, on the other hand, appeared to favor a presidential system based on the American model, in which Parliament could not remove the President and the President could not dissolve the National Assembly.

The Constitutional Problem

The French constitutional problem is sometimes described in simple institutional terms as the need to find a proper balance between executive leadership and parliamentary control. Sometimes it is expressed more profoundly, in terms of the varied and subtly distinguishable national and human needs which the liberal–democratic tradition rightly expects governmental institutions to serve.[4] But as accurate as these formulations of the French constitutional problem may be, they constitute criteria for a good constitutional system and only indirectly take into account still another dimension of the problem. This is the need to discover a constitutional system on which at least the main democratic political groups which will have to work it can agree. Indeed, one is tempted to believe that any variant of constitutional system

[3] *Le Monde*, February 9 and February 22, 1967.
[4] For a brief, eloquent statement of this sort, see Williams, *op. cit.*, p. 453.

that rested on universal suffrage and freedom of political organization would produce satisfactory results, provided that all the democratic parties approved of it, so that one or more of them were not
busy trying to replace it with another system. Still, there are impartial observers who believe that some constitutional systems, such
as that of the Fourth Republic, are inadequate to the needs of a
modern industrial society, and they may be right. It is conceivable
that a constitutional system on which all parties agreed could
still not operate satisfactorily. But that is a problem which, at
least for the moment, is academic, as no consensus on a constitutional system exists in France.

The student may well ask why there is so much controversy
among the French parties over the structure of the political system.
The explanation offered in Chapter One for the failure of the
French Third Republic to acquire legitimacy in the opinion of all
the major political groups does not apply to the Fourth or
Fifth Republics. Under the Third Republic, there was a fundamental ideological conflict between traditional democrats and traditional authoritarians which prevented them from agreeing about
the constitutional system. The two groups held fundamentally
different views about the whole organization of French society, to
which their opposing conceptions of a good political system were
incidental. One group believed in inequality and social stratification based on heredity. The other believed in equality tempered
by talent and election. The constitutional views of the opposing
groups reflected contradictory social ideals. Compromise on the
structure of the system was virtually impossible except at the
price of a concession by one group or the other on its most deep-
seated and cherished values.[5]

No such fundamental conflict over social values separates the
Gaullists from their main non-Communist opponents. The
Gaullists and their opponents of the Federation or the Democratic Center may differ over a variety of issues ranging from
foreign policy to the distribution of wealth, but there is no reason
intrinsic to their policy differences why they could not compete
with one another over those issues within the framework of any
constitutional system which permitted free political organization
and rested on universal suffrage.

[5] This analysis is based on Raymond Aron, *Espoir et peur du siècle; Essais
non partisans,* Calman-Lévy, Paris, 1957, pp. 102–103.

It may be that from the Gaullists' point of view, foreign and defense policy occupies the fundamental place among their values that equality and inequality occupied for the traditional democrats and traditional authoritarians, and that they cannot envisage the possibility of a proper foreign policy or defense policy being followed outside of their preferred framework of political institutions. General de Gaulle's argument that the French President might have acted differently in 1940 if he had been constitutionally empowered to wield emergency powers of the sort provided for in Article 16 of the Constitution of the Fifth Republic appears to reflect such a view. But the nature of a country's foreign and defense policies depends upon the reasoned preferences of the political groups which win control of whatever decision-making institutions the constitution provides for. A Gaullist majority during the Fourth Republic of the kind which existed between 1962 and 1967 would have been able to follow the same policies which were followed during those later years. Similarly, if parties with policy positions different from those of the Gaullists were to win a parliamentary majority under the Fifth Republic, they could implement their policies.

The constitutional conflict in France cannot be explained on the basis of conflicting social values. It does not appear to be explicable in terms of conflicting economic forces either. The contending parties do not reflect distinct economic groups which might find different constitutional systems particularly appropriate to their needs.

We saw in Chapter One that for about the first fifty years of the Third Republic there was an underlying compatibility between the organization of the economy and the distrust of authority that was expressed in a weak executive and institutionalized in the form of ministerial instability. Small-scale enterprises wanted neither help from nor control by the government, and larger enterprises were content to encourage this basic outlook. The essentially laissez-faire attitude of the dominant political groups probably expressed accurately the views of the large rural and small-town population.

During the 1930s, at a time of economic distress (and international danger), the régime came under attack by people who urged the need for a more authoritative executive. But the régime's opponents were notable for their diversity rather than for their coherence. There is no reason to believe that the régime's defenders were supported by groups with one set of economic characteristics while its opponents were supported by groups with different economic characteristics.

Similarly, there is no clear correlation between economic factors and support for or opposition to the Fifth Republic. The elections of 1962, 1965, and 1967, as well as the referendum of October, 1962, amending the Constitution, showed that the Gaullists were strongest in the northern half of the country and their opponents were strongest in the southern half (see Maps 3 and 4). The north is generally more economically developed than the south. But this does not mean that the electoral support for the partisans and opponents of the Fifth Republic can be sharply distinguished in terms of such indexes of economic modernity as urbanization, industrialization, or wealth. Even if we overlook the Communists, who are strong in northern industrial regions, we still find evidence that similar economic conditions do not produce similar electoral behavior. The Gaullists are strong in the richest and poorest northern regions—Paris and Brittany (see Map 5 and Table 17). Socialists compete successfully with Gaullists in northern industrial cities. Socialists and Radicals compete successfully with Gaullists in modern southern areas.

The Communists hold an economic interpretation of the Fifth Republic, as they do of all political systems. They regard Gaullism as the expression of large-scale financial and industrial capitalism. There is evidence indicating that industrialists, businessmen, upper management, and professional people were de Gaulle's strongest supporters at the second ballot in 1965, although these groups were not stratified on the basis of the scale of their enterprises (see Table 10). But de Gaulle's lead among these groups was far less commanding at the first ballot, when M. Lecanuet was a candidate. In fact, one cannot but be impressed by the heterogeneity of the occupational background of electoral supporters of each of the main candidates.

The French constitutional problem cannot be explained in terms of conflicting economic forces any more than it can be explained in terms of conflicting social values. Can it be explained on the basis of considerations of partisan advantage? Robert Dahl has advanced the proposition that "Constitutional rules are mainly significant because they help to determine what particular groups are to be given advantages or handicaps in the political struggle."[6] One can set aside the "mainly" for this discussion. That part of the proposition may or may not be correct; the concern here is simply with the part of the proposition which asserts that constitutional rules may allocate advantages and handicaps differentially to different groups.

On the basis of this proposition, it is reasonable to conclude that there will be maximum agreement on a constitution when each of the groups which will have to work within the framework it establishes believes that the constitution neither gives it excessive handicaps nor confers excessive advantages on its opponents in the competition for political power. Conversely, there will be disagreement over the constitution when one or more groups believe that it is seriously handicapped relative to its opponents. Is the Constitution of the Fifth Republic fair in this respect, or does it give advantages to some groups over others?

The question is not easy to answer because the possibility of one or another group of parties winning the presidency depends upon both the nature of the political coalitions which form and the disposition of the voters at the time of the election. In France, political coalitions and the partisan vote have traditionally been unstable. This makes it virtually impossible to calculate electoral advantages and disadvantages far in advance of any election, but it also suggests that the constitutional system is not a fundamental determining factor in the electoral outcome.

It is true that the system of direct popular election of the President confronts the Socialists and Radicals with difficult choices. Their two alternatives are to combine with the Communists, as they did in 1965, or to combine with the MRP, as Gaston Defferre had wanted them to do (see Chapter Six, pp. 163–164). The first strategy is probably the more profitable in terms of amassing electoral support, as long as the Communist Party's behavior does not arouse the latent anticommunism of the majority of the voters. The Communists, Socialists, and Radicals combined have never won a majority of the votes during the Fifth Republic, but they always did so during the Fourth Republic,[7] and they might well do so again.

[6] Robert A. Dahl, *A Preface to Democratic Theory*, The University of Chicago Press, Chicago, 1956, p. 137.
[7] Goguel, *op. cit.*, p. 457.

Such an alliance tends to place the Socialists and Radicals in dependency on an unpredictable Communist Party. The Communists made virtually no demands on M. Mitterrand in 1965 (or on the Federation of the Democratic and Socialist Left in 1967), but they may not always display such forbearance. By insisting on a common program covering all major issues, for example, the Communists could force the Socialists and Radicals to choose between an unacceptable program and a presidential victory by their Gaullist or Conservative opponents.

The alternate strategy of an alliance with the MRP, however, is also available to the Socialists and Radicals. This alliance was rejected in 1965, but some Socialists approve of it. While this coalition might not be as productive of votes as an alliance with the Communists, it is not inconceivable that such an alliance could win the presidency. The direct popular election of the President, therefore, does not necessarily disadvantage the régime's opponents.

There is another reason for believing that considerations of comparative partisan advantage are not responsible for the Socialists' and Radicals' opposition to the political system of the Fifth Republic. They opposed the concept of presidential leadership even when they could reasonably expect that they would win the presidency. The original method of electing the President of the Fifth Republic was one which, after the first election (which everyone knew that de Gaulle would win), would give a Socialist or a Radical (or a Conservative) a good chance of being elected. Those parties are heavily represented in the municipal councils which directly or indirectly furnished most of the members of the original presidential electoral college. But even so, Socialists and Radicals opposed the way in which the presidency became the main policy-making center. In accordance with the early interpretation of the Constitution, they argued that the role of the President should be limited to that of an arbitrator among the other constitutional authorities. They were unwilling to concede that executive leadership should be exercised from the presidency, even though they had a good chance of winning the office.

In the last analysis, it appears that Socialist and Radical opposition to the Fifth Republic rests on the old French Republican conviction that power should not be conferred on an individual but given only to agencies in which it must be shared: parliaments and cabinets. Such a conviction naturally leads to constitutional systems such as those of the Third and Fourth Republics.

Paradoxically, Gaullist efforts to give the Fifth Republic a firm foundation tended to intensify the opposition to it. The aggrandizement of the presidency, the amendment of the Constitution by means which were widely regarded as unconstitutional, and the President's extravagant claims for the representative character of the presidency as opposed to that of Parliament (see Chapter Three, p. 50) could only reinforce the "old" parties' mistrust of personal power. But it is precisely that mistrust of personal power which helped to produce and sustain the kind of political system which the Gaullists wanted to replace. The circle is vicious.

Unanswered Questions

The legitimacy of the Fifth Republic is not established. The opposition to the régime is divided but capable of mustering broad electoral support. Gaullist efforts to consolidate the régime feed the source of opposition to it. Still other uncertainties surround the future of the Fifth Republic because of its identification with one man. The Third and Fourth Republics were vulnerable to the appeal of a national hero in times of adversity. Is the Fifth Republic dependent on the appeal of a national hero in times of normalcy?

It was de Gaulle's contention that France required political institutions of the kind established by the Constitution of the Fifth Republic in order to counterbalance the propensity to divisions among its political leaders. Between 1958 and 1967, the French political system did, in fact, take on characteristics different from those of the Third and Fourth Republics. By early 1960, and particularly after the election of 1962, there was more unity of purpose in the Government than there had been before except on rare occasions. Ministerial instability, the characteristic phenomenon of the Third and Fourth Republics, was overcome (although not until 1962 for the Ministry of Education, which faced particularly difficult problems, both intrinsically and because of strong resistance to change within the educational system). Parliamentary support was harder to win between 1958 and 1962 than between 1962 and 1967, but the Government succeeded in main-

taining a parliamentary majority for all issues except the use of
the referendum to amend the Constitution to provide for the
direct election of the President.

But those results could hardly be attributed to the new constitutional system alone, without regard to de Gaulle's popularity
with the electorate. The Constitution was important because the
dissolution power and the possibility of holding referendums provided mechanisms by means of which de Gaulle could convert
his national popularity into effective political power. Between
1958 and 1962, the possibility that the dissolution power might
be used helped to reduce parliamentary opposition to de Gaulle's
and the Government's policies because few Deputies, particularly
among the Conservatives, wanted to have to run for re-election as
opponents of de Gaulle. De Gaulle could successfully use the
referendum in the face of widespread partisan opposition, as he
did in October, 1962, because of his own personal popularity.
The unprecedented electoral victory of the UNR-UDT in November, 1962, was due to some, if not precisely measurable, extent
to its identification in the public mind with de Gaulle. What
would the chances have been (and what would the chances be)
of another French President enjoying similar popularity?

The solidarity of the Government and the discipline of the
UNR-UDT parliamentary group cannot be dissociated from the
active leadership of de Gaulle. The Gaullists have displayed an
unusual capacity for accepting leadership. Once the struggle
within the UNR over Algerian policy was settled, both the UNR
Ministers and the UNR parliamentary group maintained impressive discipline. Even the Algerian question cost the party comparatively little in numbers, and the only high-ranking Gaullist
of long standing who left the party was Jacques Soustelle. But the
UNR's Ministers and parliamentary leaders have mainly been
men whom Jean Charlot calls "gaullistes de toujours"—abiding
Gaullists whose record of loyalty to de Gaulle began during the
Resistance and continued throughout both the bright and the dim
days of the RPF and the Social Republicans.[8] Their willingness
to accept de Gaulle's leadership has been unshakable. Is their
capacity for accepting leadership, as well as that of the newer Gaullists who are already acceding to positions of authority, transfer-

[8] Jean Charlot, *L'Union pour la nouvelle République; Étude du pouvoir au
sein d'un parti politique*, Armand Colin, Paris, 1967, pp. 233 and 239–240.

able to other leaders of less historic stature, and particularly to leaders from other parties?

To raise questions such as these is not, of course, to answer them. We cannot know what the future behavior of France's political leaders will be. But the fact that such questions can be raised at all indicates how far from stabilization the French political system is.

Possibilities

Despite the uncertainties facing the future of the Fifth Republic, the central feature of the constitutional system—the direct popular election of the President—is not likely to be changed. At the time of the referendum amending the Constitution, the opposing parties did not argue that popular election of the President was undesirable; they contended that the method of amending the Constitution was unconstitutional. The direct election of the President is popular; some three-fourths of the electorate think it is a good thing.[9]

The parties which oppose presidential authority might try to sap the powers of the office, either through selecting a candidate who would not use these powers or by trying to place a President who would use them in an intolerable situation. There are difficulties in the way of the first eventuality. The kind of presidential candidate who would be likely to win a presidential election would not also be likely to be the kind of political leader who would willingly confine himself to a placid role as ceremonial chief of state. The second possibility is a more probable one. Even a strong-willed President could be rendered powerless by a parliamentary majority opposed to him. If he dissolved in the face of a hostile majority, and that same majority were returned to the Assembly at the election, or if he lost at a referendum on a politically charged issue, he would have either to submit to the majority's wishes or to resign.

It is possible also that a President would be elected who could act as the head of a parliamentary majority, although such a majority could be based only on the Gaullists and possibly also

[9] May, 1964: 74 percent; November, 1965: 78 percent. *Sondages*, 1965, no. 4, p. 44.

on the parties of the Democratic Center, as the parties of the "left" oppose the concept of presidential leadership. This possibility, we have seen, depends upon the capacity of the Gaullists to remain united under the leadership of someone other than de Gaulle. Such a President would probably have to share power with the Premier and the Government more than is now the case, and his authority as a leader would depend upon his negotiating skill and his popular support.

That possibility shades off into the fourth and final one. This is simply that the constitutional system would operate according to the original interpretation of the Constitution of 1958. The President would not be the chief policy-maker, but would reserve his powers for use in times of emergency or when the other constitutional agencies were not functioning properly. The President might be more or less closely involved in policy-making, depending upon his estimates of his political support and the nature of the majority. He would, if he decided to resort to the dissolution power, run the risk of repudiation by the electorate. But so would the Deputies, and the mutual risk might help to give the Government the stability which it lacked under the Fourth Republic.

Appendixes

Appendixes

APPENDIX 1

The Constitution of the Fifth Republic[1]

Preamble

The French people solemnly proclaims its attachment to the Rights of Man and to the principles of national sovereignty as they were defined by the Declaration of 1789, confirmed and completed by the Preamble of the Constitution of 1946.

By virtue of these principles and that of the free determination of peoples, the Republic offers to the Overseas Territories which express the wish to adhere to them new institutions based on the common ideal of liberty, equality, and fraternity and conceived with a view toward their democratic development.

ARTICLE 1

The Republic and the peoples of the Overseas Territories who, by an act of free determination, adopt this Constitution establish a Community.

The Community is based on the equality and the solidarity of the peoples who constitute it.

Title I. Sovereignty

ARTICLE 2

France is an indivisible, secular, democratic, and social Republic. It ensures the equality before the law of all citizens without distinctions based on origin, race, or religion. It respects all beliefs.

The national emblem is the blue, white, and red tricolor.

The national anthem is the "Marseillaise."

The motto of the Republic is "Liberty, Equality, Fraternity."

[1] Author's translation.

227

Its principle is: government of the people, by the people, and for the people.

National sovereignty belongs to the people, who exercise it through their representatives and by means of the referendum.

No section of the people, nor any individual, may arrogate the right to exercise it.

The suffrage may be direct or indirect in the conditions specified by the Constitution. It is always universal, equal, and secret.

All French nationals of both sexes who are of age and enjoying civil and political rights are voters under the conditions established by law.

Political parties and groups participate in the expression of the suffrage. They are formed and carry out their activities freely. They must respect the principles of national sovereignty and of democracy.

Title II.   The President of the Republic

The President of the Republic sees to it that the Constitution is respected. He ensures, by his arbitration, the regular functioning of the public authorities as well as the continuity of the State.

He is the guarantor of national independence, of the integrity of the territory, and of respect for Community agreements and treaties.

[Amended by referendum on October 28, 1962, by application of Article 11. The original text appears in the left-hand column; the new text appears in the right-hand column.]

The President of the Republic is elected for seven years by an electoral college consisting of the Members of Parliament, of the departmental councils, and of the assemblies of the Overseas	The President of the Republic is elected for seven years by direct universal suffrage. The procedures for implementing this article are specified by an organic law.

Territories, as well as the elected representatives of the municipal councils.

These representatives are:

—the mayor for communes with fewer than 1,000 inhabitants;

—the mayor and the first deputy mayor for communes with 1,001 to 2,000 inhabitants;

—the mayor, the first deputy mayor, and one municipal councillor chosen by order on the roster for communes with 2,001 to 2,500 inhabitants;

—the mayor and the two first deputy mayors for communes with 2,501 to 3,000 inhabitants;

—the mayor, the two first deputy mayors, and three municipal councillors chosen by order on the roster for communes with 3,001 to 6,000 inhabitants;

—the mayor, the two first deputy mayors, and six municipal councillors chosen by order on the roster for communes with 6,001 to 9,000 inhabitants;

—all the municipal councillors for communes with more than 9,000 inhabitants;

—in addition, for communes with more than 30,000 inhabitants, delegates designated by the municipal council at the rate of one delegate for every 1,000 inhabitants over 30,000.

In the Overseas Territories of the Republic, the elected representatives of the councils of the administrative units also form part of the electoral college under the conditions defined by an organic law.

The participation of the member states of the Community in the electoral college for the President of the Republic is arranged by agreement between the Republic and the member states of the Community.

The terms of implementation of this article are fixed by an organic law.

ARTICLE 7

[Amended by referendum on October 28, 1962, by application of Article 11. The original text appears in the left-hand column; the new text appears in the right-hand column.]

The election of the President of the Republic takes place by an absolute majority at the first ballot. If this is not obtained, the President of the Republic is elected at the second ballot by a relative majority.

The President of the Republic is elected by an absolute majority of the valid ballots. If this is not obtained at the first ballot, there is a second ballot on the second following Sunday. Only the two candidates who received the most votes at the first ballot, not counting those candidates who ran better than they but who withdrew, may run at the second ballot.

The voting begins on notice by the Government.

[No change.]

The election of the new President takes place not less than twenty days and not more than fifty days before the expiration of the powers of the President in office.

The election of the new President takes place not less than twenty days and not more than thirty-five days before the expiration of the powers of the President in office.

In the event that the Presidency of the Republic becomes vacant, for any reason whatsoever, or if it is decided by an absolute majority of the members of the Constitutional Coun-

In the event that the Presidency of the Republic becomes vacant, for any reason whatsoever, or if it is decided by an absolute majority of the members of the Constitutional Council, to which the matter has been referred by the Government, that the Presidency is prevented from functioning, the functions of the President of the Republic, with the exception of those specified in Articles 11 and 12 below, are temporarily exercised by the President of the Senate. In the case of vacancy, or when the inability to function is declared definitive by the Constitutional Council, the voting for the election of the new President takes place, except when the Constitutional Council declares the existence of *force majeure*, not less than twenty days and not more than fifty days after the beginning of the vacancy or the declaration of the definitive character of the inability to function.

cil, to which the matter has been referred by the Government, that the Presidency is prevented from functioning, the functions of the President of the Republic, with the exception of those specified in Articles 11 and 12 below, are temporarily exercised by the President of the Senate and, if the latter is, in turn, prevented from performing these functions, by the Government.

In the case of vacancy, or when the inability to function is declared definitive by the Constitutional Council, the voting for the election of the new President takes place, except when the Constitutional Council declares the existence of *force majeure*, not less than twenty days and not more than thirty-five days after the beginning of the vacancy or the declaration of the definitive character of the inability to function.

Neither Articles 49 and 50 nor Article 89 of the Constitution may be applied during the vacancy of the Presidency of the Republic, or during the period between the declaration of the definitive character of the inability of the President of the Republic to perform his functions and the election of his successor.

ARTICLE 8

The President of the Republic appoints the Premier. He terminates his functions on the latter's presentation of the resignation of the Government.

On the proposal of the Premier, he appoints the other members of the Government and terminates their functions.

ARTICLE 9

The President of the Republic presides over the Council of Ministers.

ARTICLE 10

The President of the Republic promulgates the laws within fifteen days after the transmission to the Government of the law finally adopted.

He may, before the expiration of that period, ask Parliament to reconsider the law or some of its articles. This reconsideration may not be refused.

ARTICLE 11

The President of the Republic, on the proposal of the Government during parliamentary sessions, or on the joint proposal of the two assemblies, published in the *Journal officiel*, may submit to a referendum any Government bill bearing on the organization of the public authorities, calling for approval of a Community agreement, or providing for authorization to ratify a treaty which, without being contrary to the Constitution, would have implications for the functioning of institutions.

When the referendum results in the adoption of the bill, the President of the Republic promulgates it within the period specified in the preceding article.

ARTICLE 12

The President of the Republic may, after consultation with the Premier and the Presidents of the Assemblies, announce the dissolution of the National Assembly.

General elections take place not less than twenty days and not more than forty days after the dissolution.

The National Assembly convenes by right on the second Thursday after its election. If this meeting takes place outside the periods specified for regular sessions, a session is opened by right for a duration of fifteen days.

There may not be a new dissolution within the year following these elections.

ARTICLE 13

The President of the Republic signs the ordinances and decrees decided in the Council of Ministers.

He makes appointments to the civil and military posts of the state.

Councillors of State, the Grand Chancellor of the Legion of Honor, ambassadors and envoys extraordinary, *counseillers maîtres à la Cour des Comptes*, prefects, representatives of the Government in the Overseas Territories, general officers, *recteurs des académies*, and directors of the central administrations are appointed in the Council of Ministers.

An organic law specifies the other posts to be filled by the Council of Ministers, as well as the conditions under which the appointment power of the President of the Republic may be delegated by him to be exercised in his name.

ARTICLE 14

The President of the Republic accredits ambassadors and envoys extraordinary to foreign powers; foreign ambassadors and envoys extraordinary are accredited to him.

ARTICLE 15

The President of the Republic is the chief of the armies. He presides over the high councils and committees of national defense.

ARTICLE 16

When the institutions of the Republic, the independence of the nation, the integrity of its territory or the fulfillment of its international agreements are threatened in a grave and immediate manner, and when the regular functioning of the constitutional public authorities is interrupted, the President of the Republic takes the measures required by these circumstances, after official consultation with the Premier, the Presidents of the Assemblies, and the Constitutional Council.

He informs the nation of them by a message.

These measures must be inspired by the purpose of securing for the constitutional public authorities, in the shortest time, the means of carrying out their mission. The Constitutional Council is consulted concerning them.

Parliament meets by right.

The National Assembly may not be dissolved during the exercise of emergency powers.

ARTICLE 17

The President of the Republic has the right to pardon.

ARTICLE 18

The President of the Republic communicates with the two assemblies of Parliament by messages which are read for him and which are not followed by any debate.

When not in session, Parliament convenes specially for this purpose.

ARTICLE 19

The acts of the President of the Republic, other than those provided for in Articles 8 (first paragraph), 11, 12, 16, 18, 54, 56, and 61 are countersigned by the Premier and, when necessary, by the responsible Ministers.

Title III.   The Government

ARTICLE 20

The Government determines and directs the policy of the nation.

It has the administration and the armed forces at its disposal.

It is responsible to Parliament in the conditions and according to the procedures specified in Articles 49 and 50.

ARTICLE 21

The Premier directs the activity of the Government. He is responsible for national defense. He ensures the execution of the laws. Subject to the provisions of Article 13, he exercises the rule-making power and makes civil and military appointments.

He may delegate some of his powers to the Ministers.

When circumstances require it, he substitutes for the President of the Republic as chairman of the councils and committees referred to in Article 15.

He may, in special circumstances, substitute for him as chairman of a meeting of the Council of Ministers by virtue of an explicit delegation of authority and for a specific agenda.

ARTICLE 22

The acts of the Premier are countersigned, when necessary, by the Ministers responsible for their execution.

ARTICLE 23

The position of a member of the Government is incompatible with the exercise of any parliamentary mandate, with any position as a representative of a national professional organization, with public employment, or with any professional activity.

An organic law specifies the provisions for replacing persons holding such mandates, positions, or employment.

The replacement of Members of Parliament takes place in conformity with the provisions of Article 25.

Title IV.   Parliament

ARTICLE 24

The Parliament consists of the National Assembly and the Senate.

The Deputies to the National Assembly are elected by direct universal suffrage.

The Senate is elected by indirect suffrage. It ensures the representation of the territorial units of the Republic. French persons living outside of France are represented in the Senate.

ARTICLE 25

An organic law specifies the duration of the powers of each assembly, the number of its members, their remuneration, the terms of eligibility, and the rules concerning ineligibility and situations incompatible with membership.

It also specifies the conditions under which, when seats become vacant, persons are elected to ensure the replacement of the Deputies or Senators until the next general or partial election of the assembly to which they belonged.

ARTICLE 26

No Member of Parliament may be prosecuted, sought, arrested, detained, or tried because of the opinions expressed or votes cast by him in the performance of his functions.

During parliamentary sessions, no Member of Parliament may be prosecuted or arrested for crime or misdemeanor without the authorization of the assembly of which he is a member, except in the case of *flagrante delicto*.

When Parliament is not in session, no Member of Parliament may be arrested without the authorization of the *bureau* of the assembly of which he is a member, except in the case of *flagrante delicto*, of authorized prosecution, or of final conviction.

The detention or the prosecution of a Member of Parliament is suspended if the assembly of which he is a member demands it.

ARTICLE 27

All binding instructions on Members of Parliament [*tout mandat impératif*] are null and void.

The right of Members of Parliament to vote is personal.

Organic law may authorize voting by proxy in special circumstances. In this case, no one may be able to vote more than one proxy.

ARTICLE 28

[Amended by Parliament convened in Congress, on December 30, 1963, by application of Article 89. The original text appears in the left-hand column; the new text appears in the right-hand column.]

Parliament meets by right for two regular sessions each year.

The first session begins on the first Tuesday of October and ends on the third Friday of December.

The second session opens on the last Tuesday of April; it may not last longer than three months.

[No change.]

The first session begins on October 2; its duration is eighty days.

The second session opens on April 2; it may not last longer than ninety days.

If October 2 or April 2 is a holiday, the opening of the session takes place on the next working day.

ARTICLE 29

Parliament meets in special session at the request of the Premier or of the majority of the members of the National Assembly, to consider a specific agenda.

When the special session is held at the request of members of the National Assembly, the closure decree takes effect as soon as Parliament has exhausted the agenda for which it was called and not later than twelve days after its opening.

Only the Premier may request a new session before the end of the month following the closure decree.

ARTICLE 30

Except when Parliament meets by right, special sessions are opened and closed by decree of the President of the Republic.

ARTICLE 31

The members of the Government have access to the two assemblies. They are heard when they request it.

They may be assisted by *commissaires* of the Government.

ARTICLE 32

The President of the National Assembly is elected for the duration of the Legislature. The President of the Senate is elected after each partial election [of the Senate].

ARTICLE 33

The meetings of the two assemblies are public. The *verbatim* record of the debates is published in the *Journal officiel*.

Each assembly may sit as a secret committee at the request of the Premier or of one-tenth of its members.

Title V.   Relations Between Parliament and the Government

ARTICLE 34

Laws are voted by Parliament.
Laws establish the rules concerning:
—civil rights and the basic guarantees granted to the citizens for

the exercise of public liberties; the obligations imposed by national defense on the person and property of the citizens;

—the nationality, status, and legal situation of persons, marriage, inheritance, and gifts;

—the definition of crimes and misdemeanors as well as the penalties applicable to them; criminal procedure; amnesty; the creation of new judicial systems; and the status of magistrates;

—the base, the rate, and the methods of collection of all kinds of taxes; the system of issuing currency.

Laws also establish the rules concerning:

—the electoral system for the parliamentary assemblies and local assemblies;

—the creation of categories of public organizations;

—the basic guarantees granted to the civil servants and military personnel of the state;

—the nationalization of enterprises and the transfer of the property of enterprises from the public sector to the private sector.

Laws determine the fundamental principles:

—of the general organization of national defense;

—of the free administration of local communities, their jurisdiction, and their resources;

—of education;

—of the property system; of property rights; and of civil and commercial obligations;

—of the right to work; of trade union rights; and of social security.

The finance laws determine the resources and expenses of the state under the conditions and with the provisos specified by an organic law.

Program laws determine the objectives of the economic and social activity of the state.

The provisions of this article may be specified and completed by an organic law.

ARTICLE 35

Parliament authorizes the declaration of war.

ARTICLE 36

The state of siege is decreed in the Council of Ministers.

Its extension beyond twelve days may be authorized only by Parliament.

ARTICLE 37

Matters other than those which are in the domain of the laws are in the domain of rule-making [*ont un caractère réglementaire*].

Legislative measures concerning these matters may be modified by decrees issued after consultation with the Council of State. Those legislative measures which may be passed after this Constitution has gone into effect may be modified by decree only if the Constitutional Council has declared that they are in the rule-making domain by virtue of the preceding paragraph.

ARTICLE 38

The Government may, in order to carry out its program, ask Parliament to authorize it to issue ordinances, for a limited period, concerning matters which are normally in the domain of the laws.

The ordinances are enacted in the Council of Ministers after consultation with the Council of State. They take effect upon their publication, but become null and void if the Government bill for ratification is not placed before Parliament before the date set by the authorizing law.

At the expiration of the period mentioned in the first paragraph of this article, the ordinances concerning matters which are in the legislative domain may be modified only by law.

ARTICLE 39

The Premier and the Members of Parliament have the right to initiate legislation.

Government bills are discussed in the Council of Ministers after consultation with the Council of State and are submitted to the *bureau* of one of the two assemblies. Finance bills are submitted first to the National Assembly.

ARTICLE 40

Bills and amendments formulated by Members of Parliament are not admissible when the result of their adoption would be either a decrease in public resources or the creation or increase of public expenditure.

ARTICLE 41

If it appears in the course of the legislative procedure that a parliamentary bill or amendment is not in the domain of the laws or is contrary to a delegation of power granted pursuant to Article 38, the Government may oppose it as inadmissible.

In case of disagreement between the Government and the President of the assembly concerned, the Constitutional Council, upon the request of either party, decides the question within a period of eight days.

ARTICLE 42

The discussion of Government bills takes place, in the first assembly to which they are referred, on the text presented by the Government.

An assembly deliberates on the text that is transmitted to it when it considers a text passed by the other assembly.

ARTICLE 43

Government and parliamentary bills are, at the request of the Government or of the assembly considering them, sent for study to committees specially designated for that purpose.

Government and parliamentary bills for which such a request has not been made are sent to one of the standing committees, the number of which is limited to six in each assembly.

ARTICLE 44

Members of Parliament and the Government have the right to move amendments.

After the opening of the debate, the Government may oppose the examination of any amendment which has not previously been submitted to the committee.

If the Government requests it, the assembly considering a bill decides by a single vote on all or part of the text under discussion, retaining only the amendments proposed or accepted by the Government.

ARTICLE 45

Every Government or parliamentary bill is examined successively in the two assemblies of Parliament with a view toward the adoption of an identical text.

When, as the result of disagreement between the two assemblies, it has not been possible to adopt a Government or parliamentary bill after two readings by each assembly or, if the Government has declared the matter urgent, after a single reading by each of them, the Premier may call for the meeting of a joint-conference committee [*commission mixte paritaire*] charged with proposing a text on the matters remaining under discussion.

The text prepared by the joint-conference committee may be submitted by the Government to the two assemblies for approval. No amendment is admissible without the agreement of the Government.

If the joint-conference committee does not succeed in adopting a common text, or if this text is not adopted under the conditions specified in the preceding paragraph, the Government may, after a new reading by the National Assembly and by the Senate, ask the National Assembly to make the final decision. In this case, the National Assembly may reconsider either the text prepared by the joint-conference committee, or the last text voted by the National Assembly, modified by one or more of the amendments which may have been adopted by the Senate.

ARTICLE 46

The laws that the Constitution characterizes as organic laws are passed and amended under the following conditions.

The Government or parliamentary bill may be considered and voted on by the first assembly to which it is referred only at the expiration of a period of fifteen days after its introduction.

The procedure described in Article 45 applies. However, in the absence of agreement between the two assemblies, the text may be adopted by the National Assembly at final reading only by an absolute majority of its members.

The organic laws concerning the Senate must be passed in the same terms by the two assemblies.

The organic laws may be promulgated only after certification by the Constitutional Council of their conformity with the Constitution.

ARTICLE 47

Parliament passes finance bills under the conditions specified by an organic law.

If the National Assembly has not made a decision at the first reading within a period of forty days after a bill has been introduced, the Government refers it to the Senate, which must decide within a period of fifteen days. The procedure set forth in Article 45 is then followed.

If Parliament has not made a decision within a period of seventy days, the provisions of the bill may be put into effect by ordinance.

If the finance bill determining the resources and expenditures for a fiscal year has not been introduced in time to be promulgated before the beginning of that fiscal year, the Government immediately requests Parliamentary authorization to collect the taxes and make available by decree the funds relating to public services already voted.

The time limits referred to in this article are suspended when Parliament is not in session.

The *Cour des Comptes* assists Parliament and the Government in supervising the execution of the finance laws.

ARTICLE 48

The agenda of the assemblies includes, by priority and in the order which the Government has set, discussion of the Government bills introduced by the Government and of the parliamentary bills accepted by the Government.

One meeting each week is reserved, by priority, for questions by Members of Parliament and for answers by the Government.

ARTICLE 49

The Premier, after deliberation by the Council of Ministers, engages the responsibility of the Government before the National Assembly on its program or, possibly, on a declaration of general policy.

The National Assembly questions the responsibility of the Government by voting a motion of censure. Such a motion is admissible only if it is signed by at least one-tenth of the members of the National Assembly. The vote may not take place less than forty-eight hours after the motion has been introduced. The only votes counted are those favoring the motion of censure, which may be adopted only by a majority of the members comprising the Assembly. If the motion of censure is rejected, its signers may not propose a new one during the same session, except in the case described in the paragraph below.

The Premier may, after deliberation by the Council of Ministers, engage the responsibility of the Government before the National Assembly on the vote of a text. In this case, the text is considered adopted unless a motion of censure, introduced within the next 24 hours, is adopted in the conditions set forth in the preceding paragraph.

The Premier may ask the Senate for approval of a declaration of general policy.

ARTICLE 50

When the National Assembly adopts a motion of censure or when it disapproves the program or a declaration of general policy of the Government, the Premier must submit the resignation of the Government to the President of the Republic.

ARTICLE 51

The closure of regular or special sessions is delayed by right, should this be necessary, to permit the application of the provisions of Article 49.

Title VI.   Treaties and International Agreements

ARTICLE 52

The President of the Republic negotiates and ratifies treaties.

He is informed of all negotiations leading to the conclusion of an international agreement not subject to ratification.

ARTICLE 53

Peace treaties, commercial treaties, treaties or agreements relating to international organizations, those that commit state funds, those that modify provisions of a legislative nature, those relating to the status of persons, and those that call for the cession, exchange, or addition of territory, may be ratified or approved only by a law.

They take effect only after having been ratified or approved.

No cession, exchange, or addition of territory is valid without the consent of the populations concerned.

ARTICLE 54

If the Constitutional Council, on the appeal of the President of the Republic, the Premier, or the President of either assembly, has declared that an international commitment contains a clause contrary to the Constitution, the authorization to ratify or approve it may be granted only after amendment of the Constitution.

ARTICLE 55

Treaties or agreements duly ratified or approved have, upon their publication, higher authority than the laws, subject to the proviso, for each agreement or treaty, that it be applied by the other party.

Title VII. The Constitutional Council

ARTICLE 56

The Constitutional Council consists of nine members, whose term of office lasts nine years and may not be renewed. One-third of the members of the Constitutional Council are replaced every three years. Three of its members are appointed by the President of the Republic, three by the President of the National Assembly, and three by the President of the Senate.

In addition to the nine members provided for above, former Presidents of the Republic are members of the Constitutional Council for life.

The President of the Constitutional Council is appointed by the President of the Republic. He has the deciding vote in case of a tie.

ARTICLE 57

The office of Member of the Constitutional Council is incompatible with those of Minister or Member of Parliament. Other incompatibilities are specified by an organic law.

ARTICLE 58

The Constitutional Council sees to the regularity of the election of the President of the Republic.

It examines complaints and announces the results of the election.

ARTICLE 59

The Constitutional Council decides, in case of dispute, on the regularity of the election of Deputies and Senators.

ARTICLE 60

The Constitutional Council sees to the regularity of referendum procedures and announces their results.

ARTICLE 61

Organic laws, before their promulgation, and the rules of the parliamentary assemblies, before they go into effect, must be submitted to the Constitutional Council, which rules on their conformity with the Constitution.

To the same end, laws may be referred to the Constitutional Council, before their promulgation, by the President of the Republic, the Premier, or the President of either assembly.

In the cases specified in the two preceding paragraphs, the Constitutional Council must decide within a period of one month. However, at the request of the Government, if there is urgency, this period is reduced to eight days.

In these same cases, referral to the Constitutional Council suspends the time limit for promulgation.

ARTICLE 62

A provision declared unconstitutional may not be promulgated or applied.

There is no appeal from the decisions of the Constitutional Council. They are binding on the public authorities and on all administrative and judicial authorities.

ARTICLE 63

An organic law determines the rules of organization and operation of the Constitutional Council, the procedure which is followed before it, and particularly the time limits within which disputes may be referred to it.

Title VIII. The Judicial Authority

ARTICLE 64

The President of the Republic is the guarantor of the independence of the judicial authorities.

He is assisted by the High Council of the Judiciary.

An organic law governs the status of magistrates.

Judges may not be removed from office.

ARTICLE 65

The High Council of the Judiciary is presided over by the President of the Republic. The Minister of Justice is its Vice-president. He may substitute for the President of the Republic.

The High Council also includes nine members designated by the President of the Republic under conditions specified by an organic law.

The High Council of the Judiciary proposes nominations for judges of the Court of Cassation and for First Presidents of Courts of Appeal. It gives its opinion, under conditions specified by an organic law, on the proposals of the Minister of Justice for the appointment of other judges. It is consulted on pardons under conditions specified by an organic law.

The High Council of the Judiciary acts as the disciplinary body for magistrates. It is then presided over by the First President of the Court of Cassation.

ARTICLE 66

No one may be arbitrarily detained.

The judicial authorities, guardians of individual liberty, ensure respect for this principle under conditions established by law.

Title IX. The High Court of Justice

ARTICLE 67

A High Court of Justice is established.

It is composed of members elected in equal numbers and from their own memberships by the National Assembly and the Senate after each general or partial election of those assemblies. It elects its President from its members.

An organic law specifies the composition of the High Court, its rules of operation, and the procedure to be followed before it.

ARTICLE 68

The President of the Republic is responsible for acts performed in the conduct of his office only in case of high treason. He may be indicted only by the two assemblies deciding in the same way by roll-call votes and by an absolute majority of the members comprising them; he is tried by the High Court of Justice.

The members of the Government are criminally liable for acts performed in the conduct of their offices defined as crimes or misdemeanors at the time when they were committed. The procedure described above is applicable to them, as well as to their accomplices, in the case of a conspiracy against the security of the state. In the cases specified in this paragraph, the High Court is bound by the definition of crimes and misdemeanors, as well as by the establishment of penalties, as they are described by the criminal laws in effect at the time when the acts were committed.

Title X.   The Economic and Social Council

ARTICLE 69

The Economic and Social Council, when called upon by the Government, gives its opinion on Government bills, ordinances, or decrees, as well as on parliamentary bills submitted to it.

A member of the Economic and Social Council may be designated by it to present before the parliamentary assemblies the opinion of the Council on the Government or parliamentary bills which are submitted to it.

ARTICLE 70

The Economic and Social Council may also be consulted by the Government on any economic or social problem concerning the Republic or the Community. Any plan or Government bill concerning a program of an economic or social character is submitted to it for its opinion.

ARTICLE 71

The composition of the Economic and Social Council and its rules of procedure are specified by an organic law.

Title XI.   Territorial Units

ARTICLE 72

The territorial units of the Republic are the communes, the departments, and the Overseas Territories. Other territorial units are created by law.

These units are administered freely by elected councils and under conditions established by law.

In the departments and territories, the delegate of the Government is responsible for national interests, administrative supervision, and respect for the laws.

ARTICLE 73

The legislative system and administrative organization of the Overseas Departments may be adapted by measures required by their special situation.

ARTICLE 74

The Overseas Territories of the Republic have a special organization which takes account of their own interests within the overall interests of the Republic. This organization is defined and modified by law after consultation with the territorial assembly concerned.

ARTICLE 75

The citizens of the Republic who do not have ordinary civil status, the only status referred to in Article 34, retain their personal status as long as they have not renounced it.

ARTICLE 76

The Overseas Territories may retain their status within the Republic.

If they express the desire to do so by a decision of their territorial assembly made within the period specified in the first paragraph of Article 91, they become either Overseas Departments of the Republic or, in groups or individually, member states of the Community.

Title XII. The Community

ARTICLE 77

Within the Community established by this Constitution, the states enjoy autonomy; they administer themselves and manage their own affairs democratically and freely.

There is only one citizenship of the Community.

All citizens are equal before the law, whatever their origin, their race, or their religion. They have the same duties.

ARTICLE 78

The Community's jurisdiction includes foreign policy, defense, currency, common economic and financial policy, and policy concerning strategic raw materials.

It also includes, except when there are special agreements, the supervision of justice, higher education, the general organization of external and common transportation, and telecommunications.

Special agreements may create other common jurisdictions or govern any transfer of jurisdiction from the Community to one of its members.

ARTICLE 79

The member states benefit from the provisions of Article 77 as soon as they have exercised the choice referred to in Article 76.

Until the measures necessary for the implementation of this Title go into effect, matters within the common jurisdiction are governed by the Republic.

ARTICLE 80

The President of the Republic presides over and represents the Community.

The institutions of the Community are an Executive Council, a Senate, and a Court of Arbitration.

ARTICLE 81

The member states of the Community participate in the election of the President under the conditions specified in Article 6.

The President of the Republic, in his capacity as President of the Community, is represented in each state of the Community.

ARTICLE 82

The Executive Council of the Community is presided over by the President of the Community. It consists of the Premier of the Republic, the Heads of Government of each of the member states of the Community, and the Ministers responsible for the common affairs of the Community.

The Executive Council organizes the cooperation of the members of the Community on the Governmental and administrative levels.

The organization and operation of the Executive Council are specified by an organic law.

ARTICLE 83

The Senate of the Community is composed of delegates chosen by the Parliament of the Republic and the legislative assemblies of the other members of the Community from their own members. The number of delegates from each state depends upon its population and the responsibilities it assumes in the Community.

It holds two sessions each year which are opened and closed by the President of the Community and which may not last longer than one month each.

When called upon by the President of the Community, it deliberates on common economic and financial policy before laws on these matters are voted on by the Parliament of the Republic and, when the case arises, by the legislative assemblies of the other members of the Community.

The Senate of the Community examines the acts and treaties or international agreements referred to in Articles 35 and 53 and which commit the Community.

It makes enforceable decisions in the domains in which it has received delegations of power from the legislative assemblies of the members of the Community. These decisions are promulgated in the same form as the law on the territory of each of the states concerned.

An organic law governs its composition and specifies its rules of operation.

ARTICLE 84

A court of Arbitration of the Community decides litigation among the members of the Community.

Its composition and its jurisdiction are specified by an organic law.

ARTICLE 85

[Amended by the French Parliament on May 18, 1960, and by the Senate of the Community, on June 3, 1960, by application of Article 85. The original text appears in the left-hand column; the new text appears in the right-hand column.]

The procedure specified in   [No change.]
Article 89 notwithstanding, the

provisions of this Title which concern the operation of the common institutions are amended by laws voted in the same terms by the Parliament of the Republic and by the Senate of the Community.

The provisions of this Title may also be amended by agreements concluded among all the states of the Community; the new provisions are put into effect under the conditions required by the Constitution of each state.

ARTICLE 86

[Amended by the French Parliament on May 18, 1960, and by the Senate of the Community on June 3, 1960, by application of Article 85. The original text appears in the left-hand column; the new text appears in the right-hand column.]

A change in the status of a member state of the Community may be requested either by the Republic or by a resolution of the legislative assembly of the state concerned, confirmed by a local referendum, the organization and supervision of which are ensured by the institutions of the Community. The procedures involved in such a change are determined by an agreement approved by the Parliament of the Republic and the legislative assembly concerned.

[No change.]

Under the same conditions, a member state of the Community may become independent. It

[No change.]

thereby ceases to belong to the
Community.

A member state of the Community may also, by agreement, become independent without thereby ceasing to belong to the Community.

An independent state not a member of the Community may, by agreement, join the Community without ceasing to be independent.

The position of these states within the Community is determined by agreements concluded for this purpose, in particular the agreements mentioned in the preceding paragraphs, as well as, on occasion, the agreements mentioned in the second paragraph of Article 85.

ARTICLE 87

The special agreements concluded for the implementation of this Title are approved by the Parliament of the Republic and the legislative assembly concerned.

Title XIII.   Agreements of Association

ARTICLE 88

The Republic or the Community may make agreements with states which want to associate with it in order to develop their civilizations.

Title XIV.   Amendment

ARTICLE 89

The initiative for amending the Constitution belongs both to the President of the Republic on the proposal of the Premier and to the Members of Parliament.

The Government or parliamentary bill for amendment must be passed by the two assemblies in identical terms. The amendment is final after having been approved by a referendum.

However, the Government bill for amendment is not submitted to a referendum when the President of the Republic decides to submit it to Parliament convened in Congress; in this case, the Government bill for amendment is approved only if it is adopted by a three-fifths majority of the valid ballots cast. The *bureau* of the Congress is that of the National Assembly.

No amendment process may be undertaken or continued when the integrity of the territory is in jeopardy.

The republican form of government is not subject to amendment.

Title XV.   Temporary Provisions

ARTICLE 90

The regular session of Parliament is suspended. The term of office of the members of the present National Assembly will expire on the day that the Assembly elected by virtue of this Constitution convenes.

Until that meeting, the Government alone has the authority to convene Parliament.

The term of office of the members of the Assembly of the French Union will expire at the same time as the term of office of the members of the present National Assembly.

ARTICLE 91

The institutions of the Republic provided for by this Constitution will be established within four months after its promulgation.

This period is extended to six months for the institutions of the Community.

The powers of the President of the Republic now in office will expire only upon the proclamation of the results of the election provided for by Articles 6 and 7 of this Constitution.

The member states of the Community will participate in this first election under the conditions appropriate to their status at the date of the promulgation of the Constitution.

The established authorities will continue to perform their functions in these states according to the laws and rules applicable when the Constitution goes into effect, until the authorities provided for by their new régimes are established.

Until it is definitively constituted, the Senate consists of the present members of the Council of the Republic. The organic laws which will govern the definitive composition of the Senate must be enacted before July 31, 1959.

The powers conferred on the Constitutional Council by Articles 58 and 59 of the Constitution will be exercised, until this Council is established, by a Committee consisting of the Vice-president of the Council of State as President, the First President of the Court of Cassation, and the First President of the *Cour des Comptes*.

The peoples of the member states of the Community continue to be represented in Parliament until the measures necessary for the implementation of Title II go into effect.

ARTICLE 92

The legislative measures necessary for the establishment of the institutions and, until their establishment, for the functioning of the public authorities will be enacted in the Council of Ministers, after consultation with the Council of State, by ordinances having the force of law.

During the period referred to in the first paragraph of Article 91, the Government is authorized to determine, by ordinances having the force of law and enacted in the same way, the electoral systems for the assemblies provided for by the Constitution.

During the same period and under the same conditions, the Government may also enact measures, in all matters, which it regards as necessary to the life of the nation, to the protection of the citizens, or to the safeguard of liberties.

APPENDIX 2

Ministers, 1959–1967[a]

PREMIER	MICHEL DEBRÉ, S (U)		

CABINET FORMATION AND MAJOR REORGANIZATION DATES	JANUARY 8, 1959	FEBRUARY 5, 1960	AUGUST 24, 1961
MINISTERS OF STATE:			
Cultural Affairs	Malraux ———		
Cooperation[b]	Lecourt, D (M)	*Jacquinot*	
DOM and TOM[d]		*Lecourt*	*Jacquinot* ———
Algerian Affairs		*Joxe*[e] ———	
Scientific Research[f]	Jacquinot, D (C)		
Other	Houphouet-Boigny, D (RDA)[h]		
MINISTERS ATTACHED TO PREMIER'S OFFICE:	Soustelle, D (U)[l]	*Frey*[m]	*Terrenoire*[k]
		Guillaumat[j,q] ———	
DEPARTMENTAL MINISTERS:			
Justice	Michelet, S (U) ————————→		*Chenot*
Foreign Affairs	Couve de Murville, CS ———		
Interior	Berthoin, S (R)	Chatenet, CS[t,v]	*Frey*[w] ———
Armed Forces	Guillaumat, CS	Messmer, CS ———	
Finance	Pinay, D (C)	Baumgartner, CS[x] ———	
Education	Boulloche, CS	Joxe, CS[t,z]; Guillaumat[e] (interim)	Paye, CS[aa]
Equipment			
Public Works	Buron, D (M)[c] ———		
Industry	Jeanneney, P ———		
Agriculture	Houdet, S (C)	Rochereau, S (C)[v]	Pisani, S (R) ———
Social Affairs			
Labor	Bacon, FD (M)[c] ———		
Health	Chenot, CS ————————→		Fontanet, D (M)[t,c] ———
Construction	Sudreau, CS ———		
Veterans	Triboulet, D (U) ———		
Post Office	Cornut-Gentille, D (U)	Maurice-Bokanowski, D (U)[t] ———	
Information	Frey (U)	Terrenoire, D (U)	
Other			Foyer, D (U)[t,dd,ee]

Table footnotes appear on p. 258.

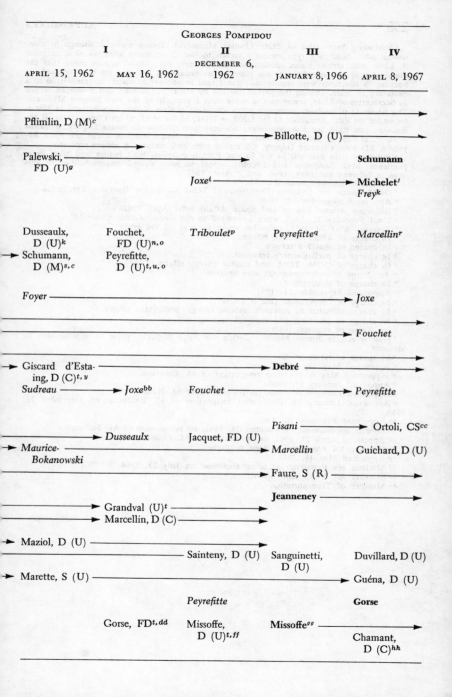

GEORGES POMPIDOU

	I	II	III	IV
	APRIL 15, 1962	MAY 16, 1962	DECEMBER 6, 1962	JANUARY 8, 1966	APRIL 8, 1967

Pflimlin, D (M)[c] ⟶

⟶ Billotte, D (U) ⟶

Palewski, FD (U)[g] ⟶ **Schumann**

Joxe[i] ⟶ **Michelet**[j] **Frey**[k]

Dusseaulx, D (U)[k]   Fouchet, FD (U)[n,o]   *Triboulet*[p]   *Peyrefitte*[q]   *Marcellin*[r]

⟶ Schumann, D (M)[s,c]   Peyrefitte, D (U)[t,u,o]

Foyer ⟶ Joxe

⟶ Fouchet

⟶ Giscard d'Esta-ing, D (C)[t,y] ⟶ **Debré** ⟶

Sudreau ⟶ Joxe[bb]   Fouchet ⟶ Peyrefitte

Pisani ⟶ Ortoli, CS[cc]

⟶ Dusseaulx   Jacquet, FD (U)

⟶ Maurice-Bokanowski ⟶ Marcellin   Guichard, D (U)

⟶ Faure, S (R) ⟶

Jeanneney ⟶

⟶ Grandval (U)[t] ⟶
⟶ Marcellin, D (C) ⟶

⟶ Maziol, D (U) ⟶

⟶ Sainteny, D (U) ⟶   Sanguinetti, D (U)   Duvillard, D (U)

⟶ Marette, S (U) ⟶ Guéna, D (U)

Peyrefitte   **Gorse**

Gorse, FD[t,dd]   Missoffe, D (U)[t,ff]   **Missoffe**[gg] ⟶

Chamant, D (C)[hh]

a Excluding Secretaries of State (Junior Ministers). Italics mean a change in ministerial post; bold face type means a return to the Government after an absence from it. Lines with arrows mean continuation in the same post. Blank spaces mean that the identical post was not filled at the time, either because it had not yet been created, or because its functions were terminated, transferred to another Minister, or transferred to a Secretary of State. During the period covered by the table, 23 men and 1 woman served as Secretaries of State, sometimes in more than 1 post; 10 of the men became Ministers. The letters in parentheses designate party affiliation at time of first appointment as Minister under the Fifth Republic: U for UNR or UDT, M for MRP, C for Conservative, R for Radical, and RDA for *Rassemblement démocratique africain*. D means Deputy, S means Senator, at time of first appointment as Minister or Junior Minister under the Fifth Republic. FD means former Deputy; CS means high civil servant; P means professor.

b Relations with and aid to the former French colonies, both before and after independence. MM. Jacquinot and Lecourt appear to have shared responsibilities in this domain between February, 1960, and August, 1961.

c All MRP Ministers resigned on May 15, 1962.

d DOM stands for Overseas Departments; TOM stands for Overseas Territories.

e Appointed November 22, 1960.

f Including Atomic Energy and Space Affairs after April 1962.

g Until February 22, 1965, when appointed to the Constitutional Council.

h Resigned May 20, 1959, upon becoming Premier of the Ivory Coast.

i In charge of administrative reform.

j In charge of the civil service.

k In charge of parliamentary relations.

l In charge of DOM, TOM, and atomic energy affairs.

m In charge of interministerial coordination.

n In charge of information.

o Appointed September 11, 1962.

p In charge of cooperation (see b above).

q In charge of scientific research, atomic energy, and space affairs.

r In charge of planning and regional development.

s In charge of regional planning.

t Had served as Junior Minister during the Fifth Republic prior to appointment as Minister.

u In charge of repatriation.

v Appointed May 28, 1959.

w Appointed May 6, 1961, on resignation of M. Chatenet.

x Appointed January 13, 1960.

y Appointed January 18, 1962, on resignation of M. Baumgartner.

z Appointed January 15, 1960, after resignation of M. Boulloche on December 23, 1959.

aa Appointed February 20, 1961.

bb Interim appointment on October 15, 1962, on resignation of M. Sudreau.

cc Appointed April 29, 1967, on resignation of M. Pisani.

dd Minister for Cooperation (see b above).

ee Appointed May 18, 1961.

ff Minister for Repatriation; office abolished on July 23, 1964.

gg Minister for Youth and Sports.

hh Minister of Transportation.

The Difference Between PR Based on the Highest Average and PR Based on the Largest Remainder

ASSUME THAT THERE ARE FIVE SEATS to be allocated and that 80,000 votes have been cast among five lists of candidates as follows:

LIST A	LIST B	LIST C	LIST D	LIST E
27,000	23,000	15,000	7,600	7,400

Under both systems of PR, the first step is to determine the electoral quotient. This is done by dividing the number of votes by the number of seats to be allocated. In this case, the electoral quotient is 16,000. Still under both systems, the next step is to see whether any lists received more votes than the electoral quotient, and if any did, to allocate to each such list as many seats as the times the quotient can be divided into each of those lists' total vote. In this case, there are two such lists, Lists A and B, and each list will receive one seat. At this point, the two systems of PR diverge.

Under PR based on the highest average, the next steps consist of dividing the vote received by each party's list by the number of seats which have already been allocated to it plus one, and allocating each successive seat to the party which shows the highest number, that is, the highest average number of votes per seat, after each division. In our illustration, the process would operate as follows:

	A	B	C	D	E
Quotient Allocations:	**27,000**	**23,000**	15,000	7,600	7,400
First Division:	13,500	11,500	**15,000**	7,600	7,400
Second Division:	**13,500**	11,500	7,500	7,600	7,400
Third Division:	9,000	**11,500**	7,500	7,600	7,400

259

Under PR based on the largest remainder, only one step follows the initial allocation of seats on the basis of the electoral quotient. This consists of subtracting the quotient from the total vote for each list which has already received a seat (or multiples of the quotient if a list has won more than one seat on the basis of the quotient) and then awarding the remaining seats to the lists in the order of the size of the numbers which remain. In our illustration, the process would operate as follows:

A	**27,000**	minus	16,000	equals	**11,000**
B	**23,000**	minus	16,000	equals	7,000
C	**15,000**				
D	**7,600**				
E	7,400				

PR based on the highest average has resulted in 2 seats for List A, 2 for List B, and 1 for List C. PR based on the largest remainder has resulted in 2 seats for List A, 1 seat for List B, 1 for List C and 1 for List D. The system of the highest average has favored the larger List B; the system of the largest remainder has favored the smaller List D.

Select Bibliography

THIS BIBLIOGRAPHY contains works which were used in the preparation of this book as well as works which should be useful to readers who wish to explore particular topics further. Brief comments have been added in some cases, particularly where the title (combined with the date of publication) does not fully describe the contents of the work.

Periodical Publications

L'Année Politique, Économique, Sociale et Diplomatique en France, Presses Universitaires de France, Paris. Published annually; contains an account of French political, economic, social, and diplomatic developments for each year, as well as documents, speeches, and statistics.

Journal Officiel de la République Française. An official publication appearing in several series containing verbatim accounts of parliamentary debates and records of roll-call votes, the text of laws and decrees, and various public documents.

Le Monde. A distinguished daily Paris newspaper which gives extensive coverage of political developments.

Revue Française de Science Politique. The leading French political science journal, published quarterly in Paris by the Fondation Nationale des Sciences Politiques; contains full-length articles and a section entitled "Les forces politiques en France" which deals more briefly with current political developments.

Sondages; Revue Française de l'Opinion Publique. Published quarterly in Paris; contains the results of public opinion surveys conducted by the Institut Français d'Opinion Publique.

General, Historical, and Interpretive Works

Aron, Raymond, *France, Steadfast and Changing: The Fourth to the Fifth Republic,* Harvard, Cambridge, Mass., 1960.

Aron, Robert, in collaboration with Georgette Elgey, *The Vichy Regime, 1940–1944,* trans. by Humphrey Hare, Putnam & Co., Ltd., London, 1958.

Bouju, Paul-M., Georges Dupeux, Claude Gérard, Alain Lancelot, Jean-Alain Lesourd, and René Rémond, *Atlas historique de la France contemporaine, 1800–1965,* Armand Colin, Paris, 1966 (Collection U, Série "Histoire contemporaine"). Contains useful political, economic, social, and other information presented cartographically.

Crozier, Michel, *The Bureaucratic Phenomenon,* trans. by M. Crozier, The University of Chicago Press, Chicago, 1964. An ingenious interpretation of French bureaucratic behavior in terms of French cultural traits; shows how other forms of behavior—including the political—may also be related to those traits.

Duverger, Maurice, *La Cinquième République,* Presses Universitaires de France, Paris, 3rd ed., 1963.

Fauvet, Jacques, *La IVe République,* Fayard, Paris, 1959.

Girard, Alain, *La Réussite sociale en France; Ses caractères—ses lois—ses effets,* Presses Universitaires de France, Paris, 1961 (Institut national d'études démographiques, Travaux et Documents, Cahier No. 38). Contains data on social mobility and the factors in professional success in France.

Goguel, François, *France Under the Fourth Republic,* Cornell, Ithaca, N.Y., 1952. The fifth chapter is particularly valuable for its interpretation of party conflict and institutional problems in historical and social terms.

Goguel, François, and Alfred Grosser, *La Politique en France,* Armand Colin, Paris, 1964 (Collection U, Série "Société Politique").

Hoffmann, Stanley, "Aspects du régime de Vichy," *Revue Française de Science Politique,* VI (January–March, 1956), 44–69.

Hoffmann, Stanley, *et al., In Search of France,* Harvard, Cambridge, Mass., 1963; Harper & Row (Harper Torchbook paperback), New York, 1965. Contains important interpretive essays by Hoffmann and Goguel.

Hoffmann, Stanley, "Succession and Stability in France," *Journal of International Affairs,* XVIII (1964), 86–103.

Laponce, J. A., *The Government of the Fifth Republic; French Political Parties and the Constitution,* University of California Press, Berkeley, 1961.

MacRae, Duncan, Jr., *Parliament, Parties, and Society in France, 1946–1958*, St. Martin's, New York, 1967. Applies statistical methods to a study of the Fourth Republic.

Micaud, Charles A., *The French Right and Nazi Germany, 1933–1939*, Duke, Durham, N.C., 1943.

Siegfried, André, *France: A Study in Nationality*, Yale, New Haven, Conn., 1930.

Thomson, David, *Democracy in France Since 1870*, Oxford, Fair Lawn, N.J., 4th ed., 1964 (Royal Institute of International Affairs). Particularly good on the historical forces affecting French politics.

Viansson-Ponté, Pierre, *Bilan de la Ve République, Les Politiques*, Calmann-Lévy, Paris, 1967.

Werth, Alexander, *The De Gaulle Revolution*, Robert Hale, London, 1960.

Werth, Alexander, *The Twilight of France, 1933–1940*, Harper & Row, New York, 1942.

Williams, Philip M., *Crisis and Compromise; Politics in the Fourth Republic*, Longmans, London, 1964. A masterpiece; indispensable to the student of French politics.

Williams, Philip, "How the Fourth Republic Died: Sources for the Revolution of May 1958," *French Historical Studies*, III (spring, 1963), 1–40.

Williams, Philip M., and Martin Harrison, *De Gaulle's Republic*, Longmans, London, 2nd. ed., 1962.

Wright, Gordon, "Reflections on the French Resistance (1940–1944)," *Political Science Quarterly*, LXXVII (September, 1962), 336–349.

Wright, Gordon, *The Reshaping of French Democracy*, Harcourt, Brace & World, New York, 1948. An account of the establishment of the Fourth Republic.

Wylie, Laurence, ed., *Chanzeaux: A Village in Anjou*, Harvard, Cambridge, Mass., 1966.

Wylie, Laurence, *Village in the Vaucluse*, Harper & Row, New York, rev. ed., 1964.

Political Institutions

Avril, Pierre, *Le Régime politique de la Ve République*, R. Pichon et R. Durand-Auzias, Paris, 1964 (Librairie Générale de Droit et de Jurisprudence).

Bauchet, Pierre, *Economic Planning, The French Experience*, trans. by Daphne Woodward, Frederick A. Praeger, Inc., New York, 1964.

Buron, Robert, *Le plus Beau des Métiers*, Plon, Paris, 1963. An interesting account of what Deputies and Ministers do by someone who served in both capacities under the Fourth and Fifth Republics.

Chapman, Brian, *Introduction to French Local Government*, G. Allen, London, 1953.

Chapman, Brian, *The Prefects and Provincial France*, G. Allen, London, 1955.

"La Constitution de la Ve République," *Revue Française de Science Politique*, IX (March, 1959). A special issue containing important articles, documents, and bibliography.

Cotteret, Jean-Marie, *Le Pouvoir législatif en France*, R. Pichon et R. Durand-Auzias, Paris, 1962 (Librairie Générale de Droit et de Jurisprudence).

Denis, Nicolas, "L'application des nouvelles règles de procédure parlementaire établies par la Constitution de 1958," *Revue Française de Science Politique*, X (December, 1960), 899–911.

Ehrmann, Henry W., "Direct Democracy in France," *American Political Science Review*, LVII (December, 1963), 883–901.

Guichard-Ayoub, Eliane, Charles Roig, and Jean Grangé, *Études sur le Parlement de la Ve République*, Presses Universitaires de France, Paris, 1965.

Harrison, Martin, "The French Experience of Exceptional Powers: 1961," *Journal of Politics*, XXV (February, 1963), 139–158.

Hoffmann, Stanley, "The French Constitution of 1958: I. The Final Text and Its Prospects," *American Political Science Review*, LIII (June, 1959), 332–357.

Parodi, Jean-Luc, *Les Rapports entre le législatif et l'exécutif sous la Ve République*, Paris, Fondation Nationale des Sciences Politiques, February, 1962.

Wahl, Nicholas, "The French Constitution of 1958: II. The Initial Draft and Its Origins," *American Political Science Review*, LIII (June, 1959), 358–382.

Political Parties

Almond, Gabriel, *The Appeals of Communism* Princeton, Princeton, N.J., 1964. A comparative study of former members of the Communist parties of several countries, including France.

Bal, Marielle, "Les indépendants," *Revue Française de Science Politique*, XV (June, 1965), 537–555.

Charlot, Jean, *L'Union pour la Nouvelle République; Étude du pouvoir au sein d'un parti politique*, Armand Colin, Paris, 1967 (Cahiers de la Fondation Nationale des Sciences Politiques, 153).

De Tarr, Francis, *The French Radical Party from Herriot to Mendès-France*, Oxford, Fair Lawn, N.J., 1961.

Duverger, Maurice, *et al.*, *Partis politiques et classes sociales en France*, Armand Colin, Paris, 1955. (Cahiers de la Fondation Nationale des Sciences Politiques, 74).

Einaudi, Mario, and François Goguel, *Christian Democracy in Italy and France*, University of Notre Dame Press, Notre Dame, Ind., 1952.

Einaudi, Mario, Jean-Marie Domenach, and Aldo Garosci, *Communism in Western Europe*, Cornell, Ithaca, N.Y., 1951.

Fauvet, Jacques, *The Cockpit of France*, trans. by Nancy Pearson, Harvill Press, London, 1960. A good general account of the parties.

Fauvet, Jacques, in collaboration with Alain Duhamel, *Histoire du parti communiste français*, Fayard, Paris, 2 vols: I. *De la guerre à la guerre 1917–1939*, 1964; II. *Vingt-cinq ans de drames 1939–1965*, 1965.

Graham, B. D., *The French Socialists and Tripartisme, 1944–1947*, George Weidenfeld and Nicolson, London, 1965.

Micaud, Charles A., *Communism and the French Left*, Frederick A. Praeger, Inc., New York, 1963.

Noland, Aaron, *The Founding of the French Socialist Party, 1893–1905*, Harvard, Cambridge, Mass., 1956.

Pierce, Roy, "De Gaulle and the RPF—A Post-Mortem," *Journal of Politics*, XVI (February, 1954), 96–119.

Purtschet, Christian, *Le Rassemblement du peuple français, 1947–1953*, Éditions Cujas, Paris, 1965.

Rémond, René, *The Right Wing in France from 1815 to de Gaulle*, trans. by James M. Laux, University of Pennsylvania Press, Philadelphia, 1966.

Viansson-Ponté, Pierre, *The King and His Court*, trans. by Elaine P. Halperin, Houghton Mifflin, Boston, 1965. Brief sketches of the leading Gaullists and a discussion of presidential rituals, done with a light touch.

Elections, Referendums, and Electoral Behavior

Butler, David E., ed., *Elections Abroad*, Macmillan, London, 1959. Contains contributions on the French election of 1958 by Philip Williams and Martin Harrison, Jean Blondel, and Merlin Thomas.

Campbell, Peter, *French Electoral Systems and Elections Since 1789*, Faber, London, 2nd ed., 1965.

Converse, Philip E., "The Problem of Party Distances in Models of Voting Change," in M. Kent Jennings and L. Harmon Ziegler, *The Electoral Process*, Prentice-Hall, Englewood Cliffs, N.J., 1966, chap. 9. A theoretical analysis of the conditions and limits of changes in partisan electoral choice in multiparty systems; based on French and Finnish data and important for understanding the operation of the French two-ballot electoral system.

Converse, Philip E., and Georges Dupeux, "De Gaulle and Eisenhower: The Public Image of the Victorious General," in Angus Campbell, Philip E. Converse, Warren E. Miller, and Donald E. Stokes, *Elections and the Political Order*, Wiley, New York, 1966, chap. 15.

Converse, Philip E., and Georges Dupeux, "Politicization of the Electorate in France and the United States," in Angus Campbell, Philip E. Converse, Warren E. Miller, and Donald E. Stokes, *Elections and the Political Order*, Wiley, New York, 1966, chap. 14.

Deutsch, Emeric, Denis Lindon, and Pierre Weill, *Les Familles politiques aujourd'hui en France*, Editions de Minuit, Paris, 1966.

Duverger, Maurice, François Goguel, Jean Touchard, *et al.*, *Les Élections du 2 janvier 1956*, Armand Colin, Paris, 1957 (Cahiers de la Fondation Nationale des Sciences Politiques, 82).

Gallagher, Orvoell R., "Rural French Voting Habits," *Social Research,* XVIII (December, 1951), 501–509.

Goguel, François, "L'élection présidentielle française de décembre 1965," *Revue Française de Science Politique,* XVI (April, 1966), 221–254.

Goguel, François, "Les élections législatives des 5 et 12 mars 1967," *Revue Française de Science Politique,* XVII (June, 1967), 429–467.

Goguel, François, *Géographie des élections françaises de 1870 à 1951,* Armand Colin, Paris, 1951 (Cahiers de la Fondation Nationale des Sciences Politiques, 27).

Goguel, François, *et al., Le Référendum du 8 avril 1962,* Armand Colin, Paris, 1963 (Cahiers de la Fondation Nationale des Sciences Politiques, 124).

Goguel, François, *et al., Le Référendum du 8 janvier 1961,* Armand Colin, Paris, 1962 (Cahiers de la Fondation Nationale des Sciences Politiques, 119).

Goguel, François, *et al., Le Référendum d'octobre et les élections de novembre 1962,* Armand Colin, Paris, 1965 (Cahiers de la Fondation Nationale des Sciences Politiques, 142).

Goldey, David B., "The French Presidential Election of 5 and 19 December, 1965, Organization and Results," *Political Studies,* XIV (June, 1966), 208–215.

Hamilton, Richard F., *Affluence and the French Worker in the Fourth Republic,* Princeton, Princeton, N.J., 1967.

Kesselman, Mark, *The Ambiguous Consensus: A Study of Local Government in France,* Knopf, New York, 1967.

Marie, Christiane, *L'Évolution du comportement politique dans une ville en expansion: Grenoble, 1871–1965,* Armand Colin, Paris, 1966 (Cahiers de la Fondation Nationale des Sciences Politiques, 148).

Touchard, Jean, *et al., L'Établissement de la Cinquième République. Le référendum de septembre et les élections de novembre 1958,* Armand Colin, Paris, 1960 (Cahiers de la Fondation Nationale des Sciences Politiques, 109).

Williams, Philip, "The French Presidential Election of 1965," *Parliamentary Affairs,* XIX (winter, 1965–1966), 14–30.

Williams, Philip M., "The French Referendum and Election of October–November 1962," *Parliamentary Affairs,* XVI (spring, 1963), 165–173.

Public Opinion, Popular Participation, and Political Personnel

Davis, Morris, and Sidney Verba, "Party Affiliation and International Opinions in Britain and France, 1947–1956," *Public Opinion Quarterly,* XXIV (winter, 1960), 590–604.

Dogan, Mattei, "Le personnel politique et la personnalité charismatique," *Revue Française de Sociologie,* VI (July–September, 1965), 305–324.

Dogan, Mattei, "Political Ascent in a Class Society: French Deputies 1870–1958," in Dwaine Marvick, ed., *Political Decision-Makers*, The Free Press, New York, 1961 (vol. 2, International Yearbook of Political Behavior Research), chap. 2.

Dogan, Mattei, and Jacques Narbonne, *Les Françaises face à la politique; Comportement politique et condition sociale*, Armand Colin, Paris, 1955 (Cahiers de la Fondation Nationale des Sciences Politiques, 72).

Dupeux, Georges, "Citizen Participation in Political Life: France," UNESCO, *International Social Science Journal*, XII (1960), 40–52.

Fougeyrollas, Pierre, *La Conscience politique dans la France contemporaine; essai*, Editions Denoël, Paris, 1963. Attempts to identify the political outlooks of the electorates of the various parties, mainly on the basis of public opinion polls.

Meynaud, Jean, and Alain Lancelot, *La Participation des Français à la politique*, Presses Universitaires de France, Paris, 2nd ed., 1965 ("Que sais-je?" No. 911).

Vedel, Georges, *et al.*, *La Dépolitisation, mythe ou réalité?*, Armand Colin, Paris, 1962 (Cahiers de la Fondation Nationale des Sciences Politiques, 120).

Interest Groups

Bosworth, William, *Catholicism and Crisis in Modern France; French Catholic Groups at the Threshold of the Fifth Republic*, Princeton, Princeton, N.J., 1962. Good on the whole background of the religious question and on the MRP, as well as on particular Catholic groups.

Brown, Bernard E., "Pressure Politics in the Fifth Republic," *Journal of Politics*, XXV (August, 1963), 509–525.

Clark, James M., *Teachers and Politics in France; A Pressure Group Study of the Fédération de l'Education Nationale*, Syracuse University Press, Syracuse, N.Y., 1967.

Ehrmann, Henry W., *Organized Business in France*, Princeton, Princeton, N.J., 1957.

Fauvet, Jacques, Henri Mendras, *et al.*, *Les Paysans et la politique dans la France contemporaine*, Armand Colin, Paris, 1958 (Cahiers de la Fondation Nationale des Sciences Politiques, 94).

Furniss, Edgar S., Jr., *De Gaulle and the French Army; A Crisis in Civil-Military Relations*, Twentieth Century Fund, New York, 1964.

Girardet, Raoul, "Civil and Military Power in the Fourth Republic," in Samuel P. Huntington, ed., *Changing Patterns of Military Politics*, The Free Press, New York, 1962 (vol. 3, International Yearbook of Political Behavior Research), chap. 5.

De la Gorce, Paul-Marie, "Histoire de l'O.A.S. en Algérie," *La Nef*, XIX (October, 1962–January, 1963), Nouvelle Série, Numéro spécial, Cahier nos. 12–13, pp. 139–192.

Lavau, Georges, "Political Pressures by Interest Groups in France," in Henry W. Ehrmann, ed., *Interest Groups on Four Continents*, The University of Pittsburgh Press, Pittsburgh, Pa., 1958.

Lorwin, Val R., *The French Labor Movement*, Harvard, Cambridge, Mass., 1954.

Meynaud, Jean, *Les Groupes de pression en France*, Armand Colin, Paris, 1958 (Cahiers de la Fondation Nationale des Sciences Politiques, 95).

Meynaud, Jean, *Nouvelles études sur les groupes de pression en France*, Armand Colin, Paris, 1962 (Cahiers de la Fondation Nationale des Sciences Politiques, 118).

Reynaud, Jean-Daniel, *Les Syndicats en France*, Armand Colin, Paris, 1963 (Collection U, Série "Société Politique").

Tavernier, Yves, *La F.N.S.E.A.*, Fondation Nationale des Sciences Politiques, Paris, March, 1965.

Wright, Gordon, *Rural Revolution in France; The Peasantry in the Twentieth Century*, Stanford University Press, Stanford, Cal., 1964.

Biographies, Essays, Memoirs, Polemics, and Speeches

Bromberger, Merry, *Le Destin secret de Georges Pompidou*, Fayard, Paris, 1965.

Debré, Michel, *Au Service de la nation; Essai d'un programme politique*, Stock, Paris, 1963.

De Gaulle, Charles, *The Complete War Memoirs of Charles de Gaulle*, trans. by J. Griffin and R. Howard, Simon & Schuster, New York, 1964.

De Gaulle, Charles, *The Edge of the Sword*, trans. by Gerard Hopkins, Criterion Books, New York, 1960. Contains de Gaulle's early views on leadership; first published in 1932.

De Gaulle, Charles, *The Speeches of General de Gaulle*, trans. by Sheila Mathieu, Oxford, Fair Lawn, N.J., 1944.

Lacouture, Jean, *De Gaulle*, trans. by Francis K. Price, New American Library, New York, 1966.

Macridis, Roy C., ed., *De Gaulle: Implacable Ally*, Harper & Row, New York, 1966. A collection of de Gaulle's writings and public statements, with commentary.

Major Addresses, Statements, and Press Conferences of General Charles de Gaulle, May 19, 1958–January 31, 1964, French Embassy, Press and Information Division, New York.

Mendès-France, Pierre, *A Modern French Republic*, trans. by Anne Carter, Hill and Wang, Inc., New York, 1963.

Mitterrand, François, *Le Coup d'état permanent*, Plon, Paris, 1964.

Mollet, Guy, *13 mai 1958–12 mai 1962*, Plon, Paris, 1962.

Tournoux, Jean-Raymond, *Sons of France: Pétain and de Gaulle*, trans. by Oliver Coburn, Viking, New York, 1966.

Werth, Alexander, *De Gaulle; A Political Biography*, Simon & Shuster, New York, 1966.

Index

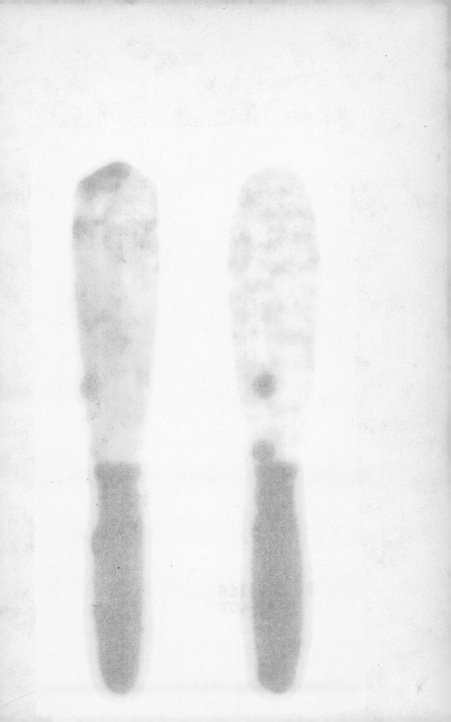

DATE DUE	